Caroline Ann

PSYCHOLOGY AND THE STU EDUCATION

CW00797072

Psychology and the Study of Education: Critical Perspectives on Developing Theories explores both the insights and applications that psychology can offer in a range of educational contexts. Introducing the reader to a wide variety of sources, from cutting edge research to key studies from the past, it offers new perspectives on the psychology of education. This includes re-examining core theories of learning, unpicking key learning processes and reconsidering the role of factors such as memory, creativity and gender in learning. Questioning myths and misconceptions, it challenges the reader to develop a critically reflective approach and asks them to reconsider the potential value of psychology in both understanding and influencing education.

With discussion points and recommended readings provided in every chapter to enhance sessions and challenge students, issues explored include:

- Reconsidering what we think we know about the psychology of education.
- Memory: How we learn by remembering and imagining.
- Creativity: Creative learning and learning creativity.
- Reading, writing and dyslexia: Understanding the myths and exploring the challenges.
- Embodiment: The entanglement of brain, body and environment in learning.
- Social understanding: Learning to relate and its role in education.
- Gender: The origins of gender identity and its impact on education.
- Behaviourism: Taking a second look at its wider relevance to learning.
- Piaget: A fresh perspective on Piagetian theory and method.
- Vygotsky: Socio-cultural theories and collective learning.

Your guide to the complex and evolving field that is psychology of education, this is an essential text for students of Education Studies, Disability Studies, Early Childhood or Childhood and Youth Studies and Teacher Education; ideal for anyone who has already been introduced to a little psychology and would like to know more, or anyone teaching psychology on an education course. Whether you are taking your first steps or looking for your next challenge, this book has something to offer anyone who wants to take their studies on the psychology of education to the next level.

Cathal Ó Siochrú is Senior Lecturer in Education Studies at Liverpool Hope University, UK.

The Routledge Education Studies Series

Series Editor: Stephen Ward, Bath Spa University, UK

The Routledge Education Studies Series aims to support advanced level study on Education Studies and related degrees by offering in-depth introductions from which students can begin to extend their research and writing in years 2 and 3 of their course. Titles in the series cover a range of classic and up-and-coming topics, developing understanding of key issues through detailed discussion and consideration of conflicting ideas and supporting evidence. With an emphasis on developing critical thinking, allowing students to think for themselves and beyond their own experiences, the titles in the series offer historical, global and comparative perspectives on core issues in education.

For a full list of titles in this series, please visit https://www.routledge.com/The-Routledge-Education-Studies-Series/book-series/RESS

Inclusive Education
Edited by Zeta Brown

Gender, Education and Work
Edited by Christine Eden

International and Comparative Education
Edited by Brendan Bartram

Contemporary Issues in Childhood
Edited by Zeta Brown and Stephen Ward

Psychology and the Study of Education
Edited by Cathal Ó Siochrú

PSYCHOLOGY AND THE STUDY OF EDUCATION

Critical Perspectives on Developing Theories

Edited by
Cathal Ó Siochrú

Routledge
Taylor & Francis Group

LONDON AND NEW YORK

First published 2018
by Routledge
2 Park Square, Milton Park, Abingdon, Oxon OX14 4RN

and by Routledge
711 Third Avenue, New York, NY 10017

Routledge is an imprint of the Taylor & Francis Group, an informa business

British Library Cataloguing in Publication Data
A catalogue record for this book is available from the British Library

Library of Congress Cataloging in Publication Data
A catalog record for this book has been requested

ISBN: 978-1-138-23764-3 (hbk)
ISBN: 978-1-138-23765-0 (pbk)
ISBN: 978-1-315-29935-8 (ebk)

Typeset in News Gothic
by Integra Software Service Pvt. Ltd.

Printed in the United Kingdom
by Henry Ling Limited

To Oisín and Dorren, my role models

Contents

Figures and tables

Figures

Tables

Contributors

Lorna Bourke is a Principal Lecturer of Psychology at Liverpool Hope University. A member of the European Literacy Network and the European Association of Research in Learning and Instruction, Special Interest Group in Writing, she has published on the development of writing in young children. Her research interests primarily lie in the cognitive skills that account for differences in the progress young people make in literacy.

Suzanne M. Egan is a Lecturer in Cognitive Psychology and Lifespan Development in the Department of Psychology, Mary Immaculate College, University of Limerick. She serves on the committee for the Division of Teachers and Researchers in the Psychological Society of Ireland (PSI) and is also member of the course advisory board for a joint honours degree in Education and Psychology. Her research examines the processes involved in thinking and imagination and the factors affecting the cognitive development of young children.

Claire Lloyd is a Lecturer in the School of Teacher Education at Liverpool Hope University, and Director of the Faculty of Education's Professional Master's and Professional Doctoral programmes. She has published in the areas of teacher decision-making and educational leadership. Her research interests are in the areas of critical animal pedagogy and qualitative research methods.

Marek McGann is Lecturer in Psychology, in the Faculty of Arts of Mary Immaculate College, University of Limerick. His research examines embodied and enactive conceptions of cognition, and the emergence of cognitive processes in social interactions. He is also a founder member of REX, the Research Expertise Exchange, a social network and online collaboration exchange for teachers, and other educational researchers.

Catherine O'Connell is a Lecturer in the Psychology of Education at Liverpool Hope University. She is Co-Director of the Centre for Education and Policy Analysis. She has worked within the higher education sector in a range of teaching, management and research roles relating to the enhancement of the student experience and internationalisation of higher education. Prior to joining Liverpool Hope she was professional development manager for the British Council's higher education team. Her research examines the influence of metrics (international and domestic) on higher education policy and practice.

Cathal Ó Siochrú is a Senior Lecturer in the Psychology of Education at Liverpool Hope University. In addition to lecturing he has extensive experience with curriculum development and has developed psychology courses and psychology of education courses for a number of different universities. His research interests include student beliefs about knowledge, student and staff views on the choice between seen and unseen exams, and student engagement.

Jim Stack is a Lecturer in Early Childhood Studies at Liverpool Hope University. His background is in the area of children's social understanding. His current research interests focus on how early years provision facilitates preschoolers' emerging social understanding and prosocial behaviour.

Stephen Ward is Emeritus Professor of Education, Bath Spa University, formerly Dean of the School of Education and subject leader for Education Studies. A founder member of the British Education Studies Association, he has published on the primary curriculum, primary music teaching and Education Studies. His research interests are education policy and university knowledge.

Chloe Shu-Hua Yeh is a Senior Lecturer in Education Studies, Bath Spa University. She specialises in interdisciplinary research involving emotion, cognition and computer gaming, publishing in psychology and education. Her most specific research interests also include creativity, perspective taking, academic motivation, emotions in learning, and academic acculturation across the fields of education, psychology and positive psychology.

Series editor's preface

Education Studies has become a popular and exciting undergraduate subject in some fifty universities across the UK. It began in the early 2000s, mainly in the post-1992 universities which had been centres of teacher training but, gaining academic credibility, the subject is being taken up by post-1992 and Russell Group institutions. In 2004 Routledge published one of the first texts for undergraduates, *Education Studies: A Student's Guide* (Ward, 2004), now in its third edition. It comprises a series of chapters introducing key topics in Education Studies and has contributed to the development of the subject.

Education Studies is concerned with understanding how people develop and learn throughout their lives, the nature of knowledge and critical engagement with ways of knowing. It demands an intellectually rigorous analysis of educational processes and their cultural, social, political and historical contexts. In a time of rapid change across the planet, education is about how we both make and manage such change. Thus, Education Studies includes perspectives on international education, economic relationships, globalisation, ecological issues and human rights. It also deals with beliefs, values and principles in education and the way that they change over time.

It is important to understand that Education Studies is not teacher training or teacher education. Its theoretical framework of psychology, sociology, history and philosophy is derived from teacher education, and undergraduates in the subject may well go on to become teachers after a PGCE or school-based training. However, Education Studies should be regarded as a subject with a variety of career outcomes, or indeed, none: it can be taken as the academic and critical study of education in itself. At the same time, while the theoretical elements of teacher training are continually reduced in PGCE courses and school-based training, undergraduate Education Studies provides a critical analysis of education for the benefit of some who will become future teachers. In a rapidly changing world, we feel that all educators need so much more than training to deliver a government-defined curriculum.

Since its inception in the late 1990s there has been continuing discussion about the roles of the disciplines within Education Studies. Some have argued that psychology, sociology, philosophy, history – and even economics – should be recognised as distinct components which combine to form the field of study known as Education Studies. Others urge that Education Studies should be seen as a 'discipline' in itself; that the other disciplines should be less prominent and may, in fact, make the study of education too difficult and complex. This book is based on the former assumption that, for a rigorous analysis of education, a strong grounding in the disciplines is essential: students should have an understanding of the nature of each of the disciplines, be aware of the theoretical issues in the subject and be au fait with recent research in education. Intended for second- and third-year undergraduates, master's students and even tutors on education-related courses, this book is the fifth in the series of Routledge publications which builds on the introductory guide and looks in depth at psychology in education.

Of course, psychology has a long history of informing teachers and educators in their practice. However, the psychology content in many education courses and textbooks has often been superficial in nature, with a lack of understanding of the nature of the discipline and based upon some popular over-simplifications. This book takes the reader to the heart of the psychology of education, dispelling popular myths and bringing us up to date with what psychology can offer the study of education.

Stephen Ward
Bath Spa University

Note

The academic network for tutors and students in Education Studies is the British Education Studies Association (BESA). It has an annual conference that shares academic practice and research in Education Studies and to which students are welcome. There are two e-journals, one designated for students and early researchers: www.educationstudies.org.uk.

Reference

Ward, S. (2004) *Education studies: A student's guide*. London: Routledge.

Abbreviations

AHELO	Assessment of Learning Outcomes in Higher Education
APA	American Psychological Association
AST	Activity Systems Theory
BIS	(Department of) Business, Innovation and Skills
BPS	British Psychological Society
CHAT	Cultural Historical Activity theory
DDAT	Dyslexia, Dyspraxia, Attention Treatment
DfE	Department for Education
DfEE	Department for Education and Employment
DfES	Department for Education and Skills
DST	Dyslexia Screening Test
EL	expressive language
ELG	Early Learning Goal
ELL	English language learners
ESL	English as a second language
EU	European Union
EHEA	European Higher Education Area
EYFS	Early Years Foundation Stage
EYFSP	Early Years Foundation Stage Profile
EYPS	Early Years Professional Status
GCSE	General Certificate of Secondary Education
HEFCE	Higher Education Funding Council for England
ICGE	International Centre of Genetic Epistemology
IMF	International Monetary Fund
KS1, 2, 3, 4	Key Stage 1, 2, 3, 4
LTM	long-term memory
LIW	Learning in and for interagency working
NACCCE	National Advisory Committee on Creative and Cultural Education
NESS	National Evaluation of Sure Start
OECD	Organisation for Economic Cooperation and Development
PISA	Programme for International Student Assessment
PPD	Phonological Processing Deficit

RAT	Remote Associates Test
RL	receptive language
SCAA	School Curriculum Assessment Authority
SRHE	Society for Research into Higher Education
SSLP	Sure Start Local Programmes
STEAM	Science, Technology, Engineering, Arts and Mathematics
STEM	Science, Technology, Engineering and Mathematics
STM	short-term memory
ToM	theory of mind
WISC	Wechsler Intelligence Scale for Children
WRAT	Wide Range Achievement Test
WTO	World Trade Organisation
ZPD	Zone of Proximal Development

1 Introduction

Reconsidering what we think we know about the psychology of education

Cathal Ó Siochrú

Introduction

What is education?

If you were to ask people to identify the time and place where they had received their 'education' they would almost all talk about their school days. Indeed, when we talk about someone being 'in education' we are usually talking about school or university. It's in school and university that we become 'educated'. These are the places where we learn things. Of course, if you pushed them, most people would acknowledge that not everything is learned in school. Practical skills, social skills, hobbies, sports, there are many things we learn outside of our formal schooling. And yet we rarely consider these to be part of our 'education'. We have to invent new terms to describe this kind of learning, calling them 'life lessons' or 'figuring things out'.

From a psychological perspective it could be argued that there is little or no difference between the learning we do in school and the learning we do outside of it. There are many definitions of learning from different psychologists. Gerrig et al. (2012: 668) define learning as 'A process based on experience that results in a relatively permanent change in behaviour or behavioural potential'. Martin et al. (2013: 769) would define learning as 'An adaptive process in which the tendency to perform a particular behaviour is changed by experience'. There are many other definitions, but they all tend to agree on a few things. The two most important things they agree on, for our purposes here, are that (1) learning results in an enduring change in the learner and that (2) this change is a result of the learner's experiences. Viewed in those terms the teacher who requires you to repeat the colours of the rainbow and the hot iron that burns your hand when you touch it are both producing learning.

This view of learning poses a number of interesting questions in terms of how we then see education. First, such a broad definition of learning necessitates a considerable expansion of the number of occasions and places where learning could be said to be taking place. This raises an important question as to whether we should also consider a similar expansion of the number of places where education could be said to be taking place. Instead, in educational psychology and elsewhere there is a tendency to distinguish between learning and education so far as to limit 'education' to those learning events where the aim to produce a change is deliberate and the subject being learned can be considered to be valuable or worthwhile (Peters, 1966). As such, the

restaurant that serves you some bad oysters, which make you ill and in turn cause you to swear off eating oysters ever again, is not a place of education.

But even with this limitation we can see that the number of places and events which would now qualify as providing us with an education extends far beyond the nurseries, schools and universities that we might have thought of as our only 'places of education' before now. It also greatly increases the number of people who we might consider as educators. For the purposes of this book, therefore, we will define education to be an event or process which has been organised with the explicit purpose of producing learning in those that participate in it and we define an educator as a role whose primary purpose is to promote and facilitate the education of others. These definitions are a good fit for describing schools and teachers but they also recognise a lot of other places and people as being 'education' and 'educators' respectively. An example of these non-traditional educational contexts would be a course run by a local council aimed at helping local residents to improve their health, or a training scheme run in the workplace by the human resources department aimed at reducing the number of workplace accidents.

From all this we can see that the study of education involves the study of learning and teaching in a variety of contexts. One approach to studying education in all these contexts is to try and understand it through the application of a number of different disciplines. Commonly, there are four disciplines that are said to contribute to our understanding of education: History, Sociology, Philosophy and Psychology. Each offers a different perspective on the factors which influence education: with history, it is the influence of the past and the stories we tell; with sociology, it is the influence of society and its structures; with philosophy, it is the influence of our fundamental beliefs and expectations. But what of psychology; what does psychology have to offer the study of education?

What is the psychology of education?

Psychology has been defined by countless people over the years. Similar to the definitions of education we have just reviewed, the specifics of these definitions of psychology may differ but there are some common elements. Most definitions would agree that psychology is (1) a scientific study (2) of human behaviour. Let us see if we can make sense of this definition and what it tells us about psychology.

First, what does it mean to define psychology as a science? Psychology's roots as a science go back to Wilhelm Wundt and his famous laboratory. Wundt and his colleagues pioneered the use of empirical methods to study mental phenomena such as reaction times, sensation and attention. There is no question that Wundt and his followers set the study of psychology on a scientific footing and it's true that the majority of contemporary psychological research uses the scientific method. The scientific method, known as empiricism, is a method used by all sciences to study the nature of reality. In a nutshell, empiricism involves proposing a theory based on the findings of previous research; coming up with a method to test that theory; gathering data through the use of structured observations and then drawing conclusions about the theory based on analysis and interpretation of that data.

To understand why it matters that psychology considers itself a science we need to consider both the advantages and limitations of empiricism. Among the advantages claimed by empiricism is that it provides us with a relatively objective method of testing the nature of reality. Empiricism requires all claims about the nature of reality to be supported by evidence. This avoids the tendency to simply follow tradition and blindly accept the beliefs of those who came before you. Scientists also use empiricism to reduce the impact that prejudice and preconceptions can have on our perceptions of the world around us. Empiricism requires scientists to predict what they will find before they gather any data. They are then required to systematically gather and record all the data relevant to the issue and then interpret that data using previously agreed methods of analysis. These safeguards make it harder for a scientist to simply ignore or overlook the evidence that doesn't confirm their theory. It's also harder to either intentionally or accidentally twist the facts to fit the theory or vice versa. Of course scientists are not perfect and care still needs to be taken to avoid preconceptions or selective interpretation of the data. Empiricism doesn't claim to make all scientists inhumanly perfect. It merely claims to offer an effective method to keep the impact of things like biases and preconceptions to a minimum and thereby to get a more accurate view of the nature of reality.

The statement that psychology is a science is widely accepted by the majority of psychologists, but not by all. There are some who feel that the scientific method is not suited to asking certain questions or finding certain answers. They propose that alongside the scientific method there are other methods of enquiry that psychologists could and should use. As a result, there are many psychologists using approaches such as qualitative research methods or ethnography to explore certain aspects of the nature of reality. (See Chapter 8 for a more detailed discussion of Piaget's use of ethnography to study cognitive development.) These psychologists might not consider themselves to be scientists, but they would almost certainly still agree to the other statement which is common across the many definitions of psychology, that psychology is primarily interested in the study of behaviour.

It might seem strange to define psychology as the study of behaviour and not to include the study of thoughts as well. This definition would seem to be contradicting the popular image of psychologists as being fascinated with 'getting inside your head' and wanting to know what you are thinking and feeling. Is 'thinking' just another type of behaviour then? Is that the 'behaviour' that psychology claims to be studying? In layman's terms, thoughts and behaviours are very different things and psychologists would agree, classifying behaviours as physical events which can be seen and measured, while thoughts are mental events which cannot be seen or measured directly. There are many in psychology who would argue that even if you were to scan someone's brain while they are thinking, all you would see is brain activity and not thought. (See Chapter 5 to learn about embodiment, a concept which suggests that 'thinking' may take place throughout the whole body and not just in the brain.)

But if you can't measure thoughts or feelings directly, then how can a psychologist study them? Empiricism requires data which is collected through observation. The solution is that psychology has developed numerous methods to study mental processes indirectly. We study the things that can't be seen, such as thoughts, by looking at the way they affect the things we can see, namely our behaviours. For this reason it makes sense to define psychology as the scientific study of behaviour; we study behaviour in order to draw conclusions about the nature of the mind as well as the structure and function of mental processes. Psychology is interested in the study of any kind of behaviour in any situation, but naturally within this general study of behaviour, areas of specialism have emerged. Sometimes the focus of the specialism is on a certain type of mental process or structure without necessarily being limited to any one context, such as those psychologists who study the function of memory or perception. Other times the focus will be on a specific context, such as those psychologists who seek to intensively study behaviour in the early years or in the workplace. One such specialism is the study of behaviour in education, known as 'educational psychology'.

Although it was first proposed more than a hundred years ago, using psychology to study education is a relatively new idea in terms of the history of education. One of the key figures in the story of how psychology was first introduced to the study of education is Edward Thorndike (1874–1949). As a follower of the behaviourist school of psychology, Thorndike had used scientific methods to study learning in animals and used his findings to draw conclusions about learning in humans as well. It's not hard to see how this led him to the conclusion that the study of education could benefit considerably from the application of scientific methods. It may seem obvious to us now, but it needs to be remembered that the idea to base the study of education on empirical evidence was revolutionary in its day. Before Thorndike there had been many writers who explored what we would now call educational psychology, but their insights and theories tended to based either on practical experience or philosophical reflection. Working with others in 1910 to establish the first journal in field of educational psychology, Thorndike sought to show how empirical research of education could provide insights and inspirations which would help to advance our understanding of education immeasurably. (See Chapter 9 to learn more about Thorndike's contributions to both the behaviourist model of learning and educational psychology as a whole.)

Although psychology has been involved in the study of education in this way for many years, it is still working hard to establish itself as a major influence on policy and practice in education. A lot of the public debates about education are still based primarily on personal beliefs or ideological models. The use of the scientific method in educational psychology means that it can make use of empirical evidence to contribute to those debates and influence pedagogical practice. It's not surprising then that psychology is a common element on most degree courses related to education. Of course, psychology is quite often only a very small part of these courses and in such situations it is usually being taught by staff with no background in psychology. This raises an interesting question as to how psychology is presented on those courses and what impression of psychology is created in the minds of the students.

How do students learn about psychology in the study of education?

One of the many interesting things about psychology as a subject is how broad its appeal appears to be. Mention that you are studying psychology to most people and the response you will so often hear is something along the lines of 'I did a bit of psychology in my course and it was really interesting' or 'I've always wanted to know more about psychology'. It's not hard to understand why the study of psychology might be an attractive proposition to so many. Psychology deals with human nature and human behaviour. It promises to help us understand ourselves and the world around us; in other words, it's something we can all relate to. It's relatively easy to find links and make connections between the concepts discussed in psychology and our everyday lives, both personal and professional. This potential for psychology to make connections with professional practice is very widespread and it's possible for psychology to have an application in the most unlikely of places. To take one example, even a structural engineer whose primary concern is with materials, forces and the physical world may well need to consider how people will use the things they design (or in some cases misuse them). This extremely broad potential for application may well be the reason for psychology cropping up in some small way within so many different university degree courses. From courses in accounting to zoology, it's very possible that at some point in their degree most students will be taught a little (or even a lot) that is drawn from the discipline of psychology.

This is especially true with courses that relate to education. The relevance of psychology in education is hard to miss. Education is an interpersonal process and so the psychology surrounding both the educator and the student is going to have a big impact on that process. Furthermore, important elements of the education process such as reading, writing, communicating, learning, memorising, problem-solving and so on are all areas of study in their own right within the discipline of psychology. For this reason it would be uncommon to find an education course that didn't include some elements of psychology. Of course it's not always the case that the elements of psychology included in the course are highlighted as 'psychology'. They may simply be presented as isolated theories which explain certain elements of human behaviour or thought. In such cases, the theories are presented without including any of the context within psychology that surrounds them, such as competing theories or later developments of the theory itself. This stripped down and somewhat simplistic presentation of psychology theory can be further exacerbated by the fact that many of the staff tasked with delivering 'a bit of psychology' within a non-psychology degree have little or no background or training in psychology.

And therein lies one of the key issues that this book hopes to tackle. If the psychology theories are presented in isolation and the person delivering the psychological content is not trained as a psychologist, then the way in which psychology is encountered can give a very misleading impression of how psychology works. Presented in isolation, with no context or links to the developments that preceded it or followed it, any psychology theory can appear arbitrary and absolutist. For a student to hear, 'Psychology says ...' can give the impression that there is only one view on this issue within the whole of psychology. Similarly, to hear 'Theory X states ...' can give the impression that the theory is claiming that all people are the same; that all of us do the same things for the same reasons and that this will never change. Impressions like these couldn't be further from the truth. Psychology is a science, and like all sciences the theories it proposes to explain the world are limited, contextual, conditional and evolving. To put it another way, there are no theories in psychology on which all psychologists agree, which are universally applicable or which are immune to being challenged or changed.

A typical example of how psychology can be misunderstood or misrepresented is the way that Piaget is often presented to students on education-related degree courses. Piaget's model of cognitive development is often held up as the 'definitive psychological explanation' of how children learn. But it is typically presented as a rigid, unvarying set of stages which all children must experience in the same way and in the same order. Not surprisingly, this 'straw man' version of Piaget and cognitive development in general doesn't match the experiences of the students either as learners or as educators, and so in their eyes it is quickly discredited. The fact that Piaget's model, despite being an important theory, is by no means the beginning and end of psychological research in this area often fails to get a mention, a victim in some cases of the limited time available to discuss this topic on the course. As such, students might never learn that Piaget's model has evolved, been challenged by competing theories and, as we will see in Chapter 8, that even Piaget himself didn't see children's learning in quite the rigid and simplistic terms habitually attributed to his model. Often these details are omitted because the staff member delivering the psychology content is unaware of them. There are no villains here, no one is deliberately trying to misrepresent psychology. More likely, it's an unfortunate and possibly inevitable side-effect of the limited space given to psychology in the degree course in question, and staff constrained by the limitations of their knowledge and experience in psychology.

This book, then, is aimed at both staff and students who already know a little psychology but who would like to learn more. In each chapter we discuss what you are likely to know or have heard about the area that the chapter is focusing on. We will then spend the remainder of the chapter trying to take you further; guiding you through some of the key developments and discoveries in that area made by researchers in psychology past and present. It's our intention that throughout each chapter, as well as introducing you to developments and how they have advanced our understanding of that area, we will also seek to link those developments back to education. This book is aimed at those who are interested in psychology for its ability to help us better understand and positively influence the process of education. We will be making a case for the relevance of the advances in psychological theory that we are discussing by showing you how they apply to education. It should be remembered though, that education is not limited to schools and classrooms. As such, we invite you to consider applications in a broad range of educational contexts which would include education in schools, but also education in the workplace, the community, the health system and many other places as well.

Overview of chapters

Starting with Chapter 2, Suzanne M. Egan provides an insight into both the structures and processes involved in memory, as well as discussing how memories of past experiences can be used to enhance future performance. The chapter begins by taking the reader through some of the key points and key theories in the long and interesting history of research on memory. This includes some of the earliest memory research which dates to the late 1800s but whose findings are still relevant to education today. The multi-store model by Atkinson and Shiffrin which brought us the concepts of short- and long-term memory will be explored, as will its evolution and refinement over the last five decades. Different types of memory will also be discussed, such as memory for meaningful personal events, facts and skills. The chapter concludes by discussing a number of methods by which memory can potentially be used and improved in an educational context. This includes reviewing mnemonic methods which produce a deeper processing of information to be learned, a consideration of the benefits of thinking about what could have happened rather than remembering what did happen (called 'counterfactual thinking'), and exploring the effects of mentally practising a physical skill. Research will show the potential learning benefits from each of these techniques for learners in a variety of contexts including pilots, prisoners, athletes and musicians, not forgetting ordinary students of course. Ultimately, this chapter aims to show that theories of memory provide a useful framework for understanding how people remember and think about the past, while also discussing the implications of these theories in a variety of educational contexts.

In Chapter 3, Chloe Yeh seeks to challenge some common beliefs regarding the nature of creativity, seen as an innate ability, relevant only to the arts and threatened or stifled by education. Instead, this chapter presents an image of creativity as psychology sees it: a set of cognitive processes, accessible to all and applicable to almost any problem or question, from profound issues whose impact is society-wide to personal concerns and challenges we all face in our day-today lives. The first section explores some foundational models of creativity such as the four-stage theory and the primary-secondary thinking process theory in order to share a basic understanding of the nature of creativity as the psychologist sees it. The second section discusses two under-lying factors, defocused attention and emotions, which may have a significant influence on creative thinking. Here we will learn that defocused (broadened) attention, which can be achieved through broadening perceptual attention or inducing positive emotions among other things, can lead to enhanced creativity. Having established the psychological perspective on creativity, the chapter will then seek to make a case for the role of education in enhancing an individual's creative potential. Thus, the final sections of the chapter explore both the challenges in nurturing creativity in education and the strategies, aimed at fostering creativity, which can be applied to a wide vari-ety of educational contexts. Ultimately, this chapter will show that with a better understanding of the nature of creativity and the factors that affect it, fostering creativity both can and should be a goal of any educator.

In Chapter 4, Lorna Bourke considers the central role of language within the context of literacy development and instruction programmes in school. The chapter initially considers the relationship between understanding vocabulary and the sound patterns within words which form the focus for much of children's learning in the early school years. Many people have contributed to key debates surrounding the content of this instruction and how it is assessed. Primarily centring on exploring the difference between analytic and synthetic phonics programmes, the chapter evaluates both approaches in the context of psychological theory and evidence. Psychological theories of reading and writing are reviewed; the contribution of cognitive processes, such as working memory, are considered; all in order to develop a fuller understanding of the interplay between the inner voice, self-regulation and phonics, as well as difficulties associated with creating structure and coherence in text-based writing. The chapter also considers how psychologists and educators recognise the challenges that some children face over and above the general developmental phases of master-ing literacy. Therefore the final part of the chapter discusses the main perspectives associated with understanding some of the complexity involved in diagnosing dyslexia. The perspectives link with biological, cognitive and behavioural explanations but also suggest the importance of recognising issues related to self-esteem, self-efficacy and motivation. Overall, the chapter urges the reader to determine the richness of accomplishment that occurs during literacy development and to cele-brate the joy of the mastering the various milestones that it involves.

In Chapter 5, Marek McGann steps back to take in some of the big picture of the science of psychology: how our general understanding of the nature of the mind has been revolutionised in the past, and may be in the throes of a new revolution now. Looking briefly at some historical context, the chapter explores how a shift in emphasis away from studying immediate physical behaviour led to a conceptualisation of the mind as a computational system, a view that has shaped decades of psychological research and is still dominant in the discipline today. However, we will also see that research within the inter-disciplinary field of 'Cognitive Science' (which draws on evidence from psychology, philosophy, neuroscience, computer science, robotics, anthropology, and more) is now suggesting that the pendulum has swung too far. It is time, once again, to pay a little more attention to bodily actions, and the physical world, in order to understand cognition and learning. This realisation is typically captured under the rubric of 'embodiment'. The chapter out-lines research which indicates that our emotional, visceral, bodily responses play a role in the way we make decisions, as well as how the gestures we make while explaining things can affect not only how other people understand what we're talking about, but change how we understand it ourselves. Also explored are findings indicating that apparently abstract cognitive skills, such as reading or scientific thinking, can be significantly affected by physical props or the arrangement of illustrations. Whether psychology will ever complete a paradigm shift away from computational thinking, toward some form of embodied perspective, remains to be seen, but this chapter provides a point of entry into the complex and intriguing literature of bodies.

In Chapter 6, Jim Stack widens the debate around children's education by critically assessing how children make sense of their social worlds. The chapter introduces the term 'social understanding' and then provides an overview of the different components that make up this construct and the various ways that it could be used by children in educational settings. The chapter then investigates the way in which this understanding of others appears compromised in children with autism. Moving outside the confines of the school, the chapter explores the home environment and the impact that quality of interactions with parents, siblings, peers and friends can have on children's emerging social understanding. These findings are important as they provide a wider lens through which educators can make sense of children's engagements with others in educational settings. Following this, the chapter reviews a number of positive and negative ways in which social understanding can be used in social situations. Finally, an overview of how social understanding can be supported and enhanced within school settings, particularly during early periods of development, is presented. Overall, the chapter is designed to inform the reader as to the importance to education of children's understanding of their social worlds.

In Chapter 7, Cathal Ó Siochrú critically evaluates the common belief that there are fundamental differences between the two genders in terms of abilities, personality and behaviour. As we will see later on in the chapter, these beliefs extend into the realm of education where there are different expectations directed at the two main genders in terms of their likely behaviours and even those subjects at which they will excel. The impact of these assumptions on the men and women in our education system is real, but are differences themselves real? This chapter draws on key studies and reviews of the research on gender differences to show that our gender identity is a combination of biological and social factors, all of which have an impact both on our gender and our education. The impact of biological differences is evaluated, including evidence for the impact of hormonal differences and differences between the genders in terms of brain structures. The social element of gender identity is explored through key concepts including gender roles, social learning and gender schemas. The picture that emerges from this review of the research is an image of gender differences as more learned than innate. We see how our experiences in the education system and the expectations of our educators are a major factor in shaping and reinforcing these gender identities. We also see how the relationship between gender and education may well be reciprocal, with the beliefs of parents and teachers regarding gender leading to gender differences in educational performance and the emergence of 'gendered' subjects. Ultimately, this chapter aims to show that, despite a considerable amount of time and effort spent searching for gender differences, there are relatively few strong differences between the genders in either thought or behaviour. Furthermore, those differences that have been found appear to be learned through socialisation and the education system itself. This places an important responsibility on educators to better understand their role in this process.

In Chapter 8, Claire Lloyd rediscovers Piaget's theory of cognitive development. This chapter shows that the popular representation of Piaget's theory, the widely cited and often heavily criticised 'stage theory' found in most textbooks, is actually a poor representation of his theory based on misconceptions about his work. Instead, this chapter presents a fresh perspective framed around two different, but related, strands of Piaget's body of work. The first strand concerns Piaget's study of the nature of knowledge development, also known as his 'epistemological project'. The chapter explores Piaget's belief that children co-ordinate their actions at progressively more complex levels through a series of internally related operative structures. The chapter reviews two such operative structures: 'action-schemes', the most basic type of operative structures which gives rise to practical knowledge; and 'operational structures, a more sophisticated operative structure involved in deductive reasoning. The development of these operative structures through the cognitive mechanisms of equilibrium, equilibration, assimilation and accommodation is also considered. The second strand concerns Piaget's approach to the study of children, critically evaluating the methods he used to carry out his research. The chapter questions the validity of critiques of Piaget's methodology; couched in assumptions originating in the positivist tradition, they take the 'view from without' – separating his method from its epistemological grounding. Instead, the chapter reconsiders Piaget's method from a qualitative perspective, characterising his approach as 'ethnographic' given his use of thick descriptions of children's actions to reveal the underlying cognitive structures of their thoughts. Ultimately this chapter seeks to demonstrate how Piaget's interpretive approach, which is both rigorous and systematic, can provide enduring insights into the development of knowledge.

In Chapter 9, Cathal Ó Siochrú explores the behaviourist perspective on learning, investigating what lies beyond the image best known to most educators: 'black box' theories which fail to acknowledge any mental processes and whose relevance is mainly in the areas of behaviour management and maintaining discipline. This chapter takes a fresh look at well-known early behaviourists like Skinner and Watson, while also considering some who are less well known but still influential, such as Edward Thorndike. We will see how the pursuit of functionalism and rejection of structuralism by some key figures came to define the early behaviourist model, but that this view was not shared by all early behaviourists or those that came after them. Following on from this, the chapter explores developments of the behaviourist model of learning, ranging from the well-regarded social learning and self-efficacy theories of Albert Bandura, to less widely known but nonetheless significant work done by Kazdin on token economies, or Tomasello and Carpenter's work on intentionality and behaviour. These developments show that behaviourism has grown beyond its strict functionalist origins and reintroduced mental concepts like self-efficacy in order to broaden the scope of behaviourism's relevance to education. Finally, the chapter considers some examples of recent research on educational practices and important social issues which draw on the behaviourist model of learning to achieve their insights, such as 'token economies', 'gamification' or the effects of videogames on children's behaviour. Ultimately, this chapter aims to show that the behaviourist model of learning is an applied model, a sophisticated and flexible tool which can help us to understand and positively influence many kinds of learning in a wide range of educational contexts.

In Chapter 10, Catherine O'Connell presents the socio-cultural viewpoint on learning, beginning with one of the best known theorists in the area, Lev Vygotsky. Although more widely known than many other socio-cultural theorists, Vygotsky is often only presented in brief and only as a counterpoint to Piaget. The chapter explores Vygotsky in full, presenting him as a fully fleshed-out theorist with his own distinct view on the nature of both cognition and learning. In addition to

Vygotsky, the chapter also introduces some contemporary socio-cultural theories of cognitive development. Among those considered is the work of Engeström and his collaborators, who build upon the Vygotskian idea that both cognition and learning are collective endeavours; a field of research they refer to as 'activity systems theory'. These theorists help us to see learning as being shaped by the divisions of labour and shared objectives of a learning community, which need to be considered first if we wish to then understand the educational behaviours and goals of an individual within that community. The chapter also explores the work of Holland, Lachicotte, Skinner and Cain, who focus on the impact of different social contexts of education through the concept of 'figured worlds'. Their theories explore the way that cultural practices and norms of any social group can both enable and constrain learning activity and can shape learner identities. Ultimately this chapter seeks to show us that our cognition, our thinking, is a social phenomenon which is shared among those we know.

It is our ultimate aim that by the end of this book you will have a fresh perspective, not just on the aspects of education we have discussed but also on the wider contribution that psychology can make to education. Furthermore, we hope that by the end of any of the chapters in this book you will feel both inspired and able to engage in self-directed further study into the ever-evolving body of psychological research in that area. Or to put it another way, it is our ambition that this book will help you to take a big step forward in your studies into the psychology of education and, having taken that step with you, we hope it won't be your last.

References

Gerrig, R.J., Zimbardo, P., Svartdal, F., Brennen, T., Donaldson, R. and Archer, T. (2012) *Psychology and life.* 1st edn. Harlow: Pearson Education.
Martin, G.N., Carlson, N.R. and Buskist, W. (2013) *Psychology.* 5th edn. Harlow: Pearson Education.
Peters, R.S. (1966) *Ethics and education.* London: Allen & Unwin.

Part I

Processes: an exploration of key learning processes

2 Memory and learning

How we learn by remembering what happened and imagining what could have happened

Suzanne M. Egan

Introduction

If you mention the word 'memory' most people will exclaim some anecdotal 'fact' about their own or someone else's memory ability. Declarations about memory are common, such as 'I have a great memory for faces but not for names', 'my husband is so forgetful', 'I remember the names of all my teachers in school but not what I did last Wednesday' or 'everyone's memory gets worse as they get older'. Beliefs about the usefulness of memory also crop up in our folk beliefs about learning, such as the belief that reflecting on past successes and failures is a good way to learn from them, or that we shouldn't waste time daydreaming about what might have been. But are any of these folk beliefs about memory accurate? How does the anecdotal picture we have of memory, and its role in learning, compare to the psychological models of memory resulting from many years of research in this field?

The goal of this chapter is to introduce you to the psychological research and theories of memory and imagination. We'll begin by considering what memory is, why it is important and discussing some findings from early studies on memory. Following that we'll move on to describe some of the structures and processes of memory and different theoretical approaches to it. In the final section, we'll discuss some practical applications of memory research that may be useful in a variety of educational settings. Ultimately, we'll seek to identify ways we can use memory research, and our memories of past experiences, to help ourselves and others to improve their memory and future learning.

Why is memory important?

'Without memory, we could never learn from our experience and would operate aimlessly, without plans or goals. Motor skills and language ability would be lost. Even the sense of personal identity we all possess would be gone' (Smith and Kosslyn, 2007: 193). This quote highlights the importance of memory and some of the many everyday behaviours and abilities it underlies. Without memory, we wouldn't be able to recognise any of our family or friends, or even ourselves. We couldn't have conversations if we couldn't remember what someone just said to us, or remember the meaning of the words they uttered. We wouldn't have a memory for how to drive, what a screwdriver is for or that lions are dangerous creatures. Life would be very difficult without memory, and so our understanding of the way in which memory operates has relevance for almost all aspects of our lives, including our education.

Contemporary research has identified four factors that are important in memory function; these are the encoding process for memories, the retrieval process for memories, the type of event or information involved in the memory and the person trying to remember it (Roediger, 2008). How well memories are maintained and stored over time depends on all of these factors. Furthermore, individual differences, such as age, memory disorders, expertise and existing knowledge base, all influence these memory related factors. For example, how much attention we pay in the first place to the information we are trying remember affects how we encode (i.e. memorise) the incoming information, and how we try to retrieve it (see box below). However, all of these insights into memory have only emerged after many years of research into memory, the way it is structured and the way it operates. To understand our current views on memory it is useful to first consider how those views have evolved over the course of the long history of research in the area.

Research focus: the importance of context in memory

The context in which we learn information is one important factor in memory and recall. The context can either be the external physical environment or our internal state. Both of these contexts have been shown to have an effect on our memory ability. For example, Godden and Baddeley (1975) looked at the impact of external context on the memory ability of deep-sea divers using a list of 40 words to be learned by the divers either underwater or on land. They discovered that recall of the word list was better when the environment in which the divers had to recall the words was the same as the environment in which they had learned the words (i.e. if they learned the words on land, recall was better if they recalled the words on land rather than underwater, and vice versa).

This effect also occurs for internal states such as mood, physiological arousal and how much alcohol an individual has drunk (e.g. Miles and Hardman, 1998). These findings may be worth bearing in mind for students studying for exams. Where possible both the external and internal context of learning should be as similar as possible to the external and internal context in which the exam will take place in order to account for the effect of context. If this is not possible, however, Smith and Vela (2001), in a review of context-dependent memory research, note that recalling the context when trying to recall a memory can reduce the effect of context.

Early memory studies

Humans have long been interested in understanding the nature of memory. Dating back to the time of Aristotle, memory was principally the interest of philosophers until the discipline of psychology developed in the nineteenth century and a more systematic experimental approach to studying it was undertaken. Early key studies on memory, and theoretical ideas relating to it, sowed the seeds for the thriving field of memory research that exists today.

One of the first memory researchers was Herman Ebbinghaus, a German philosopher who conducted experiments on his own memory in the 1880s. In order to systematically test his memory he devised lists of nonsense three-letter consonant-vowel-consonant words such as 'dax', 'zug' and 'teh' and set himself a challenge of remembering them under different conditions.

Ebbinghaus (1885/1913) found that the sharpest decline in the number of words he could correctly recall occurred in the first few hours after he learned the material. After that, the rate of
decline decreased and levelled off. While Ebbinghaus was the only participant in his own experi-
ment, his discovery of this exponential reduction in the amount of material recalled, known as the
forgetting curve, was an important contribution to the psychology of memory and a finding that
has stood the test of time. Much of what you attempt to learn fades quite rapidly and so additional
learning sessions are usually necessary in order to retain information over the long term.

A few years after Ebbinghaus' discovery of the forgetting curve, an American psychologist, William James (1890) postulated that there were at least two types of memory, which he called primary memory and secondary memory. Primary memory is material that is currently in
consciousness, what we are thinking about at this moment. In contrast, secondary memory contains material that can be recalled to consciousness if required. This distinction between these
different aspects of memory laid the foundations for later memory research and theories. One of
the dominant theoretical approaches in memory in the last few decades, the Multi-Store Model
(Atkinson and Shiffrin, 1968), drew on the work of James. We will return to this approach later in
the chapter.

Another early memory researcher, an Englishman named Frederick Bartlett, took a different
approach to studying memory. Rather than focusing on meaningless materials such as nonsense
syllables like Ebbinghaus, or on different types of memory like James, he thought it was important
to examine how we remember complex materials. Bartlett (1932) asked people to recall a short
tale called 'War of the Ghosts' and was particularly interested in the types of mistakes that people
included in their memories of the tale, as well as seeing which bits of the tale they had forgotten.
He found that where parts of the tale may have been difficult for people to understand, the participants' memory of the tale omitted these parts or contained altered details, so that those parts
now made more sense to the participants given their existing knowledge. It seemed that people
were remembering the general gist of the story they had heard, rather than every exact detail.
Bartlett called these representations 'schemas'. (See Chapter 7 for a discussion of gender schemas.) Schemas are a useful mental framework to have because they allow us to recall complex
things without having to remember every detail which could overwhelm our memory. However, as
Bartlett showed, schemas can also lead to errors in memory.

In 1960, George Sperling began to conduct experiments on visual memory. He presented participants with a grid of letters for less than one second and then asked them to recall as many
letters as they could. Even though the letters were only flashed very briefly before the participant
(using a piece of equipment called a tachyscope) it seemed that the participants had a brief visual
memory trace of the full grid of letters. This memory trace allowed them to recall about three or four
letters of the 12 or 16 presented, before the memory trace faded. Interestingly, when participants
were asked to report one specific part of the grid and were told which row of letters to report
immediately after they were flashed up, they could recall whichever row had been chosen with a
high level of accuracy. This finding suggested that they initially had a memory trace of all of the
letters that were presented, but that the trace faded so rapidly that by the time they had reported
one line of the grid, the memory for the others had already faded.

In conclusion, one of the principal things that this early memory research highlighted was that
memory is a complex phenomenon. The findings showed that there seemed to be a number of
different types of memory, such as the very brief retention of information as discovered by

Sperling (1960) but also longer-term memory for past events and knowledge that could be called to mind whenever needed, as described by James (1890). Additionally, the amount of information we can recall and the errors we make in recalling it might depend on a number of factors. These factors, as Ebbinghaus and Bartlett showed, include the content of the information we are recalling, how well it fits in with our schemas or existing knowledge, and the length of time between the point when we learn the information and the point when we are trying to recall it. In the next section we describe how some of the findings from these studies helped to shape later theories and research on memory.

Memory structures and processes

As we saw, early psychological research on memory suggested that rather than one global memory system there are many different memory structures and processes responsible for different types of memories. Memory research in recent decades has focused on discovering and defining the extent of these different memory systems and on exploring the capabilities and limits of each system. This is a dominant approach in the psychological study of memory and one which we examine in detail in this section.

The Multi-Store Model of Memory

In 1968 Atkinson and Shiffrin proposed the Multi-Store Model of Memory, building on earlier memory research by William James (1890) and combining it with advances of the time in cognitive psychology and computing. (See Chapter 5 for a critique of the limitations of the computing or 'information processing' model for thought.) In the multi-store model, drawing on computing language, information is thought to enter into memory by a process known as 'encoding' and information can then be later 'retrieved' when necessary. Atkinson and Shiffrin suggested that there are three memory stores, each with its own characteristics: sensory memory, short-term memory and long-term memory. Over the last few decades, the characteristics of these different stores and the processes by which they operate have been revised and refined in the face of new evidence and they have inspired other approaches to memory beyond the multi-store model itself.

Sensory memory

Drawing on Sperling's (1960) work, Atkinson and Shiffrin (1968) proposed that all environmental stimuli are first processed by sensory memory. Have you ever waved a sparkler in a dark room and seen the apparent trail of light it briefly leaves in its wake? This is your Iconic Memory in action, the sensory store for visual information that Sperling discovered, recording the passage of the sparkler from one location to another and all points in between. This effect with the sparkler lasts only for a moment because information is held only briefly in sensory memory before it begins to fade (Baddeley et al., 2015).

Similarly, have you ever asked someone to repeat themselves only to realise that despite not really listening to them the first time around you have still somehow managed to remember what they said? This is your Echoic Memory (Neisser, 1967) in action. It is the sensory store for auditory information and it allows us to remember any auditory information as long as we access it within a couple of seconds. According to Atkinson and Shiffrin (1968) there is a separate store for each of our senses to process all incoming information, although the stores for our other senses have been researched far less than those for incoming auditory and visual stimuli. No matter which sensory store it is in, sensory memory fades quickly unless it is attended to and processed further by short-term memory.

Short-term memory

Short-term memory is a memory store which is limited in both the duration and capacity of what it can retain. Similar to James' (1890) notion of primary memory, short-term memory contains only what we are thinking about or processing at the moment. Information that enters short-term memory is only retained for about 18 seconds before it fades (Peterson and Peterson, 1959).

In addition to a limited duration, short-term memory also appears to have a limited capacity for the information it can hold. Atkinson and Shiffrin (1968) proposed that the amount of information that can be retained in this store is restricted to about seven chunks (Miller, 1956). A chunk is a unit of meaningful information which might be a single digit, the name of a television show, an entire sentence or even larger. In fact, the size of a chunk can vary from person to person depending on their existing knowledge and how related the information is that they are trying to store. Information that is related to a single theme or concept may end up as chunk but the exact limits are flexible. However, even allowing for this rule, the variability in the size of different chunks raises interesting questions about what the upper storage limit of short-term memory really is. Even the number of chunks we can store is not universally agreed upon. Although Miller reported in 1956 that we could remember seven chunks, plus or minus two chunks, more recent research has questioned this idea (e.g. Ma *et al.*, 2014) and suggested a lower number of chunks, such as four or fewer, may be more realistic (Cowan, 2001).

Whatever the ultimate capacity of short-term memory might be, the life span of information in that store is still numbered in seconds. However, if the information is repeated, rehearsed or focused on before it fades (e.g. saying a phone number over and over) it can be retained for longer or may even move into the final store in Atkinson and Shiffrin's model: long-term memory.

Long-term memory

The final memory store proposed by Atkinson and Shiffrin (1968), long-term memory, is apparently unlimited in both capacity and duration, similar to James' (1890) notion of secondary memory. The variety and amount of information we can retain in long-term memory is quite remarkable. We can remember things such as the name of our childhood music teacher, where we went on holidays last summer, how to cycle a bike, or that Rome is the capital city of Italy. These memories are often retained for many years or even for a lifetime.

So why then do we forget some things and not others in long-term memory? Or remember some things for a lifetime but forget others after a few years? The answers to these questions are not fully understood but there are some possible explanations, and it may be that more than one mechanism accounts for different types of forgetting. One possibility is that the information we are trying to remember was not encoded properly in our long-term memory in the first place. Perhaps we were not paying as much attention to something as we should have been so the encoding was not complete. Another reason for forgetting may simply be the passage of time where the memory trace gradually becomes weaker and weaker until the memory can no longer be recalled. This is called 'trace decay' (e.g. see Baddeley *et al.*, 2015).

Another possible reason for forgetting is due to the number of experiences we have every day. It seems we forget some things because other memories may interfere with our recall ability. For example, have you ever tried to type in your current password only to find you've typed in your old one instead? When older memories interfere with recalling newer memories this is called 'proactive interference' (Underwood, 1957). In contrast, 'retroactive interference' is when newer memories interfere with recalling older memories (Baddeley and Hitch, 1977). You can probably remember what you had for dinner yesterday, but remembering what you had for dinner a week ago, a month ago or a year ago may be more difficult because there have been quite a few meals in the intervening period.

Further developments

The multi-store model was very effective in bringing together previous memory research and theories into a single coherent model, but it was not without its critics. While evidence existed for a basic distinction between the three memory stores (Atkinson and Shiffrin, 1968) chief among the criticisms were that it oversimplified the memory stores and the processes involved in them (Baddeley and Hitch, 1974). Research over the last 50 years has focused on examining the stores in more detail, making revisions to them or devising alternative theoretical approaches (Baddeley, 2012).

Reflections

Why is it important that theories are regularly tested? Why is it necessary to keep up to date with theoretical developments in your field and the latest research findings?

Working memory

One criticism of the multi-store model related to the short-term memory store. It soon became apparent that it did not operate as the unitary or passive store that Atkinson and Shiffrin had suggested. Baddeley and Hitch (1974) proposed a more complex model of short-term memory, called working memory, consisting of three components: the phonological loop, the visuo-spatial sketchpad and the central executive. A fourth component was later added: the episodic buffer (Baddeley, 2000).

One of the major changes that the working memory model proposed, which contrasted with the image of short-term memory that we have from the multi-store model, was a more active role for short-term memory. The working memory model posited that we use short-term memory as our 'workshop' when performing complex tasks (anything from performing mental arithmetic to following a recipe for chocolate chip cookies). In tasks like these, you need to do more than just store and rehearse information in your short-term memory. You need to keep track of what you have already completed on the task thus far (such as noting that you've already added the water to the flour), as well as monitoring progress towards the outcome of the current step (making cookie dough), while also preparing to move on the next step (adding chocolate chips) once the current step is finished. It's this ability to juggle all these bits of information, acting on some of them, keeping track of others, all while planning the next steps, that gave short-term memory its new name of 'working' memory.

As well as a fresh perspective on what we do with information located in working memory, Baddeley and Hitch proposed that we store and manipulate information differently at this stage depending on whether it is auditory or visual information. It is here that we encounter some of working memory's new structures, namely the visuo-spatial sketchpad and the phonological loop.

The phonological loop

The phonological loop is basically a type of auditory short-term memory within the working memory model. It briefly retains sequences of speech-based sounds and other acoustic stimuli. It seems that the phonological loop is important in both native- and second language acquisition (Gathercole and Baddeley, 1990; Nicolay and Poncelet, 2013). It assists with learning vocabulary, language comprehension and skills like reading. In addition to supporting language skills the phonological loop may also be important in action control (see box below), particularly in performing an action which requires a set of sub-vocal instructions to keep us on track. For example, when learning to drive a car we may sub-vocalise the steps required to start the vehicle in our head without actually saying them out loud: first check the car is in neutral, then start the engine, check the mirrors and so on. The phonological loop is an important component of working memory that plays a role in many aspects of learning.

Research focus: attention, task performance and the phonological loop

Studies have shown that where a task involves switching attention, any disruption to the phonological loop (such as requiring people to repeat a word over-and-over out loud) slows down performance. The reason for this is that the disruption makes it harder for them to store sub-vocal instructions on their phonological loop. Since they can no longer use the loop, they need to stop and remind themselves what the next step is.

This finding may have implications in educational contexts. If a learner is engaged in a complex task and using sub-vocalised instructions to keep themselves on track (e.g. learning to drive or attempting long division), additional auditory information could disrupt their learning. Anything from background noise, to the teacher asking questions of the learner during the task or stating additional instructions may interfere with the student's ability to use the phonological loop to process the sub-vocalised instructions (e.g. Baddeley *et al.*, 2001; Saeke *et al.*, 2013).

The visuo-spatial sketch pad

Baddeley and Hitch (1974) proposed that visual and spatial information is processed by a component of working memory called the visuo-spatial sketch pad. Our visual and spatial environments are rather complex. For example, look around the room you are in at the moment. You may see different types of furniture, items hanging on walls, things sitting on shelves, someone moving. Out the window there may be trees blowing in the wind or birds flying in the sky. Although we have a sense of smoothly scanning our visual environments, our eyes make discreet movements (little jumps called 'saccades') to focus on one part of a visual scene and then another part. Our visual short-term memory, the visuo-spatial sketchpad, integrates these different fragments to give us a sense of one whole, unified and seamless visual memory of our environment.

There are two sub-components of the visuo-spatial sketch pad: the visual cache and the inner scribe (Logie, 1995). The visual cache stores information about the colour and form of objects (i.e. 'what' information). The inner scribe processes movement and spatial information (i.e. 'where' information). Evidence that 'what' and 'where' information in our visual environments is processed separately comes from psychological experiments in laboratory settings (e.g. Smith and Jonides, 1997; Klauer and Zhao, 2004), neuroscience (e.g. Zimmer, 2008) and from patients with damage to one aspect of the visuo-spatial sketch pad but not the other (e.g. patient LE, Wilson *et al.*, 1999).

The knowledge that 'what' and 'where' information is processed separately can help us better understand some features of our memory. In memory that is functioning normally, information can still get lost and so it's possible we might lose one part of the 'what' and 'where' memory information for an object in our environment but retain the other. Thus, we may be able to remember seeing a book we needed just a minute ago in our messy study area but not recall where in the jumble of papers, books and other objects that we saw it.

This differentiation between 'what' and 'where' information is just one example of the complexity of the structures within working memory. Given the complexity of this new model, Baddeley and Hitch proposed that more was needed in the model than just a greater variety of stores and detailed a part of the model whose role was to manage all these stores and the information they contained called the 'central executive'.

Central executive

The central executive is the most versatile and important component of working memory and is involved in most complex tasks. It does not store information itself but directs attention to the other components as required and is the central controller of working memory. Basically, it coordinates all of the information coming into, and being manipulated by, working memory. It consists of various separate but related processes in order to do this. Miyake *et al.* (2000) suggested these processes involve an inhibition function to resist distraction, a shifting function to switch between tasks and an updating function to monitor the contents of working memory, adding or deleting content as necessary. Baddeley (2012) also speculated that the central executive processes include focusing attention on one task, dividing attention between two tasks, switching attention from one task to another and drawing useful information from long-term memory. These different types of executive functions are important in many of our daily activities and in educational settings (e.g. focusing attention on a teacher, dividing attention between a visual presentation and making notes on it, avoiding distraction from background noise).

This structure, with the central executive managing both the phonological loop and visuo-spatial sketchpad, represented the core of the original working memory model. While this original version of the model was considered an important development in our understanding of memory, working memory had its critics. In order to address these criticisms Baddeley and others are continually reviewing and occasionally revising the model to address its limitations. This is a common practice for all scientific theories and models. Indeed, it is one of the foundations of the scientific method that limitations in theories are addressed through such additions and revisions. One such example of an important revision to the working memory model was the addition of the episodic buffer.

Episodic buffer

The episodic buffer was a later addition to the working memory model (Baddeley, 2000) which addressed a limitation of the original model, namely that the original model was unable to account for the apparent use of long-term memories in working memory processes. An example of this is the fact that our recall for a set of words is much greater when those words are presented in a coherent sentence than as a list. With a sentence, we can recall up to 15 words correctly but for a list of unrelated words our recall is typically only five or six words (Brener, 1940). One explanation is that when remembering the words in a sentence we remember them in meaningful phrases or 'chunks' (e.g. [The man with the brown hair] [went to the shop] [and bought a carton of milk] [and a loaf of bread]). We can use the rules of grammar to break down a sentence into phrases in this way, but the rules of grammar reside within long-term memory. In order to make use of them for recall tasks such as this, they need to be available to working memory.

The original working memory model did not include a way that long-term memories might be used in working memory. The episodic buffer is hypothesised to be used to do this (Baddeley, 2012). However, it is a relatively recent addition to working memory and more research is needed to determine its exact functions and relationships with the other components.

Reflections

Do you think working memory is a useful model for educators to be aware of? How might knowledge of the working memory model prove beneficial in an educational context?

Overall, the working memory model accounts for many psychological findings and has contributed greatly to our understanding of short-term memory. However, research on working memory and its components is ongoing. It may need additional components, interactions between components may need to be better specified or an entirely different approach to working memory may be adopted in the future (Baddeley *et al.*, 2015).

It is worth noting, though, that short-term memory is not the only aspect of the original multi-store model that has undergone refinement and revision as researchers discover new findings related to its structure and function. The same is true of long-term memory, and in the next section we explore the proposal that there are different long-term memory systems for memories of different types of experience.

Long-term memory systems

Atkinson and Shiffrin (1968) originally proposed that long-term memory was a single system, like a storage chest in which all types of memories were stored together. However, evidence emerged that in fact long-term memory may be divided into a number of sub-systems for different types of memories. One source of evidence for the refinement of the long-term memory store comes from neuroimaging studies. These studies show that different parts of the brain are active when healthy adults recall different types of memories or use different memory processes (e.g. Henke, 2010). Another source of evidence for different types of long-term memory comes from patients with amnesia, which we discuss in more detail below.

Amnesia and long-term memory

Henry Molaison (known as patient HM prior to his death in 2008) suffered from severe epilepsy since childhood. He underwent surgery in 1953 to improve his condition. This involved the removal of part of his brain, including a part called the hippocampus, which is now known to play an important role in memory (Milner, 1962). The effect on HM's memory was devastating. After the surgery, and for the remainder of his life, he was incapable of retaining new information such as what he had for dinner yesterday, the name of a new doctor he met or even the fact that he had met a new doctor; a condition known as anterograde amnesia.

However, it seemed that he retained some ability to learn and remember new physical skills, such as drawing objects only seen in reflection, despite not remembering the sessions where he practised these skills. He also retained a good memory of events occurring before the surgery took place. These different effects of the surgery on different aspects of long-term memory seemed to indicate that not all aspects of long-term memory are part of one unitary system or stored in one location in the brain.

Findings from amnesia patients such as HM suggest that different types of memory may be stored in different systems. Squire (1992) later labelled the form of memory that was disrupted by HM's surgery as explicit memory (or declarative memory) because it involves explicitly recalling events or facts that you have experienced or learned. However, HM's case reveals that another type of memory exists that may be classified as implicit (or non-declarative) memory. This type of memory often involves a physical skill that is acquired through practice and is sometimes called procedural memory. It can be seen as 'implicit' because although you remember the skill you don't consciously bring to mind the events connected to learning that skill every time you use it.

Other researchers have also made a distinction between different types of implicit and explicit memories. For example, Tulving (1972) highlighted the difference between memories for events and episodes in a person's life (e.g. remembering what you had for breakfast this morning, your first kiss or where you went on holiday last summer) in contrast to memories for knowing abstract or academic facts or pieces of information (e.g. Paris is the capital of France, sugar is sweet, a chair is for sitting on). He called these different types of memory 'episodic' and 'semantic' long-term memory respectively. Clive Wearing, another patient with severe amnesia, similarly displays differential loss of different types of memory. He has little episodic memory of his life prior to the onset of his amnesia but his procedural memory of how to play the piano or conduct a choir are undiminished, and he still retains semantic knowledge. Patients such as Henry Molaison and Clive Wearing illustrate that when it comes to long-term memory it seems that we have multiple systems.

In this section, we have explored some different perspectives on memory, in particular the multi-store model, which built on earlier memory research and served as the foundation of so much that followed it. We've also investigated how evidence which indicated that our short-term and long-term memory are not single systems and so led to the conception of working memory and other developments of the multi-store model.

Although the multi-store model and its descendants are the dominant models for memory in psychological research on this area today, it is worth noting that radically different approaches to the study of memory also exist within psychology. Not all models of memory examine memory from the perspective of different types of memory stores and subcomponents. For example, neuroanatomical perspectives draw on advances in brain imaging techniques which emphasise the brain structures or processes involved in memory (e.g. Henke, 2010; Cabeza and Moscovitch, 2013). Other approaches, such as embodied perspectives, do not view memory as stored information in different systems and instead emphasise changes in skilled behaviour (Glenberg, 1997). (See Chapter 8 for more detail on the 'embodied' perspective.)

Irrespective of how it is modelled, one of the driving forces behind the study of memory is the desire to use our understanding of memory to improve our memory performance. In the next section, we look at how we can improve our memory and future performance on learning tasks by using research on memory and imagination in applied settings.

Using and improving memory

As we have seen, our memory ability is essential to our daily lives. While memory theorists have uncovered much regarding the structures and processes of memory, it is clear that understanding memory is an ongoing and complex challenge. But what about improving our memory? Can we use memory research to help us remember more information for longer and recall it more accurately? Furthermore, is there any way that reviewing of past memories can be used to improve future performance?

In this section, we consider some methods that can aid in the encoding and retrieval of semantic memories (knowledge about the world), and discuss how existing episodic and procedural memories (memories of our experiences and skills) can be used by our imaginations to improve future performance.

Improving semantic memory

Depth of processing

In the previous section we mentioned that some of the information stored in working memory will eventually end up in long-term memory, but we didn't consider how this happens or what factors make it more or less likely to happen. A number of researchers have explored the processes by which information is transferred from short-term to long-term memory. For example, Craik and Lockhart (1972) suggested that the level of processing of the information was important in determining whether the information faded from short-term memory or was transferred to long-term memory.

Information can be processed at a superficial level for surface meaning or at a deeper level for semantic meaning. For example, when trying to learn a list of words, or vocabulary for a second language, one method is to sound out the words or repeat them over and over. Another way to learn them, however, is to process them more deeply. This might involve thinking about the meaning of the words, how the words relate to each other, whether they could be put into a story, or how they can be organised within existing knowledge or within a schema. What a number of studies on memory have found is that the deeper information is processed the more likely it is to be transferred to, and retained in, long-term memory (e.g. Craik and Tulving, 1975; Roediger, 2008).

In an example of these principles in action, Chase and Ericsson (1982) reported that a student, who was a keen runner, was able to increase his digit span through training to recall long series of digits by linking them to his existing extensive knowledge of running times. He was able to recall more information than he might otherwise by drawing meaning from a random sequence of digits, processing it more deeply, and linking it to existing long-term knowledge and memories. Noice (1992) found that actors use a similar technique. The actor would attempt to achieve a deeper understanding of her character's beliefs and motivations in order to help her remember why that character would choose those exact words to express themselves. Elaboration of the script in this way enabled retention of the words so that they could be recalled often for many months afterwards (Schmidt *et al.*, 2002).

Many techniques commonly used to improve memory, called 'mnemonics', rely on some form of elaboration of the material in order to increase the depth of processing. This in turn increases the connection of the new knowledge to existing knowledge already stored in long-term memory. Often these techniques involve visual imagery, or making explicit links between what is known already and what is to be learned.

Research focus: three methods to improve your semantic memory

One method, called 'the method of loci', is based on visual imagery. First, the learner recalls a set of connected places that they are already very familiar with. For example, this might be the rooms in your home, the route you take to college or work every day, or even a special memory palace you have thought of specifically for this purpose. You then imagine placing items to be remembered at different locations in your home. In order to later recall the items you mentally walk through your home, noting the items as you go. Studies have shown that it is a very effective memory technique both for lists of items (Bower, 1973) and for longer passages of text (De Beni *et al.*, 1997).

A second, similar technique is 'the pegword system'. This allows people to remember a list of up to ten items in the correct order by associating a rhyming pegword with a number, such as bun for 1, shoe for 2, tree for 3 and so on. By picturing the pegwords with the items to be recalled (e.g., a cabbage inside a shoe or eggs growing on a tree) the information has been elaborated upon and recall improves. This technique has been shown to be as effective as the method of loci (Wang and Thomas, 2000).

A third technique that involves elaborating on the information to be learned is known as 'concept maps' or 'mind maps'. The mapping of the relations between elements of what needs to be recalled assists with elaboration of the information and improves recall. Studies have shown greater recall of medical information for students using these techniques than students not using them (Farrand *et al.*, 2002). A review of studies also found that medical students who used concept maps showed enhanced critical thinking abilities and an increase in meaningful learning (Daley and Torre, 2010).

The testing effect

While increasing the depth of processing by elaborating on information as it is being learned is one way to improve your memory for it, another way to improve your memory for material is to test yourself on what you have learned thus far. This is called the 'testing effect' and a number of studies have provided evidence of its effectiveness as a learning technique (Roediger and Karpicke, 2006). Most people, when asked a question about the effectiveness of studying versus test-taking, say that they would rather do extra study of material (57 per cent), than have a test on it (18 per cent), or use some other study method (21 per cent) (Karpicke *et al.*, 2009). Possible reasons why repeated study of material may be attractive to students are that it may seem less effortful than being tested (Baddeley *et al.*, 2015) and because it does seem to produce benefits in short-term recall (Roediger and Karpicke, 2006).

However, in a review of ten different learning techniques, repeated studying was rated as one of the least useful techniques while testing was rated as the most useful (Dunlosky *et al.*, 2013). This clearly supports the effectiveness of the 'testing effect' as a method for enhancing memory. Bear this in mind when trying to learn something new yourself or when supporting learning in others! One mechanism which might explain the testing effect is that repeated testing helps with the organisation of information in long-term memory and encourages more associations between elements of the material to be learned and existing knowledge (Pyc and Rawson, 2010). In many ways, this resembles the impact of elaboration.

Using memory

In this section thus far, we have considered how you can improve your ability to create new long-term memories (encoding) and recall them, particularly in relation to remembering semantic information (e.g. facts and knowledge about the world). Next, we will explore the possibility of using your existing memories of past events, combined with your imagination, to improve learning and future performance.

Reflections

Is it really useful to make a distinction between different types of memory, such as for personal events, facts or skills? Why do you think it is helpful or unhelpful to categorise these different types of memory?

Imagination and episodic memories

When we engage in a task such as sitting an exam, solving a crossword puzzle or cooking a meal we often retain an episodic memory of completing the task. Memories of episodes in our lives are important and help shape who we are. Of course, not all events in our day-to-day lives are important or life-changing. For example, not all meals we cook are special and not every single one will be remembered in detail, but there's a good chance we'll retain a memory of particular meals such as the first meal we cooked for our future in-laws or of situations where things did not turn out as expected.

Reflecting on these episodic memories can be helpful to learn lessons for future situations. We can think about a task we completed, an event we organised or a meal we cooked and consider if the situation turned out as planned, if were we happy with the outcome, or if there was anything we could have done differently that might have made the outcome better or worse.

This ability to think about how things could have turned out differently is called 'counterfactual thinking'. Counterfactual thinking is an important and pervasive part of everyday thought that seems to develop early in life (Harris, 2000). Previous research shows that people regularly and spontaneously generate counterfactual thoughts about all sorts of events (Roese, 1997). For example, after recalling an episodic memory of a time when they failed an exam someone might think 'If only had studied more I would have done better'. Likewise, after winning the lottery some-one might think 'If I hadn't stopped to buy a lottery ticket I wouldn't have won'. Although counter-factual thinking is a ubiquitous human ability, one might question what use there is in thinking about what might have been.

In fact, thinking about what might have been has many uses and functions (Byrne, 2016; Epstude and Roese, 2008). It plays a role in emotions such as guilt, shame and regret (Mandel, 2003) and it also helps to give our lives meaning by reflecting on memories of pivotal experiences such as 'If I hadn't decided to study education my life would be very different' (Kray et al., 2010). Another function of counterfactual thinking is that it allows us to learn from our memories of past experiences and to potentially avoid mistakes in the future in similar situations (Epstude and Roese, 2008). Research suggests that these types of thoughts, particularly about actions within our control, are useful in learning from past mistakes, possibly avoiding them in the future and potentially improving performance.

For example, Morris and Moore (2000) reviewed near-miss accident logs of aeroplane pilots. They found that pilots who generated counterfactuals about controllable events had better learning outcomes that those who didn't (e.g. 'If I had begun the descent earlier and deployed the flaps, the plane would not have skidded on the runway'). Maloney and Egan (2017) also showed that there was greater improvement on a cognitive task following counterfactual thinking about a controllable aspect of behaviour, compared to thinking about an uncontrollable aspect of behaviour or not engaging in counterfactual thinking at all. Similarly, Mandel and Dhami (2005) found that in pris-oners, those encouraged to generate self-focused counterfactuals (e.g. 'If I hadn't broken into the house I wouldn't be in prison now') had intensified attributions of self-blame and feelings of guilt. This may lead to lower rates of reoffending.

Nasco and Marsh (1999) examined the impact of counterfactual thinking in an academic setting. Students sat an exam and after receiving their grade they were asked to think about how it could have turned out better (i.e. think counterfactually). A month later they had another exam as part of the module and the findings showed that those who had thought about how their first grade could have been better, improved more on the subsequent test than those who hadn't thought counter-factually. This illustrates that we can use our memories of experiences to learn from them and improve in the future.

What this research indicates is that it is useful to reflect on past failures, as well as successes, in order to figure out how we might do better in future. This technique can be applied in a variety of educational settings, whether a student is taking a biology exam or learning to fly a plane. Simi-larly, teachers can also encourage counterfactual thinking in their students so that students may think about factors within their control that they can focus on for the future.

Imagination and procedural memories

Much of what we learn, or try to teach others, relates to semantic memory with the principal goal being to increase knowledge in a particular area such as English, engineering or education. However, as described earlier, not all of our memories are for facts and figures. Much of our learning involves acquiring a physical skill through practice. This may include sports such as football or tennis, or activities such as driving a car or riding a bicycle. In an educational context, it may involve physical skills such as the competent use of a piece of equipment or technology, or learning handwriting. These types of memory, known as procedural memories, are typically formed through repeated physical practice.

With semantic memories, we can enhance our learning outside of the classroom through study, linking information to existing knowledge and testing ourselves. Often the opportunity to learn is limited only by the time we have available to study. By contrast, physical skills can sometimes offer limited opportunities to practise that skill. We may not have access to equipment, technology, musical instruments or surgery patients in order to practise the skill. However, in recent years research has emerged which suggests that practising a skill in our imagination can lead to real improvements in future physical performance of the skill.

Brain imaging studies suggest that similar parts of the brain are involved in imagining an action, as in performing that action (Ganis *et al.*, 2004; Kosslyn *et al.*, 2006). This may, in part, explain why recalling previous physical practice of a skill, and using it as the basis to mentally practise that skill, could be beneficial in developing it. Indeed, mental practice (or motor imagery) has been demonstrated to be beneficial in a number of areas. These areas include sports performance (Moran *et al.*, 2011), stroke rehabilitation (Liu *et al.*, 2014), musical performance (Bernardi *et al.*, 2013) and reducing motor clumsiness in children (Wilson *et al.*, 2002). Research is also under way to examine if mental practice might be helpful for children with developmental coordination disorder, a condition where the control of movements is impaired (Adams *et al.*, 2016).

Depending on the physical skill that is being practised, mental practice may work best when there is physical practice available to the individual as well. However, where access to equipment, technology or sports facilities is limited, recalling and mentally performing an action or behaviour can have significant positive impacts on the later physical performance of the action or behaviour. This technique may be a useful addition to the methods employed by any educator seeking to support students trying to learn a physical skill.

In conclusion, what this section has shown us is that our memory is a dynamic system. Far from being at the mercy of a 'good memory' for names or 'bad memory' for faces we can consciously direct and enhance our memory to serve us better through the use of encoding techniques. Furthermore, the studies on counterfactual thinking and mental practice show us that memory's effectiveness as a tool in our learning goes far beyond simply storing and retrieving the facts that we learn. In truth, it seems the usefulness of memory in learning is limited only by our imagination.

Conclusion

Ultimately, one of the key goals of education is to change the knowledge or skills that are available to us in our memories. The aim of this chapter was to provide you with a greater understanding of memory theory and research by exploring the ways in which perspectives on memory have changed and evolved over the last six decades. From the foundations of the Multi-Store model of memory, through working memory and beyond, we can see how psychological theories regarding memory are constantly evolving, offering us new insights into memory processes and the potential roles for memory in our learning.

By exploring some of the practical applications of these theories I've also, I hope, given you a taste of some of the ways in which these theories can be useful to you, whether you apply the information you have learned here as a student or as an educator.

Key points

- The scientific study of memory has been ongoing for over a century in order to better understand how our memory works.
- There are different types of memory stores for information that is retained only for a short period of time (short-term memory) and information that is retained for longer periods (long-term memory).
- On the basis of new evidence, refinements have been made to both short-term memory (e.g. working memory) and long-term memory (e.g. different types of long-term memories).
- Thinking about information more deeply and making connections between new information and information already in long-term memory can assist with learning and with later memory recall.
- By using imagination (e.g. building a memory palace, thinking counterfactually or engaging in mental practice) we can use and improve our memory and future performances.

Recommended reading

Baddeley, A., Eysenck, M.W. and Anderson, M.C. (2015) *Memory*. Hove: Psychology Press.
Byrne, R.M. (2016) Counterfactual thought. *Annual Review of Psychology*, **67**, pp. 135–157.
Karpicke, J.D. and Roediger, H.L. (2008) The critical importance of retrieval for learning. *Science*, **319**, pp. 966–968.
Moran, A., Guillot, A., MacIntyre, T. and Collet, C. (2011) Re-imagining motor imagery: Building bridges between cognitive neuroscience and sport psychology. *British Journal of Psychology*, **103**(2), pp. 224–247.

References

Adams, I.L.J., Steenbergen, Lust, J.M. and Smits-Engelsman, B.C.M. (2016) Motor imagery training for children with developmental coordination disorder: Study protocol for a randomised controlled trial. *BioMed Central*, **16**(5), pp. 1–9.
Atkinson, R.C. and Shiffrin, R.M. (1968) Human memory: A proposed system and its control processes. In K.W. Spence and J.T. Spence, *The psychology of learning and motivation*. Vol. **2**. New York: Academic Press.
Baddeley, A. (2000) The episodic buffer: A new component of working memory? *Trends in Cognitive Science*, **4**(11), pp. 417–423.
Baddeley, A. (2012) Working memory: Theories, models, and controversies. *Annual Review of Psychology*, **63**, pp. 1–29.
Baddeley, A., Chincotta, D. and Adlam, A. (2001) Working memory and the control of action: Evidence from task switching. *Journal of Experimental Psychology: General*, **130**(4), pp. 641–657.
Baddeley, A., Eysenck, M.W. and Anderson, M.C. (2015) *Memory*. Hove: Psychology Press.
Baddeley, A.D. and Hitch, G. (1974) Working memory. In G.H. Bower (ed.) *The psychology of learning and motivation: Advances in research and theory*. Vol. **8**. New York: Academic Press.
Baddeley, A.D. and Hitch, G. (1977) Recency re-examined. In S. Dornic (ed.) *Attention and performance*. Hillsdale, NJ: Lawrence Erlbaum Associates.
Bartlett, F.C. (1932) *Remembering: A study in experimental and social psychology*. Cambridge: Cambridge University Press.

Bernardi, N.F., De Buglio, M., Trimarchi, P.D., Chielli, A. and Bricolo, E. (2013) Mental practice promotes motor anticipation: Evidence from music performance. *Frontiers in Human Neuroscience*, **7**(451), pp. 1–14.

Bower, G. H. (1973) How to. .. uh. .. remember. *Psychology Today*, **7**(5), pp. 63–70.

Brener, R. (1940) An experimental investigation of memory span. *Journal of Experimental Psychology*, **26**, pp. 467–483.

Byrne, R.M. (2016) Counterfactual thought. *Annual Review of Psychology*, **67**, pp. 135–157.

Cabeza, R. and Moscovitch, M. (2013) Memory systems, processing modes, and components: Functional neuroimaging evidence. *Perspectives on Psychological Science*, **8**(1), pp. 49–55.

Chase, W.G. and Ericsson, K.A. (1982) Skill and working memory. In G.H. Bower (ed.) *The psychology of learning and motivation*. Vol. **16**. New York: Academic Press.

Cowan, N. (2001) The magical number 4 in short-term memory: A reconsideration of mental storage capacity. *Behaviour and Brain Science*, **24**, pp. 87–114.

Craik, F.I.M. and Lockhart, R.S. (1972) Levels of processing: A framework for memory research. *Journal of Verbal Learning and Verbal Behaviour*, **11**(6), pp. 671–684.

Craik, F.I.M. and Tulving, E. (1975) Depth of processing and the retention of words in episodic memory. *Journal of Experimental Psychology*, **104**(3), pp. 268–294.

Daley, B.J. and Torre, D.M. (2010) Concept maps in medical education. *Medical Education*, **44**(5), pp. 440–448.

De Beni, R., Moe, A. and Cornoldi, C. (1997) Learning from texts or lectures: Loci mnemonics can interfere with reading but not with listening. *European Journal of Cognitive Psychology*, **9**, pp. 401–415.

Dunlosky, J., Rawson, K.A., Marsh, E.J., Nathan, M.J. and Willingham, D.T. (2013) Improving students' learning with effective learning techniques: Promising directions from cognitive and educational psychology. *Psychological Science in the Public Interest*, **14**(1), pp. 4–58.

Ebbinghaus, H. (1885) *Über das Gedächtnis* [Memory: A contribution to experimental psychology]. Translated by Henry A. Ruger and Clara E. Bussenius (1913). New York: Teachers College, Columbia University.

Epstude, K. and Roese, N. (2008). The functional theory of counterfactual thinking. *Personality and Social Psychology Review*, **12**(2), pp. 168–192.

Farrand, P., Hussain, F. and Hennessy, E. (2002). The efficacy of the 'mind map' study technique. *Medical Education*, **36**(5), pp. 426–431.

Ganis, G., Thompson, W.L. and Kosslyn, S.M. (2004) Brain areas underlying visual mental imagery and visual perception: An fMRI study. *Cognitive Brain Research*, **20**(2), pp. 226–241.

Gathercole, S. and Baddeley, A. (1990) The role of phonological memory in vocabulary acquisition: A study of young children learning new names. *British Journal of Psychology*, **81**(4), pp. 439–454.

Glenberg, A.M. (1997) What memory is for: Creating meaning in the service of action. *Behavioural and Brain Sciences*, **20**(1), pp. 41–55.

Godden, D.R. and Baddeley, A. (1975) Context-dependent memory in two natural environments: On land and under water. *British Journal of Psychology*, **66**(3), pp. 325–331.

Harris, P.L. (2000) *The work of the imagination*. Oxford: Wiley-Blackwell.

Henke, K. (2010) A model for memory systems based on processing modes rather than consciousness. *Nature Reviews Neuroscience*, **11**, pp. 523–532.

James, W. (1890) *The principles of psychology*. New York: Henry Holt.

Karpicke, J.D., Butler, A.C. and Roediger, H.L. (2009) Metacognitive strategies in student learning: Do students practise retrieval when they study on their own? *Memory*, **17**(4), pp. 471–479.

Klauer, K.C. and Zhao, Z. (2004) Double dissociations in visual and spatial short-term memory. *Journal of Experimental Psychology: General*, **133**, pp. 355–381.

Kosslyn, S.M., Thompson, W.L. and Ganis, G. (2006) *The case for mental imagery*. New York: Oxford University Press.

Kray, L., George, L.G., Liljenquist, K.A., Galinsky, A.D., Tetlock, P.E. and Roese, N. (2010) From what might have been to what must have been: Counterfactual thinking creates meaning. *Journal of Personality and Social Psychology*, **98**(1), pp. 106–118.

Liu, H., Song, L. and Zhang, T. (2014) Changes in brain activation in stroke patients after mental practice and physical exercise: A functional MRI study. *Neural Regeneration Research*, **9**(15), pp. 1474–1484.

Logie, R.H. (1995) *Visuo-spatial working memory*. Hove: Lawrence Erlbaum.

Ma, W.J., Husain, M. and Bays, P.M. (2014) Changing concepts of working memory. *Nature Neuroscience*, **17**, pp. 347–356.

Maloney, D.M. and Egan, S.M. (2017) The effect of autonomy on counterfactual thinking about controllable events. *Journal of Cognitive Psychology*, **29**(3), pp. 337–351.

Mandel, D. (2003) Counterfactuals, emotions, and context. *Cognition and Emotion*, **17**(1), pp. 139–159.

Mandel, D. and Dhami, M.K. (2005) 'What I did' versus 'what I might have done': Effect of factual versus counterfactual thinking on blame, guilt, and shame in prisoners. *Journal of Experimental Social Psychology*, **41** (6), pp. 627–635.

Miles, C. and Hardman, E. (1998) State-dependent memory produced by aerobic exercise. *Ergonomics*, **41**(1), pp. 20–28.

Miller, G.A. (1956) The magical number seven. *Psychological Review*, **63**, pp. 81–97.

Milner, B. (1962) Les troubles de la mémoire accompagnant des lésions hippocampiques bilatérales. In P. Passouant (ed.) *Physiologie de l'hippocampe*. Paris: Centre National de la Recherche Scientifique.

Miyake, A., Friedman, N.P., Emerson, M.J., Witzki, A.H., Howerter, A. and Wager, T.D. (2000) The unity and diversity of executive functions and their contributions to complex 'frontal lobe' tasks: A latent variable analysis. *Cognitive Psychology*, **41**(1), pp. 49–100.

Moran, A., Guillot, A., MacIntyre, T. and Collet, C. (2011) Re-imagining motor imagery: Building bridges between cognitive neuroscience and sport psychology. *British Journal of Psychology*, **103**(2), pp. 224–247.

Morris, M. and Moore, P. (2000). The lessons we (don't) learn: Counterfactual thinking and organizational accountability after a close call. *Administrative Science Quarterly*, **45**(4), pp. 737–765.

Nasco, S. and Marsh, K. (1999) Gaining control through counterfactual thinking. *Personality and Social Psychology Bulletin*, **25**(5), pp. 556–568.

Neisser, U. (1967) *Cognitive psychology*. New York: Appleton-Century-Crofts.

Nicolay, A.C. and Poncelet, M. (2013) Cognitive abilities underlying L2 vocabulary acquisition in an early L2-immersion educational context: A longitudinal study. *Journal of Experimental Child Psychology*, **115**, pp. 655–671.

Noice, H. (1992) Elaborative memory strategies of professional actors. *Applied Cognitive Psychology*, **6**(5), pp. 417–427.

Peterson, L. and Peterson, M.J. (1959) Short-term retention of individual verbal items. *Journal of Experimental Psychology*, **58**(3), pp. 193–198.

Pyc, M.A. and Rawson, K.A. (2010) Why testing improves memory: Mediator effectiveness hypothesis. *Science*, **330**, p. 335.

Roediger, H.L. (ed.) (2008) *Cognitive psychology of memory*. Vol. 2 of Learning and memory: A comprehensive reference (J. Byrne, ed.). Oxford: Elsevier.

Roediger, H.L. and Karpicke, J.D. (2006) Test-enhanced learning: Taking memory tests improves long-term retention. *Psychological Science*, **17**(3), pp. 249–255.

Roese, N. (1997). Counterfactual thinking. *Psychological Bulletin*, **121**(1), pp. 133–148.

Saeke, E., Baddeley, A., Hitch, G. and Saito, S. (2013) Breaking a habit: A further role of the phonological loop in action control. *Australian Journal of Psychology*, **65**, pp. 163–171.

Schmidt, H.G., Boshuizen, H.P. and van Breukelen, G.J. (2002) Long-term retention of a theatrical script by repertory actors: The role of context. *Memory*, **10**(1), pp. 21–28.

Smith, E.E. and Jonides, J. (1997) Working memory: A view from neuroimaging. *Cognitive Psychology*, **33**(1), pp. 5–42.

Smith, E.E. and Kosslyn, S.M. (2007) *Cognitive psychology: Mind and brain*. Harlow: Prentice Hall.

Smith, S.M. and Vela, E. (2001) Environmental context-dependent memory: A review and meta-analysis. *Psychonomic Bulletin and Review*, **8**(2), pp. 203–220.

Sperling, G. (1960) The information available in brief visual presentations. *Psychological Monographs: General and Applied*, **74**(11), pp. 1–29.

Squire, L.R. (1992) Memory and the hippocampus: A synthesis from findings with rats, monkeys, and humans. *Psychological Review*, **99**(2), pp. 195–231.

Tulving, E. (1972) Episodic and semantic memory. In E. Tulving and W. Donaldson (eds) *Organization of memory*. New York: Academic Press.

Underwood, B.J. (1957) Interference and forgetting. *Psychological Review*, **64**(1), pp. 49–60.

Wang, A.Y. and Thomas, M.H. (2000) Looking for long-term mnemonic effects on serial recall: The legacy of Simonides. *American Journal of Psychology*, **113**(3), pp. 331–340.

Wilson, B.A., Baddeley, A. and Young, A.W. (1999) LE, a person who lost her 'mind's eye'. *Neurocase*, **5**(2), pp. 119–127.

Wilson, P.H., Thomas, P.R. and Maruff, P. (2002) Motor imagery training ameliorates motor clumsiness in children. *Journal of Child Neurolology*, **17**(7), pp. 491–498.

Zimmer, H.D. (2008) Visual and spatial working memory: From boxes to networks. *Neuroscience and Biobehavioural Reviews*, **32**, pp. 1373–1395.

3 Creative learning and learning creativity

Scrutinising the nature of creativity and developing strategies to foster creativity in education

Chloe Shu-Hua Yeh

Introduction

Creativity is often viewed as a gift rather than a learned skill. From this perspective, individuals who are creative are seen to have the creative 'spark' in particular abilities, often focusing on the so-called 'creative arts' such as literature, painting or sculpture. Therefore, the role of education and the educator in such a process is limited or even seen as a threat to creativity due to the conventions of education which may stifle individuals from developing their creativity (Craft, 2001).

The overall aims of this chapter are to challenge these common views on the nature of creativity and to make a case for the role of education in enhancing an individual's creative potential. The first section explores some foundational models of creativity, such as the four-stage theory (Wallas, 1926) and the primary-secondary thinking process theory (Kris, 1952), which shape the basic understanding of the nature of creativity. The second section moves on to discuss two underlying factors, defocused attention and emotions, which may have a significant influence on creative thinking. The final section articulates the challenges in fostering creativity and provides several strategies aimed at fostering creativity in educational contexts.

The nature of creativity

There are many definitions of creativity but one of the most widely cited comes from Sternberg and Lubart (1999), who define creativity as 'the ability to produce work that is both novel (i.e., original, unexpected) and appropriate (i.e., useful, adaptive concerning task constraints)' (Sternberg and Lubart, 1999: 3). In line with this definition, Mayer (1999) suggests there are two key characteristics of creativity: 'Originality' and 'Usefulness'. Here, 'Originality' refers to the concept of novelty or novel features of creative products, and 'Usefulness' to the concept of utility, appropriateness, significance or the degree to which the features of a creative product are valued by society. The 'originality' dimension of creativity tends to be how the general public would recognise something as creative; however, the 'usefulness' dimension is sometimes neglected when creativity is discussed.

Creativity is also often considered as a property of thinking processes. Torrance (1966: 6) defined creativity as:

> a process of becoming sensitive to problems, deficiencies, gaps in knowledge, missing elements, disharmonies, and so on; identifying the difficulty; searching for solutions, making guesses, or formulating hypotheses about the deficiencies: testing and retesting these hypotheses and possibly modifying and retesting them; and finally communicating the results.

In this respect, Torrance (1966) suggests that creative thinking involves multiple cognitive thinking processes primarily distinguished into two states. One state involves the processes of generating ideas; identifying unusual and innovative approaches to problems and ordinary situations. Some would see this state as being similar to divergent thinking, a concept which also describes a process of generating potential creative thoughts (Runco and Chand, 1995), but as we will see later this view is contested by others. The other state in Torrance's definition involves a critical evaluation of these new and unusual ideas or perspectives, estimations of their acceptability and further considerations for creative outcomes. We will encounter this dual-state definition of creative thinking in the next section where certain models see creativity as alternating between these states in order to produce something both original and useful.

Reflections

What is divergent thinking and what are the similarities and the differences between divergent thinking and creative thinking?

Different researchers have proposed their own models of creative thinking, often with similar viewpoints but using different terminologies for the thinking states which are described as sub-processes of creative thinking. To get a better understanding of the nature of creativity, four such models which are important to education, namely the four-stage theory by Wallas (1926), the Primary-Secondary process by Kris (1952), the three-component model of creativity by Amabile (1983; 2013) and, the Little C and Big C theory by Gardner (1993), are all explored in the next section.

Four-stage theory of creativity

In his four-stage theory of creativity, Wallas (1926) attempted to understand creativity from the perspective of creative problem solving. He suggested that creativity could be broken down into four sequential creative thinking processes in search of a solution to a problem, including Preparation, Incubation, Illumination and Verification.

In the Preparation stage, the problem is analysed with attempts to provide possible solutions. It involves a preliminary analysis of the problem, including defining and setting up the problem, and obtaining sufficient raw materials for creative idea generation (Lubart, 2001). In this stage, individuals work to obtain problem-relevant knowledge, consciously develop familiarity with the existing elements, and then analyse them seeking new creative combinations. This means that there is a time requirement for the Preparation stage; sufficient time is needed to learn the necessary domain-related knowledge before an individual can be creative. The greater the diversity of domain-related knowledge an individual accumulates in this time, the greater are the opportunities in terms of broader associations for creative idea generation (Martindale, 1995).

After Preparation is complete, if a solution has not presented itself and an impasse is reached then the next stage, Incubation, may be triggered (Finke *et al.*, 1992). In the Incubation stage, the creative individuals usually set the problem aside to work on other tasks, so the problem solving processes occur below the conscious level (Wallas, 1926). Therefore attention is not focused on the problem. Often, creative individuals take time off from their focused work when impasses are encountered to simply relax, take a break, and engage in an unrelated activity. Unconsciously, however, the mind continues to work on the problem, forming train-of-thought associations which generate further creative solutions or ideas (Lubart, 2001). This indicates that defocused (broadened or diffused) attention benefits further creative performance as it provides the opportunity for new associations to appear in our thinking processes (Finke *et al.*, 1992; Kounios *et al.*, 2008).

The final two stages, Illumination and Verification, are closely linked. In the Illumination stage, creative individuals usually find the solution to the problem as a sudden insight (Wallas, 1926). Therefore, it is also referred to as a period of 'insight', in which creative ideas jump up to the surface of consciousness from existing elements incubated with a preceding and intuitive feeling that an idea is coming (Sawyer, 2006). After insights emerge into consciousness, the stage of Verification is triggered where the creative individuals seek to make sure that a given solution works (Wallas, 1926). After evaluating the appropriateness of the insights, they are then refined and developed into a complete creative product or idea.

The four-stage theory offers two important insights into the nature of creativity. First, it highlights the critical importance of domain-relevant knowledge as a foundation for creativity. This shows a clear role for education in promoting creativity through providing that foundation and challenges the validity of the popular image of education as something that stifles creativity. Second, by proposing the incubation and illumination stages, the four-stage model suggests a role for subconscious processes in the production of creative ideas and solutions. In that, 'defocused attention' is an important cognitive process which provides opportunities to develop related teaching and learning pedagogies that would facilitate the generation of original ideas. The concept of defocused attention is elaborated in a later section of this chapter.

Primary-Secondary process

Wallas's (1926) four-stage model was highly influential on the theories that followed it while adding their own unique spin. One of the better known theories is the Primary-Secondary process model of Kris (1952). In essence, Kris has taken the four stages and divided them into two cyclical stages labelled 'Primary Process' and 'Secondary Process'. Kris defined primary process thinking as free-associative, analogical, uninhibited, abstract and less conscious. This is very much in line with the specification for incubation and illumination stages; new combinations of mental elements or ideas are freely associated in an uninhibited and often less conscious manner. There is a tendency to fantasise during this process, which is believed to facilitate the discovery of creative ideas (Fromm, 1978). By contrast, the secondary process is defined as thinking which is logical, associated with concrete images and knowledge, reality-oriented thought occurring in fully 'waking consciousness'. This is very much in line with the verification stage in that cognitive elements of ideas are analysed logically and reoriented with goals. This model is also similar to what Torrance (1966) defined as 'dual-state' creative thinking processes that involve creative individuals generating original ideas and critically evaluating their ideas or perspectives for creative outcomes.

An important distinction that the Primary-Secondary process model makes is to present creativity as a more cyclical process overall than the four-stage model. The process described in the four-stage model is more linear, from new ideas being generated to the productions of a creative output at the end. By contrast, Kris (1952) suggested that we alternate back and forth between primary and secondary processes many times before a solution is reached. Creative individuals possess a better ability to alternate more flexibly between primary and secondary process than uncreative individuals.

Following on from Wallas and Kris, research on the concept of creativity continued to explore and expand our understanding of the nature of creativity during the 1960s, 1970s and 1980s, as psychology entered a period known as the 'Cognitive Revolution' (Gardner, 1987), and the computational model emerged as the dominant paradigm. (See Chapter 5 for a critical evaluation of the computational model.) During this time, Rhodes (1961) proposed the '4 P's of creativity', four strands which have influence on creativity, namely Person, Process, Press and Product. The 4 P's model and others are influential in creativity research because they see creativity as one of the cognitive processes such as memory, motivation or attention which are all intertwined and influence each other (Torrance, 1966).

Three-component model of creativity

Another example of a creativity model which was influenced by the cognitive research of the time is Amabile's (1983; 2013) three-component model of creativity. Amabile proposed three key elements of creativity: *domain-relevant skills, creativity-relevant processes* and *intrinsic task motivation*. This model suggests that creativity, rather than a single ability, is a collection of skills and knowledge possessed by creative individuals. She characterised domain-relevant skills as knowledge, expertise, technical skills, intelligence, and talent in the particular domain where the problem-solver is working. Creativity-relevant processes refer to interactions between cognitive processes and creative individuals' characteristics. The cognitive processes include the ability to use a wide range of flexible categories for synthesising information and to break out of perceptual and performance scripts. The characteristics include self-discipline, risk-taking and projecting a tolerance for ambiguity during creative processes. Finally, intrinsic task motivation is characterised as the passion and intrinsic motivation to undertake a task or solve a problem because it is interesting, enjoyable, personally challenging and satisfying, rather than being externally motivated by rewards, surveillance, competition or evaluation (Amabile, 1983; 2013).

Amabile's model provides a detailed analysis on the interconnections of these three essential components of creativity within creative individuals and their interactions with external tasks and environments. The three-component model could be seen as an update of Wallas's (1926) four-stage theory for the cognitive era, incorporating a good deal of the key cognitive concepts and research of the time. It has continued to develop and remains highly influential in educational contexts right up to the present day. It is used as the basis for a number of educational practices aimed at fostering creativity among students.

Little C and Big C

Research on the scope of creativity emerging in the 1990s and early 2000s considered the different levels of impact that a creative output had on individuals and society. Gardner (1993) explores this phenomenon in his notion of Little C and Big C theory. Big C refers to the impact of one's creative output being recognised by a wider society as an eminent contribution which has made a fundamental and historically novel contribution to a particular field. By contrast, Little C refers to creativity at the personal level, regardless of whether many others have produced similar ideas or innovations; something any individual might produce on a regular basis in the process of solving problems and adapting to changes in daily life (Runco, 2004).

Gardner's (1993) Little C and Big C theory provides two insights on creativity in relation to education. First, it shows that the characteristics of creativity – originality and usefulness/appropriateness (Sternberg and Lubart, 1999; Mayer, 1999) – are contextual. That is, an output or idea might be original or significant in one area but not the other (e.g. local versus global). In this way, something can be known to others but newly 'discovered' by one individual and still qualify as an example of creativity on his or her own part. Second, the Little C concept challenges educators to consider how variable the processes of evaluating originality in students' work and learning progress can be. Each educator may have their own 'thresholds' in mind when it comes to making a judgement on the originality of students' work (e.g. one may consider that an idea in an essay is not original if it's also in the textbook, but others may disagree). Educators need to be consciously aware of these thresholds, as they could affect how students are evaluated and whether their creativity is encouraged under such practice.

In summary, this section shows that creativity can be seen as the product of processes that produce the features of 'originality' and 'appropriateness' which characterise creative thought. It has also been demonstrated that creative thinking is more complex than merely thinking divergently and creating new ideas. The next section will show that these complex creative thinking processes are interconnected with other factors which influence creativity both positively and negatively.

Underlying factors that influence creativity

Creativity should not only be considered in isolation from other dimensions of human ability and experience (Sternberg, 2010). Previous reviews on the nature of creative thinking have identified two significant underlying factors which have a direct impact on the creative processes: defocused (broadened) attention and emotions.

Defocused (broadened) attention

Attentional breadth is defined by Kasof as 'the number and range of stimuli attended to at any one time' (Kasof, 1997: 303). The links between attentional breadth and creativity have been explored in a number of studies (e.g. Fredrickson and Branigan, 2005; Friedman *et al.*, 2003; Kasof, 1997; Kounios *et al.*, 2008). In the context of creativity, attentional breadth determines the number of mental elements or cognitive units to be triggered for idea generation. A defocused (broadened) attentional breadth, which allows more of these mental elements to come to mind, is thought to be beneficial to creative thinking (Kasof, 1997). Mendelsohn stated that 'The greater the attentional capacity, the more likely the combinational leap which is generally described as the hallmark of creativity' (Mendelsohn, 1976: 366).

Attentional breadth determines the range of stimuli to be attended to and thereby has an effect on the degree to which extraneous or less relevant stimuli or information will be filtered from awareness (Kasof, 1997). If breadth of attention is consistently narrowed (or focused) on a relatively small range of stimuli or information, individuals tend to filter greater amounts of less relevant information away from their consciousness. In contrast, if breadth of attention is broadened (or defocused) on a large range of stimuli or information, less relevant information has a greater chance of gaining our attention. In other words, a defocused or broadened breadth of attention enlarges the possibility for remotely associated ideas, information or cognitive units to enter into consciousness, resulting in facilitating creative performance (Mendelsohn, 1976; Runco and Sakamoto, 1999). In this line of thought, defocused (broadened) attention would be more of an asset during the incubation stage (Wallas, 1926) or primary process (Kris, 1952) where ideas are generated and a greater attentional capacity is required; whereas focused (narrowed) attentional breadth would be of more use in the evaluation stage or secondary process where ideas are to be evaluated and an attention to detail is required.

Friedman and Förster (2005; 2010) further developed the concept of attentional breadth by distinguishing between perceptual and conceptual attention and attributing a 'breadth of attention' to both facets. Breadth of perceptual attention refers to 'the degree to which attention is trained on central as opposed to peripheral perceptual cues', while breadth of conceptual attention refers to 'the degree to which attention is trained on internal cognitive representations as opposed to external percepts' (Friedman and Förster, 2005: 263). Friedman and Förster believed that the two kinds of attentional breadth were positively associated with each other. Narrowed or broadened breadth of perceptual attention may correspondingly expand or constrict breadth of conceptual attention, which in turn may influence creative generation (Friedman et al., 2003). It is interesting to note that according to the study by Friedman and his colleagues (2003), physically directing visual attention to a wider or a narrower visual area could broaden or narrow breadth of perceptual attention (for more details, see the first 'Research focus' box below). This shift in visual attentional breadth could subsequently engender a corresponding shift in internal breadth of conceptual attention, increasing or undermining creative generation correspondingly. This phenomenon could have implications for developing creative teaching strategies, which are discussed in the final part of this chapter.

In summation, the above discussion suggests that creative individuals utilise a form of defocused or broadened attentional breadth at certain stages of the creative process to achieve a wider, cognitively remote association for the generation of ideas. In addition, Friedman and Förster suggest that achieving defocused attention in one area (visual attention) may be linked to achieving defocused attention in other areas (conceptual attention). Interestingly, in the next section emotion is shown to be another factor which influences this defocused (broadened) attention-creativity link.

Research focus: can breadth of perceptual attention affect breadth of conceptual attention?

In order to explore the relationship between breadth of perceptual attention and breadth of conceptual attention, Friedman et al. (2003) first examined whether manipulating an individual's breadth of perceptual attention would have an influence on the breadth of their conceptual attention. Participants' breadth of perceptual attention was manipulated by a visual searching task which had participants search for a specific digit (e.g. '3') in either a broader or narrower size of digital display. A second method of altering perceptual attention was also used involving facial muscles. To broaden the breadth of perceptual attention, participants were asked to contract their frontalis facial muscle by raising their eyebrows associatively.

To narrow attentional breadth, they were asked to contract their corrugators muscle by furrowing their eyebrows. Measuring creativity involved participants generating alternative uses or titles for several objects, with the originality of their suggestions being rated by several independent scorers. Results of these experiments yielded consistent evidence that a broadened or narrowed breadth of perceptual attention was positively related with a broad or a narrow breadth of conceptual attention respectively, suggesting a corresponding enhancement or impairment of creativity.

Emotions

Emotions are thought by some to serve as a gate which unconsciously widens or narrows attentional breadth and thereby affect the range of stimuli or information which may be brought to mind during the creative process. This means that emotional stimuli such as targets, rewards, competitions, a relaxing environment or anything else which might affect an individual's emotions would influence subsequent creative cognition (Howard-Jones, 2002). The means by which external emotional stimuli may influence creative thinking can be explained via the breadth of attention theories previously mentioned. For example, more relaxed emotional states are associated with broader attentional breadth benefiting idea generation. By contrast, reduced relaxation (i.e. stress) induced by extrinsic goals or competitive environmental settings may lead individuals to fixate upon a limited set of ideas, hindering idea generation (Howard-Jones, 2002). It has been emphasised that even mild fluctuations in emotions from daily life events and activities can have very significant influences on cognitive abilities (Mitchell and Phillips, 2007). For example, a different extent of arousal might affect creativity differently (Martindale, 1999).

A large body of research on the cognitive effects of positive emotions has suggested that both artificially induced and naturally occurring positive emotional states will generally lead to greater cognitive flexibility and facilitate performances on creative problem-solving activities (for reviews, see Ashby et al., 1999; Ashby et al., 2002; Isen et al., 1987). These studies have provided evidence to support the notion that positive emotions broaden our access to alternative cognitive perspectives and facilitate creative problem-solving skills across a broad range of situations, from young children at play to adults in organisational settings. In many of these studies, the remote associates test (RAT) (Mednick, 1962) has been used to provide evidence that positive emotions improve cognitive flexibility (Ashby et al., 1999; Isen et al., 1987). In this test, participants are presented with three cue words and a blank line and are asked to respond with a fourth word that is related to each of the three cue words. An example of one set of cue words is GOWN, CLUB and MARE, and the correct response was NIGHT (i.e. nightgown, nightclub and nightmare). Research using this test has shown that individuals in the positive emotions condition responded with a broader range of more unusual word associations than those in the neutral emotions condition (Isen et al., 1985).

In another set of studies, participants in the positive emotions condition produced a wider range of possible solutions and perspectives in an innovative problem-solving task – Duncker's candle task (Isen et al., 1987). Participants viewed comedy film clips before being presented with an innovative problem-solving task (the candle task) to complete. Their performance on the task was compared to two other groups with different conditions: those who had watched a neutral film, and those who were presented with a 'separated-cue'. The candle task was presented to them as three objects: a box of tacks, a candle and a box of matches placed on a table next to a cardboard wall. The problem was how to attach the candle to the cardboard wall in such a way that the candle could burn properly without dripping wax on the table or the floor beneath. In the separated-cue condition the display of the objects in the task was changed by separating the tacks from their box as a cue for alternative uses for each item (i.e. the box could be a separate tool rather than just being a container for the tacks). The solution to this task was usually to empty the box, then tack it to the wall and use it as a platform or a holder for the candle. The results from this study showed that participants in both the comedy film condition and the separated-cue condition showed higher levels of creativity in their solutions compared to those in the neutral film condition. It's worth noting, however, that although most kinds of positive emotions are likely to enhance creative generation, there may be some kinds of positive emotions that do not.

Research focus: will positive emotions always lead to broader attentional breadth?

Gable and Harmon-Jones (2010) challenged the view that positive emotions always broaden attentional breadth when they proposed the Motivational Dimensional Model of Affect, which explored the way that both positive and negative emotions vary in motivational intensity (i.e. high or low). They argued that a combination of the valence (positive or negative) of an emotion as well as its motivational intensity is what determines the effect that emotions would have on breadth of attention and creative cognition. This is in contrast to previous studies which only considered the valence of an emotion and in doing so implied that all positive emotions would broaden attention. Instead, Gable and Harmon-Jones (2010) suggested that only positive emotions that are low in motivational intensity (e.g. relaxation) will lead to a broadening of attention; whereas, positive emotions which are high in motivational intensity (e.g. desire) actually narrow attention. In the same way, negative emotions high in motivational intensity (e.g. anger) will narrow attention, yet negative emotions low in motivational intensity (e.g. sadness) which actually broaden attention. What all this shows us is that the relationship between emotions and creativity may be more complex than we originally thought.

To summarise the above discussions on the underlying factors that influence creativity generation, it can be understood that defocused (broadened) attention may facilitate remote associations leading to creative ideas being generated. Furthermore, by defocusing or broadening perceptual attention, creative idea generation may also be enhanced and encouraged. In addition, emotions play a significant role in determining breadth of attention, and that is likely to thereby influence levels of creative thinking too. As we will see later, the above concepts lend themselves to application through educational techniques aimed at enhancing creativity. Before we can review those techniques, in this next section the challenges and strategies of fostering creativity in education are first discussed.

Encouraging creativity in education

While on the one hand education has often been criticised for spoon-feeding and killing creativity (Kaila, 2005; Robinson, 2009), ironically, it is also in demand to provide educated and creative graduates to respond to global changes in politics and economics as well as the sociocultural and environmental landscapes (Shaheen, 2010). When unforeseen and unpredictable challenges and problems emerge, creativity is seen as the solution (Gaspar and Mabic, 2015). Thus, educational institutions are increasingly expected to encourage creativity in a wide range of students from early years to higher education (Shaheen, 2010; Walberg, 1988). In light of this chapter's discussion of the nature of creativity and the factors that influence it, it can be argued that creativity can be developed as part of an individual's life-long development (Craft, 2001) and that everyone can be creative (Lin, 2011). Creativity exists not only within the extraordinary but, most importantly, also within the ordinary (Craft, 2003; NACCCE, 1999). To investigate how creativity can be fostered in education, this section first discusses common challenges in promoting creativity in education today. Several educational strategies to encourage creativity in the twenty-first century are then articulated.

Challenges in fostering creativity

There have been many discussions in the literature regarding the challenges in fostering creativity in a wide variety of educational contexts (e.g. Craft, 2005; Jeffrey, 2006; Lin, 2011). From these reviews, this section identifies four common challenges in fostering creativity: (1) misconceptions regarding the nature of creativity and creative pedagogy, (2) limitations of a pre-designed curriculum, (3) lack of teacher training in fostering creativity, and (4) overvaluing the grading and assignment systems.

Misconceptions regarding the nature of creativity and creative pedagogy

A common misconception regarding the nature of creativity found in both teachers and students is the belief that to be 'creative' is merely to form new ideas and think divergently (Rinkevich, 2011). This misconception leaves teachers and students with incomplete educational practices which do not lead to enhancing creative outcomes. The notion that creativity has two characteristics, originality and usefulness/appropriateness (Mayer, 1999), would change those practices dramatically. It reinforces the idea that both teachers and students should see the development of creativity as learning not only to create new ideas but also to scrutinise these ideas and form them into useful outcomes which have value either at a personal level or on a wider scale.

In addition, misconceptions in relation to the concepts and terminology surrounding creative pedagogy may sometimes cause 'slippage of the language' used to describe creativity in educational practices and thereby hinder the development of creative teaching and learning (Craft, 2003). In England, a report by the National Advisory Committee on Creative and Cultural Education (NACCCE, 1999) sought to distinguish between teaching creatively and teaching for creativity. Teaching creatively is referred to as 'using imaginative approaches to make learning more interesting and effective' (NACCCE, 1999: 89), whereas teaching for creativity is defined as the 'forms of teaching that are intended to develop young people's own creative thinking or behaviours' (Jeffrey and Craft, 2004: 81). The former focuses on developing the teacher's practices, while the latter focuses on developing the student's creativity (Craft, 2005). Craft (2003) and Lin (2011) further argued that creative teaching and teaching for creativity are also distinct from the concept of creative learning. These concepts of creative teaching, teaching for creativity and creative learning are all explored in

Lin's (2011) model, which is elaborated in a later section in this chapter. It's important that educators understand these differences: that an initiative which promotes one kind of creativity (e.g. creative teaching) is not guaranteed to promote the other (e.g. student creativity).

Limitations of a pre-designed curriculum

Many courses in the education system are based on a pre-designed curriculum, one designed by a central authority and not by the teacher who delivers the course itself. The curriculum plays an important role in fostering creativity on a course because teaching and learning practices are often based directly on its design and content. Although a pre-designed curriculum provides a starting-point for educators and students to then maximise their best practices according to learning goals and expected outcomes, it can also cause limitations that hinder creativity development. One limitation is the tendency of many pre-designed curricula to place restrictions on teachers' practice, forcing them to follow all the instructions provided and so lose sight of the goal of fostering creativity. Creativity is not usually listed among the prescribed goals on most courses and so many teachers see it as not within their discretion in terms of which teaching pedagogies/ strategies they adopt (Rinkevich, 2011; Craft, 2003). Another issue is time constraints arising from the time allocated in the curriculum to a given class or topic. Also, the way in which the curriculum is presented and organised to meet a certain assessment criterion can cause limitations to teachers' practice in fostering creativity (Craft, 2003). Ultimately, these time and regulation constraints that teachers face may lead them to see creativity as something 'extra' and so optional rather than necessary.

Lack of teacher training in fostering creativity

Teachers' behaviours can be a significant factor in encouraging or discouraging creativity through their acceptance or rejection of the unusual and imaginative. Although educators generally claim to recognise the importance of encouraging creativity in their classroom practice, they often hold negative views about certain characteristics of students that are associated with creativity (e.g. nonconformity, autonomy) (Westby and Dawson, 1995). Many teachers tend to view novel (unexpected) responses as disruptive, so they prefer 'relevance' over 'uniqueness' in students' responses during classroom discussions (Beghetto, 2007).

Teachers may find it difficult to value creative and non-conforming behaviours due to their lack of training in fostering creativity and dealing with these behaviours (Rinkevich, 2011). Without such training teachers may simply wish to avoid the stress and potentially unpleasant emotional feelings of being seemingly disrespected by creative students' 'disruptive behaviours' (Chang and Davis, 2009). They need help to develop the level of trust in their relationships with students that is necessary to foster a creative learning environment (Rinkevich, 2011).

Overvaluing the grading and assignment systems

Exams and grading systems, peer competitions and external rewards are commonplace techniques for achieving motivation in education. However, extrinsic rewards such as these may hinder intrinsic motivation if not managed appropriately (Hennessey and Amabile, 1987).

Reflections

How does focusing on the goals set in assessments help students to learn? In what ways may that help be a hindrance to creativity development?

Assessments can and should be used to facilitate students' intrinsic as well as extrinsic motivation. Unfortunately, when high performance in assessments is presented as the goal of a student's learning, both teachers and students tend to miss the potential for assessments to facilitate and support a student's learning. Achievement in assessments is then overly emphasised and learning or creativity are relegated to little more than the means-to-an-end, seen only as methods for increasing the level of that achievement. By contrast, an individual's own enjoyment of or involvement in the course, their satisfaction in their work, ungraded learning, and mastery of their subject are all instrumental in the emergence of intrinsic motivation. Both intrinsic and extrinsic motivations are important to the development of creativity. However, with performance in assessments increasingly valued by both students and teachers (who are themselves evaluated on the performance of their students), a focus on assessment performance comes to dominate teaching and learning interactions. Thus, intrinsic motivations are sidelined, creating a missed opportunity for creativity development.

Research focus: culture and creativity in education

It is possible that in some cultural contexts where levels of choices and personal autonomy are culturally defined, education may face constraints which hamper creativity. For example, Chinese educational traditions are heavily influenced by Confucianism (Wu *et al.*, 2014) where 'maxims of modesty' are seen as a social norm for teachers' and students' interactions. The general rule of being modest in a Chinese social context is the expectation that children do not to show off or ask questions, irrespective of how much they know or are curious, but instead they keep quiet and listen to the adult's instructions (Hui and Yuen, 2010). The social hierarchy is also another dominant culture at all levels of Chinese society. For the young to respect the elder and the novice to respect the experienced are common practices, particularly in educational contexts. The young and the novice are expected not to argue with the elder and the experienced in order to sustain a social harmony in society. Thus, under such cultural constraints, in educational contexts, creativity is implicitly discouraged and instead students conform compliantly to externally prescribed standards such as learning outcomes and grades. This cultural element presents an additional challenge for both teachers and students who wish to introduce and adapt creative practices in educational contexts involving those Chinese learners who are influenced by the Confucian educational culture.

Strategies for fostering creativity

This section provides four strategies for fostering creativity in learners. These are based on a combination of the models of creativity, the factors that influence creative thinking and an awareness of the challenges of creativity which have been reviewed in the previous section.

Integrating creativity into the curriculum

In both the four-stage model (Wallas, 1926) and the three-component model (Amabile 1983) of creativity, the development of domain-relevant knowledge is seen as an important first step. Thus, in order to build creativity into the curriculum, schools should provide an environment where each student can learn the fundamental knowledge, technical skills and intellectual abilities related to a few domains based on their personal interests. Educators should create a curriculum which provides opportunities for students to enhance their cognitive complexity, which is paramount to creative idea generation (Runco and Chand, 1995).

'Cognitive complexity' refers to a cognitive space which allows for a great diversity of relevant domain knowledge or information to create interrelationships with each other, facilitating remotely associated ideas to merge into generative thinking processes. A greater level of cognitive complexity influences the production of both the quality and quantity of these ideas. This can be done in education by designing activities that exercise and expand the capacity of thinking. For example, an up-to-date curriculum should integrate the use of technology into teaching practices to create a virtual learning environment which helps to expand thinking capacity. Many students today have long been 'habitués' of a multidisciplinary world, informational omnivores owing to the empowerment of living in a digital environment which stimulates their creativity (Livingston, 2010). An example of this can be found in research by Yeh (2015), which looked at the cognitive effects of out-of-school videogame play on creativity, and found evidence that games which demand a greater attentional breadth and expending cognitive complexity in visual forms appear to facilitate creativity.

Another way to enhance cognitive complexity is to create interdisciplinary subject knowledge integrated from several different subject domains, an approach that is not often supported in most educational systems (Kandiko, 2012). Today's students face challenges that require multidisciplinary knowledge, and problems that cannot be fully addressed by discipline-specific approaches, all of which shows the need for providing interdisciplinary course elements in the curriculum. Curriculum design could stimulate creativity through the use of interdisciplinary teaching approaches such as introducing elements of the arts into other more traditionally academic subjects (Treffinger *et al.*, 1971), including what are known as the STEAM subjects: Science, Technology, Engineering, Arts and Mathematics (e.g. see Barrett *et al.*, 2015).

Encouraging creative pedagogy

Lin (2011) developed a framework of creative pedagogy to illustrate the relationships and interplay between 'teaching creatively', 'teaching for creativity' and 'learning creatively'. He emphasised that the best creative pedagogy requires teachers to practise all these three aspects of teaching and learning. To foster creativity, teachers should 'teach creatively' by providing imaginative, dynamic, and innovative approaches to inspire (Jeffrey and Craft, 2004). The teachers can 'teach for creativity' by identifying learners' creative potential as well as encouraging and providing opportunities for the development of those capacities, for example, promoting strategies of learning how to learn, arousing curiosity and learners' motivation (Lin, 2011). The interplay between creative teaching and teaching for creativity is fluid and teachers are encouraged to seek collaborative co-construction of knowledge and classroom practices with students.

One teaching strategy which can be classified as 'teaching for creativity' is to promote collaborative thinking and interaction through group work. Both class discussions and group assignments help to develop the skills of teamwork and group acceptance (Fasko, 2001; Livingston, 2010). Evidence also showed that, when working in a group, students were more active, constructive and improvisational (Sawyer, 2004) and revealed a greater willingness to take risks (Rinkevich, 2011). However, it's important that these group activities do not merely become another way to focus on goals such as good grades and assessments, as that can undermine their usefulness in the development of creative potential. Lin (2011) suggests that fostering creativity can be achieved by linking learning to ungraded activities such as questioning, searching, experimenting and aimless play.

Developing creativity through character development

Schooling and education are often seen as contexts which encourage students to develop the skills and abilities related to creativity such as learning to work collaboratively, broadening the scope of their attention or learning new approaches to problem solving. However, education should also provide a space to develop personal characteristics which are key to creativity, such as self-motivation, self-discipline, tolerance of ambiguity (Kieran, 2014), openness, curiosity, risk-taking, resilience, playfulness, humour, dedication, and so on (for reviews, see Zhou and Oldham, 2001). In particular, the four categories of classroom practices created by Treffinger and his colleagues (2002: 7) can be used to nurture creativity characteristics. This includes encouraging individuals or groups to 'generate many ideas', to be 'able to dig deeper into those ideas', to be 'willing and able to listen to their own inner voice', and to 'have the motivation, openness, and courage to explore new and unusual ideas'. Ultimately, through practices such as these educators should aim to develop individuals whose creative outcomes and behaviours consider social justice and promote the common good (Livingston, 2010).

Providing a positive learning environment

Given that breadth of attention affects creative performance and positive emotions appear to facilitate breadth of attention (Ashby *et al.*, 1999), creating a positively charged learning environment may be helpful in fostering creativity. Teaching and learning in a relaxing learning environment often means that there are positive emotional experiences for both teachers and students during educational practices. There are a number of ways in which this can be achieved. For example, a relaxing learning environment can be encouraged by offering short breaks, or changing contexts which could also broaden attentional breadth and facilitate new idea generation, or by offering a safe environment where students are free to make mistakes without suffering negative consequences. Fasko (2001) argued that the most effective teaching and learning techniques for creativity are those which stimulate both cognitive and emotional factors as well as provide active learning opportunities. Bringing the classroom outdoors is another way to stimulate positive emotions during learning, and broadens perceptual and cognitive attentional breadth to the benefit of creative idea generation.

Conclusion

By reviewing relevant models of creativity and examining the underlying factors which influence creative thinking processes, this chapter provides a number of insights into both the nature of creativity and its relevance to education. Far from being the exclusive remit of certain subjects or 'gifted' individuals, creativity can be seen as any output which contains the two key elements, originality and appropriateness, and can be produced in almost any subject or situation by any ordinary individual. Creativity could be seen as an outcome of a complex combination of remotely associated information and knowledge, as well as the analysis and evaluation of ideas in a circular process. This conceptualisation of creativity as a cognitive process has allowed researchers to explore its relationship with other cognitive processes like attention and emotions. Thus, it also enables educators to develop strategies for fostering creativity in education. With all this in mind, although there are challenges in fostering creativity in educational contexts, it has been shown in that education can be a safe place for creativity development when the appropriate strategies are put in place.

Ultimately, this chapter shows that creativity both can and should be fostered by education. It is important to foster creativity, particularly in today's fast-changing world where there are many unforeseen challenges, such as tackling ambiguous problems in an uncertain future or achieving economic stability in a competitive global market (Shaheen, 2010). With enhanced creative thinking skills, students today will be better equipped with the fundamental life skills which are vital not only to survive but to thrive in the twenty-first century.

Key points

- Creativity represents the ability to produce work that is both original and useful. While originality is a widely recognised characteristic of creativity, usefulness is often overlooked.
- Creative thinking involves either alternating between or progressing through the processes of generating new ideas and a critical evaluation of these new ideas.
- The scope of creativity can range from a historical impact on issues faced by a wider society to a personal impact on problems and changes faced in daily life.
- A defocused (broadened) attentional breadth, which allows more mental elements to come to mind, is thought to be beneficial to creative thinking.
- Emotions serve as a gateway which unconsciously widens or narrows attentional breadth, thereby affecting which information is brought to mind during the creative process.
- There are various ways in which creativity can be fostered in education: by introducing cognitive complexity, encouraging group work, promoting the development of personal characteristics such as self-discipline or tolerance for ambiguity, and creating a relaxing, low-stress learning environment.

Recommended readings

Friedman, R.S., Fishbach, A., Förster, J. and Werth, L. (2003) Attentional priming effects on creativity. *Creativity Research Journal*, **15**(2 and 3), pp. 277–286.

Ho, D.Y.F. and Ho, R.T.H. (2008) Knowledge is a dangerous thing: Authority, relations, ideological conservatism, and creativity in Confucian-heritage cultures. *Journal for the Theory of Social Behaviour*, **38**(1), pp. 67–86.

Newton, D. (2012) Moods, emotions and creative thinking: A framework for teaching. *Thinking Skills and Creativity*, **8**, pp. 33–44.

Shaheen, R. (2010) Creativity and education. *Creative Education*, **1**(3), pp. 166–169.

References

Amabile, T.M. (1983) The social psychology of creativity: A componential conceptualization. *Journal of Personality and Social Psychology*, **45**, pp. 357–376.

Amabile, T.M. (2013) Componential theory of creativity. In E.H. Kessler (ed.) *Encyclopaedia of management theory*. Thousand Oaks: Sage.

Ashby, G., Isen, A.M. and Turken, A.U. (1999) A neuropsychological theory of positive affect and its influence on cognition. *Psychological Review*, **106**, pp. 529–550.

Ashby, G., Valentin, V.V. and Turken, A.U. (2002) The effects of positive affect and arousal on working memory and executive attention: Neurobiology and computational models. In S. Moore and M. Oaksford (eds) *Emotional cognition: From brain to behaviour*. Amsterdam: John Benjamins.

Barrett, T., Webster, P., Guyotte, K.W., Sochacka, N., Costantino, T.E. and Kellam, N.N. (2015) Collaborative creativity of STEAM: Narratives of art education students' experiences in transdisciplinary spaces. *International Journal of Education and the Arts*, **16**(15), pp. 1–38.

Beghetto, R.A. (2007) Does creativity have a place in classroom discussions? Prospective teachers' response preferences. *Thinking Skills and Creativity*, **2**(1), pp. 1–9.

Chang, M.-L. and Davis, H.A. (2009) Understanding the role of teacher appraisals in shaping the dynamics of their relationships with students: Deconstructing teachers' judgments of disruptive behavior/students. In P. A. Schutz and M. Zembylas (eds) *Advances in teacher emotions research*. New York: Springer.

Craft, A. (2001) *An analysis of research and literature on creativity in education*. London: Qualifications and Curriculum Authority.

Craft, A. (2003) The limits to creativity in education: Dilemmas for the educator. *British Journal of Educational Studies*, **51**(2), pp. 113–127.

Craft, A. (2005) *Creativity in schools: Tensions and dilemmas*. Abingdon: Routledge.

Fasko, D. (2001) Education and creativity. *Creativity Research Journal*, **13**(3 and 4), pp. 317–327.

Finke, R.A., Ward, T.B. and Smith, S. (1992) *Creative cognition: Theory, research and applications*. Cambridge, MA: MIT Press.

Fredrickson, B.L. and Branigan, C. (2005) Positive emotions broaden the scope of attention and thought-action repertoires. *Cognition and Emotion*, **19**, pp. 313–332.

Friedman, R.S., Fishbach, A., Förster, J. and Werth, L. (2003) Attentional priming effects on creativity. *Creativity Research Journal*, **15**(2 and 3), pp. 277–286.

Friedman, R.S. and Förster, J. (2005) Effects of motivational cues on perceptual asymmetry: Implications for creativity and analytical problem solving. *Journal of Personality and Social Psychology*, **88**(2), pp. 263–275.

Friedman, R.S. and Förster, J. (2010) Implicit affective cues and attentional tuning: An integrative review. *Psychological Bulletin*, **136**(5), pp. 875–893.

Fromm, E. (1978) Primary process and secondary process in waking and in altered states of consciousness. *Journal of Altered States of Consciousness*, **4**, pp. 115–128.

Gable, P. and Harmon-Jones, E. (2010) The motivational dimensional model of affect: Implications for breadth of attention, memory, and cognitive categorisation. *Cognition and Emotion*, **24**(2), pp. 322–337.

Gardner, H. (1987) *The mind's new science: A history of the cognitive revolution*. New York: Basic Books.

Gardner, H. (1993) *Creating minds*. New York: Basic Books.

Gaspar, D. and Mabic, M. (2015) Creativity in higher education. *Universal Journal of Educational Research*, **3**(9), pp. 598–605.

Hennessey, B.A. and Amabile, T.M. (1987) *Creativity and learning: What research says to the teacher*. West Haven: National Education Association, Professional Library, PO Box 509, 06516.

Howard-Jones, P.A. (2002) A dual-state model of creative cognition for supporting strategies that foster creativity in the classroom. *International Journal of Technology and Design Education*, **12**, pp. 215–226. http://doi.org/10.1023/A:1020243429353.

Hui, A.N.N. and Yuen, T.C.M. (2010) The blossoming of creativity in education in Asia: Changing views and challenging practices. *Thinking Skills and Creativity*, **5**(3), pp. 155–158.

Isen, A.M., Daubman, K.A. and Nowicki, G.P. (1987) Positive affect facilitates creative problem solving. *Journal of Personality and Social Psychology*, **52**(6), pp. 1122–1131.

Isen, A.M., Johnson, M.M., Mertz, E. and Robinson, G.F. (1985) The influence of positive affect on the unusualness of word associations. *Journal of Personality and Social Psychology*, **48**(6), pp. 1413–1426.

Jeffrey, B. (2006) Creative teaching and learning: Towards a common discourse and practice. *Cambridge Journal of Education*, **36**(3), pp. 399–414.

Jeffrey, B. and Craft, A. (2004) Teaching creatively and teaching for creativity: Distinctions and relationships. *Educational Studies*, **30**(1), pp. 77–87.

Kaila, H.L. (2005) Democratizing schools across the world to stop killing creativity in children: An Indian perspective. *Counselling Psychology Quarterly*, **18**(1), pp. 1–6.

Kandiko, C.B. (2012) Leadership and creativity in higher education: The role of interdisciplinarity. *London Review of Education*, **10**(2), pp. 191–200.

Kasof, J. (1997) Creativity and breadth of attention. *Creativity Research Journal*, **10**(4), 303–315.

Kieran, M. (2014) Creativity as a virtue of character. In S.B. Kaufman and E.S. Paul (eds) *The philosophy of creativity*. New York: Oxford University Press.

Kounios, J., Fleck, J.I., Green, D.L., Payne, L., Stevenson, J.L., Bowden, E.M. and Jung-Beeman, M. (2008) The origins of insight in resting-state brain activity. *Neuropsychologia*, **46**, pp. 281–291.

Kris, E. (1952) *Psychoanalytic explorations in art*. New York: International Universities Press.

Lin, Y.-S. (2011) Fostering creativity through education: A conceptual framework of creative pedagogy. *Creative Education*, **2**(3), pp. 149–155.

Livingston, L. (2010) Teaching creativity in higher education. *Arts Education Policy Review*, **111**(2), pp. 59–62.

Lubart, T.I. (2001) Models of the creative process: Past, present and future. *Creativity Research Journal*, **13**(3–4), pp. 295–308.

Martindale, C. (1995) Creativity and connectionism. In S.M. Smith, T.B. Ward and R.A. Finke (eds) *The creative cognition approach*. Cambridge, MA: MIT Press.

Martindale, C. (1999) Biological basis of creativity. In R.J. Sternberg (ed.) *Handbook of creativity*. New York: Cambridge University Press.

Mayer, R.E. (1999) Fifty years of creativity research. In R.J. Sternberg (ed.) *Handbook of creativity*. New York: Cambridge University Press.

Mednick, S.A. (1962) The associative basis of the creative process. *Psychological Review*, **69**, pp. 220–232.

Mendelsohn, G. (1976) Associative and attentional processes in creative performance. *Journal of Personality*, **44**, pp. 341–369.

Mitchell, R.L.C. and Phillips, L.H. (2007) The psychological, neurochemical and functional neuroanatomical mediators of the effects of positive and negative mood on executive functions. *Neuropsychologia*, **45**(4), pp. 617–629.

NACCCE (1999) *All our futures: Creativity, culture and education*. London: DfEE.

Rhodes, M. (1961) An analysis of creativity. *Phi Delta Kappan*, **42**, pp. 305–310.

Rinkevich, J.L. (2011) Creative teaching: Why it matters and where to begin. *The Clearing House*, **84**(5), pp. 219–223.

Robinson, K. (2009) Ken Robinson: Do schools kill creativity? [Online]. Available from: www.ted.com/talks/ken_robinson_says_schools_kill_creativity (Accessed 30 October 2016).

Runco, M.A. (2004) Creativity. *Annual Review of Psychology*, **55**, pp. 657–687.

Runco, M.A. and Chand, I. (1995) Cognition and creativity. *Educational Psychology Review*, **7**(3), pp. 243–267.

Runco, M.A. and Sakamoto, S. O. (1999) Experimental studies of creativity. In R.J. Sternberg (ed.) *Handbook of creativity*. Cambridge: Cambridge University Press.

Sawyer, R. (2006) *Explaining creativity: The science of human innovation*. New York: Oxford University Press.

Sawyer, R.K. (2004) Creative teaching: Collaborative discussion as disciplined improvisation. *Educational Researcher*, **33**(2), pp. 12–20. http://doi.org/10.3102/0013189X033002012.

Shaheen, R. (2010) Creativity and education. *Creative Education*, **1**(3), pp. 166–169.

Sternberg, R.J. (2010) The nature of creativity. *Creativity Research Journal*, **18**(1), pp. 87–98.

Sternberg, R.J. and Lubart, T.I. (1999) The concept of creativity: Prospects and paradigms. In R.J. Sternberg (ed.) *Handbook of creativity*. Cambridge: Cambridge University Press.

Torrance, E.P. (1966) *The Torrance tests of creative thinking*. Princeton: Personnel Press.

Treffinger, D.J., Renzulli, J.S. and Feldhusen, J.F. (1971) Problems in the assessment of creative thinking. *The Journal of Creative Behavior*, **5**, pp. 104–111.

Treffinger, D.J., Young, G., Selby, E. and Shepardson, C. (2002) *Assessing creativity: A guide for educators*. Storrs, CT: National Research Center on the Gifted and Talented.

Walberg, H.J. (1988) Creativity and talent as learning. In R.J. Sternberg (ed.) *The nature of creativity: Contemporary psychological perspectives*. Cambridge: Cambridge University Press.

Wallas, G. (1926) *The art of thought*. New York: Harcourt Brace and Co.

Westby, E.L. and Dawson, V.L. (1995) Creativity: Asset or burden in the classroom? *Creativity Research Journal*, **8**(1), pp. 1–10.

Wu, H.-Y., Wu, H.-S., Chen, I.-S. and Chen, H.-C. (2014) Exploring the critical influential factors of creativity for college students: A multiple criteria decision-making approach. *Thinking Skills and Creativity*, **11**, pp. 1–21.

Yeh, C.S.-H. (2015) Exploring the effects of videogame play on creativity performances and emotional responses. *Computers in Human Behavior*, **53**, pp. 396–407.

Zhou, J. and Oldham, G.R. (2001) Enhancing creative performance: Effects of expected developmental assessment strategies and creative personality. *Journal of Creative Behavior*, **35**(3), pp. 151–167.

4 Reading, writing and dyslexia

Understanding the myths, supporting education

Lorna Bourke

Introduction

Reading and writing are complex skills that require effective instruction and practice. The main aim of this chapter is to outline some common assumptions that are made about how these skills develop. This includes notions regarding the effect that the development of spoken language has on literacy development, the impact of different methods of instruction on reading and writing, and the contested nature of dyslexia. The chapter will evaluate the evidence that supports those assumptions and the teaching practices that have arisen from them. In order to do this, a number of sources (e.g. newspapers, peer-reviewed journal articles, Department for Education documents) are used to compare and contrast theoretical and practice-based perspectives in education and psychology. Ultimately, this chapter aims to show that being equipped with a better understanding of the complex cognitive processes involved in literacy will enable the improvement of life chances and experiences for a great many children and encourage them to enjoy reading and writing irrespective of the many challenges.

Learning to talk and literacy

> Children who are not fluent speakers will always face difficulty writing, while those children who enjoy reading are likely to become more sophisticated speakers.
>
> (Sweetman, 1996: 16)

It is widely assumed in educational literature that most of what children need to know about literacy can be gleaned from their experience in developing spoken language skills. Whilst spoken language is quite sensibly identified as one of the primary avenues for cognitive development (e.g. Vygotsky, 1976; see Chapter 10 to learn more about Vygotsky's views on the relationship between language and thought), there are other complex interactive processes involved in the development of both reading and writing. They include developmental changes in the internal mechanisms that support learning through memorisation and recall. For example, from around the age of 5–6 years, a greater capacity to store and manipulate phonological (sound based) information in working memory (Baddeley, 1986; see Chapter 2 for more about working memory and the phonological loop) is closely aligned to the development of inner speech (sub-vocal articulation) skills. This corresponds with children's increased tendency to decode (reading) and encode (writing) information in their environment in a phonological form (Hitch *et al.*, 1988). In other words, what appears as a visible improvement in their literacy is actually driven by invisible improvements in their memory. We will explore this relationship between memory and literacy in more detail later on. For now, suffice it to say that recognising these hidden elements and building them into our understanding of the teaching of reading and writing could help us to account for the widely different rates at which children progress in literacy (Bourke and Adams, 2003; 2010; Bourke *et al.*, 2014).

Both psychologists and educators recognise the primary importance of the association between vocabulary and literacy. Put simply, it is a lot easier to read a word if the word is already known to the reader. Alongside an awareness of the phonological composition of words (e.g. syllables, onset and rime [explained later], phonemes), vocabulary knowledge could be considered a key foundation behind complex cognitive activities such as reading and writing, at least in the early stages of instruction. From Sweetman's (1996) perspective there appears to be a causal relationship between spoken language production and writing. The importance of spoken language is evident in the three main teaching approaches associated with writing instruction outlined in the National Literacy Strategy (NLS) (i.e. Talk for writing, Shared writing, and the Development of transcription skills to an automatic level). When talking for writing, children are encouraged to develop their ideas, think about the ways in which language is structured and include a more diverse range of vocabulary (DfES, 2001). Although the potential underlying internal processes are not specified, the practice is based on the idea that there are common factors that unite spoken and written language. In effect, these approaches demonstrate a belief that much of what young children need to learn about story-writing can be gained from story-telling.

We have, up until now, been viewing language development as single entity when in fact it could be conceptualised as two separate processes, the production of language and the comprehension of language. Although there is typically a strong relationship between an individual's abilities in relation to these two processes (see Bryant *et al.*, 1990), they can also be dissociated. Thus, it is possible to produce words and phrases without actually knowing what they mean, a phenomenon which can be observed in both spoken and written form. In psychological terms this is known as the difference between *expressive* and *receptive* language.

Receptive (comprehension) (RL) and expressive (production) (EL) language abilities are both thought to be factors which explain individual differences in children's educational outcomes (Bryant *et al.*, 1990). Although this relationship impacts on educational outcomes for all children, research has shown it to be a key factor in determining academic attainment in low-income families in the UK and USA. According to Ann Fernald (Fernald *et al.*, 2013) from Stanford University, USA, a language 'gap' (measured using assessments of expressive and receptive vocabulary) between low and higher income families emerges in infancy between 18 and 24 months of age. This is despite programmes and initiatives, including Head Start in the USA from 1965 (Currie and Thomas, 1995), the Nursery Voucher scheme introduced by the Conservative government in 1996 (SCAA, 1996) and Sure Start Local Programmes (SSLPs) by the Labour government in the UK from 1998 which have sought to reduce this inequality by fostering close relationships between parents, education and health within communities.

Research focus: challenges in shrinking the languages 'gap'

Despite an emphasis on the development of expressive language (EL) skills in many Sure/Head Start pre-school programmes, the language gap between lower and higher income families continues to be pervasive and is one of the enduring predictors of attainment once children are in the school system (Hemphill and Tivnan, 2008). Consequently, an important question remains regarding whether children actually benefit from such interventions. A national evaluation of Sure Start found that the programme had no clear effects on children in terms of school readiness (Early Years Foundation Stage Profile measuring language, numeracy and social skills) (NESS, 2010; see also Currie and Thomas, 1995 for critique of Head Start, USA). One reason for this may be that it is only in the early stages of formal schooling that we can start to make progress on this issue. Currently, 94 per cent of children participate in government-funded early education (DfE, 2014a). A rich language experience for children at this stage would be one where they are able to hear a diversity of words being spoken from parents and caregivers from which they can learn. However, this speech needs to be *child directed*, which encompasses paying attention to children, using words with the specific intention of building their vocabulary and, critically, it means engaging the child in conversations, especially by asking them questions (Peterson and Roberts, 2003).

The influence of language on literacy can be explored in more depth through studying the development of private speech or 'self-talk'. Lev Vygotsky (1976) noticed that from the ages of 2 to 7 years children could be heard talking to themselves without the intention of it being for the information of others. He determined that this was a form of self-directed communication that was crucial for providing guidance and regulating behaviour when children were performing tasks. This form of talk is known to enhance literacy skills in the early stages of development, but then tends to be replaced by 'inner speech' processes whereby the 'self-talk' occurs within the mind and is not audible to others. This is particularly useful when encountering difficult tasks in education; by the keeping the mind focused on the goals of the task, and/or increasing motivation to complete the task educational outcomes can improve. One noticeable variation to this rule is that young children are less likely to use private speech when a teacher is present (Vygotsky, 1976). There are a number of reasons why this might be the case. For example, the expectation that children remain silent whilst undertaking their work could be one factor and, therefore, this developmental phase may need to become more 'normalised' within education settings. The externalisation of thought through speech in young children occurs when tasks are more difficult and self-regulation (e.g. focusing attention and keeping on task) becomes more important. However, the appropriateness of the task is determined by teachers and may on occasion be too difficult or too easy for them to use this innate strategy (Behrend et al., 1989).

Building on the concepts of 'self-talk' and 'inner speech', Hitch et al. (1988) have studied what they call 'sub-vocal based processes' and their use in information processing and retention. More specifically, the application of a phonological code to information (e.g. phonics) occurs through the development of active speech processes in working memory. This ability is crucial to the alphabetic phase of reading and writing. At this point children's writing becomes increasingly recognisable to the reader because of a more systematic application of phoneme-grapheme rules (i.e. the way a word sounds compared to how it is written). Prior to this there is a tendency to apply a visual code to words during which strings of letters and words are produced which can bear little resemblance to the target word.

One means of assessing whether the strategy the children are using for processing visual representations (e.g. words on a page) is visual or phonological is to look at the errors they make with visually and phonologically similar stimuli. If visually similar items (key/spade, knife/saw) are being confused with each other then they are using a visual representation method, whereas if phonologically similar items (bar/car, mat/rat) are confused, then they are applying predominantly phonological representations to information. Hitch and colleagues established that children younger than 4 years of age tended to process incoming pictorial information in a visual format rather than using phonological information acquired through the sub-vocal naming or labelling of the images they were presented with (i.e. silently saying the names to themselves, in which case vocabulary knowledge would be important). As children become older the phonological similarity effect is increasingly evident, suggesting more sophisticated manipulation of phonological representations via sub-vocalisations (Henry, 1991). Furthermore, McNeil and Johnston (2004) found that poor readers were on average more likely to demonstrate a larger visual similarity effect, and a smaller phonological similarity effect than typically developing readers at an older age (i.e. 8–9 years). This confirms that the ability to process and retain information into phonological form through inner speech processes is related to the level of literacy achieved by the student. It suggests that not only can we use tests of sub-vocalisation to monitor literacy development, but that there are also implications of a link between sub-vocalisation, literacy development and methods of reading instruction (e.g. synthetic phonics) which are worthy of further examination (Palmer, 2000).

In conclusion, we can see from this research that the development of memory processes, spoken vocabulary knowledge and the use of sub-vocalisations were all found to be important predictors of both literacy development and, by extension, educational outcomes over time. However, in the early stages of literacy development, progress is not only accounted for by spoken language fluency but also print knowledge (letter identification and reading) and children's sensitivity to the sound structure (phonology) of words (Dickinson *et al.*, 2003). In combination, all these factors represent a more comprehensive language approach to early literacy, and this is recognised in the instructional programme for children in the UK (Early Years Foundation Stage Profile [EYFSP], DfE, 2014b). Therefore, since there is evidence that the strongest impact on a child's writing skills is their ability to read (independent of EL and RL), it is worth considering the dominant method of reading instruction currently used in UK schools, the synthetic phonics method, and evaluating its effectiveness.

Reflections

Can you remember how you learnt to read? Were you 'taught' in a formal sense (flashcards with words accompanied by associated pictures, sounding out words into their individual sounds) or through more informal methods?

How might a teacher use established methods of instruction to support a child who has struggled to learn to read through more informal methods?

Learning to read and phonics

> Literacy development involves encouraging children to link sounds and letters to begin to read and write. Children must be given access to a wide range of reading materials (books, poems, and other written materials) to ignite their interest.
>
> (DfE, 2014b: 8)

In 2005, it was announced by the Education Secretary, Ruth Kelly, that the main approach to teaching reading was to be synthetic phonics. This involves children learning the individual sounds of letters and then blending those sounds from the very beginning of reading instruction. Since phonics instruction had declined in popularity since the 1960s, it was more typical for children to learn to read words by sight (e.g. whole-word 'look say' method) and to focus on their meaning. With more and more evidence being presented detailing the relative advantages of phonics methods, a teaching strategy based on analytic phonics became more widely practised in the UK. This relies on both encouraging children to read by sight and to learn letter sounds at the beginning (onset), the end (rime) and then the middle of words. It is not until they are at the end of their first or in their second year of instruction that they will be taught how to blend letter sounds together to decode unfamiliar words (DfEE, 1999). The application of phonics instruction (e.g. synthetic phonics) remains controversial, with arguments presented on both sides of the debate between a choice of these and whole-word approaches to reading. The Department for Education's (DfE, 2014b) perspective is clearly suggesting that the development of literacy skills in the classroom involves both instruction by phonics and exposure to different genres to increase motivation and understand the purpose of reading. Sir Jim Rose, who led an Independent Review of the Teaching of Early Reading in 2006, as well as an Independent Review of the Primary Curriculum and Dyslexia in 2008, came out very heavily in favour of a systematic approach to teaching phonics through the synthetic phonics method. Furthermore, the Rose Report (2006) accused critics of trying to 'destroy' phonics programmes which in turn would cause damage to children's education.

The evidence on which Rose based his report came from a study conducted by the now Emeritus Professor Rhona Johnston, University of Hull, and her colleagues. They have continued to conduct longitudinal research and have found over a number of years that children taught by the synthetic phonics approach demonstrate superior reading and spelling abilities compared to those taught via analytic phonics (i.e. both traditional 'whole-word' and some application of phonics) methods. This shows that despite English being such an irregular language, children are not disadvantaged when taught an approach to reading that is common in more regular languages (Johnston *et al.*, 2012). Regardless of the support for phonics programmes, there still seems to be a sense of outrage among some members of the public, best represented by the views of Michael Rosen, a leading children's author. His most famous book, *We're Going on a Bear Hunt*, is widely admired for the expression of sound through language. However, according to Rosen the focus on phonics is inhibiting the development of a love for reading:

> Is it any wonder children are leaving school unable to read? Synthetic phonics is being presented as a cure-all but will never be enough to teach kids to read. Let's stop pretending phonics will solve everything, and develop a book-loving culture.
>
> (Michael Rosen, as reported in *The Telegraph*, 17 June 2012)

Termed the 'Reading Wars' in the USA in recognition of the strong feelings associated with the issue, it seems incredible for those feelings to be directed at an evidence-based instructional programme. They appear to be further compounded by the introduction of a controversial checklist to assess children's ability to decode *nonwords* in order to estimate their progress on the synthetic phonics programme. This involves children reading aloud to the teacher 40 words, of which 20 are nonwords (e.g. *stin, proom, sars*) (DfE, 2013). Why use nonwords if there is so much controversy over this? For cognitive developmental psychologists like myself the use of nonwords in itself is not controversial and represents a well-established methodology first introduced by Ebbinghaus (1885/1913). Ebbinghaus used nonwords in order to assess someone's ability to learn something new (i.e. a short-term/working memory process) without the aid of knowledge gained through prior experiences (i.e. long-term memory). When a child reads a word they have encountered before it is hard to know if they are phonically decoding that word each time they read it or simply remembering the pronunciation of the word from long-term memory. Through the use of nonwords we eliminate the possibility of them accessing a long-term memory for the pronunciation of the word, since they will not have heard anyone say it before. Therefore, as the DfE (2013) explains, using nonwords allows teachers and parents to identify which children could use the phonics decoding strategy they have learnt in order to read an unfamiliar word for which they would have no advantage from prior experience of encountering it.

One concern with regard to the phonics screening check (i.e. the checklist of nonwords) which has more serious psychological connotations is the idea that children who perform badly on this checklist could be labelled as 'failures' from a young age. This criticism stems, in part, from the EYFSP (DfE, 2014b) and DfE (2016) statistics which indicate that some children are not meeting the standards outlined previously for their reading (total meeting standards 77 per cent, 72 per cent boys and 83 per cent girls) and their writing (total meeting standards 72.6 per cent, 66 per cent boys and 80 per cent girls). Yet, it is worth recognising that the figures have improved steadily from 2013 (reading, 70.5 per cent and writing, 61.9 per cent). Furthermore, it's interesting to note that although girls are outperforming boys on both tasks, Johnston *et al.* (2012) found evidence for synthetic phonics benefitting boys over girls in terms of their reading performance by the end of their third year. This, suggests that this method of instruction could provide a way to ameliorate differences. It is particularly important as boys are, on average, less accomplished at literacy based tasks at all levels of assessment (e.g. EYFS Profile, SATs at all Key Stages, and GCSE). If it is possible to redress this imbalance by the time children reach Year 4 (KS2) with a synthetic phonics programme then this should surely be considered, especially at the earliest stages of education before statutory education begins, as reading and writing could be more challenging to boys based on the evidence presented in the EYFS Profile assessment. If action is not taken to find effective ways to reverse the trend, then the poorer performance by boys will undoubtedly impact on their motivation, self-efficacy and self-esteem, despite excellent male role models in a multitude of writing genres beyond school, including song-writing. (See Chapter 7 for a critical perspective challenging our interpretation of 'gender differences' in education like this one.) Ultimately, they could typify this within themselves, as '*boys not being good at language*' in its widest sense (see also Bourke and Adams, 2012, for a fuller discussion).

Research focus: self-esteem and reading

It is important to enhance the self-esteem of both genders in relation to their literacy abilities, and this can be done through timetabled opportunities to discuss reading and writing. Children who are encouraged to express ideas, feelings and emotions will also become more motivated through a belief that they can succeed (self-efficacy) and through 'demonstrating their understanding [comprehension] when talking to others about what they have read' (DfE, 2014b: 11). In positive circumstances, the sense of mastery in being able to decode previously unknown words can no doubt be made to feel like fun. Debbie Hepplewhite (2016), author of the *No Nonsense Phonics Skills* programme, makes very clear that synthetic phonics can be an all-round effective method of teaching reading and spelling skills. Her programme aims to be fun, motivational and stimulate a joy of reading while also providing an opportunity for children to practise applying their decoding skills to unfamiliar real words.

The ability to manipulate sound and understand its meaning within the context of words inherent in the phonics approach is a lifelong skill that will assist students not only in the early stages of reading but also when they are in higher education and are introduced to unfamiliar terminology. As Rhona Johnston suggests, although synthetic phonics is common across other countries using an alphabetic system (e.g. Europe and the USA), analytic phonics was more widely practised in the UK. One of the main reasons cited for an emphasis on this traditional 'whole-word' approach was the differences between the English orthography (writing system) and others. The English writing system contains many more words with irregular sound patterns (e.g. *hint, tint, pint*) and is described as a 'deep orthography'. Alternatively, in a language with a transparent orthography (e.g. Finnish or German) the direct spelling [grapheme] to sound [phoneme] correspondences will help students to learn the one-to-one relationship between graphemes and phonemes in a more systematic and consistent way. However, as we saw earlier in this section, the research by Johnston and colleagues (2012) presented evidence for the longitudinal positive impact of synthetic phonics on children's reading skills even in a UK group learning to read English. This was especially evident for children from low-income families who would normally underperform in reading, but with the synthetic phonics method performed, on average, just as well as those from more socially advantaged circumstances.

In conclusion, despite the mountain of evidence to support it, critics of the synthetic phonics approach remain opposed to what they see as an artificially limited and overly technical approach to learning how to read. From an evidence-based perspective, there are some merits to their concerns. There is no doubt that children need motivation to read and authors such as Michael Rosen, Philip Pullman and J.K. Rowling capture this through their imaginative writing. From a psychological perspective the developmental progression through understanding the relationship between sound and print can be enhanced by the programmes of synthetic phonics instruction that schools have been encouraged to employ. The current perspective of the DfE (2014b) seems to bridge the gulf between children's authors and education experts by suggesting that children should be exposed to myriad examples of literature as well as gaining an understanding of a phonological decoding approach to reading.

Working memory and learning to write

Near the start of this chapter we touched on the idea that there is a relationship between literacy and language, and the use of what is known as 'inner speech' or sub-vocalisations. To properly understand the link between inner speech and literacy, it is important to understand the role of working memory in the development of what is known as phonological awareness (e.g. the understanding that spoken words and syllables are composed of a specific sequence of individual sounds) and coding skills (e.g. the ability to produce, discriminate and manipulate the sound structure of language that might be presented in various forms including print and is distinct from its meaning) (Torgesen and Burgess, 1998). Working memory is a concept that was developed in the 1970s to explain how we flexibly employ various cognitive processes (i.e. visuospatial 'sketchpad', phonological 'loop', attention) to store and process information in our limited capacity short-term memory (STM) (Baddeley, 1986; 2000; see also Cowan, 2010). The working memory model is our basis for understanding how a variety of complex mental activities, including language, reasoning and problem-solving, are thought to operate. (See Chapter 2 to learn more about the proposed mechanisms of the working memory model.)

Reading and writing are considered to be supported by two main strategies which utilise working memory: sub-vocal rehearsal (saying words inside our head) which requires the phonological loop and chunking (taking smaller units of information, e.g. phonemes, and converting or binding them into larger units of information, e.g. syllables and words) which is supported by the episodic buffer through integrating or binding together the various associated features.

Chunking involves thinking about the relationships between individual components (e.g. combining the verb 'walk' with the suffix 'ed' to produce the past tense verb 'walked', or the sound that is associated with the shape of a letter or word). When processes like chunking are not automatic (i.e. well-practised) they will also require conscious direction from the central executive. When searching and retrieving information from long-term memory is required this will also be directed by the central executive, which helps to monitor and regulate the process through focusing attentional resources on the current goal (e.g. story components, vocabulary, spelling, handwriting). The involvement of the central executive in these processes tells us that they will require conscious effort and concentration; to do this effectively on demand and reduce the overall cognitive load, implied in the viewpoint of the DfEE (2001) below, will require practice.

> Like Ben, many children find independent writing a struggle because they are faced with too many hard things to do at once. He has to plan what he will write, think about which words to choose and how to order them into sentences, work out the spellings for each and transcribe them all onto the page. For experienced writers, much of this is automatic, and only occasionally requires conscious control.
>
> (DfEE, 2001: 10)

Thus, the ability of an individual to marshal all these working memory processes and resources is likely to be a major factor in determining their ability to produce a piece of written work. Consequently, one of the best known cognitive models of writing by Kellogg (1996) explores how the various components of working memory interact with the six different processes of writing described by Hayes (1996).

Let us imagine a scenario where a child is asked by their teacher to write down what they did during their summer holidays as a class exercise. In this scenario, if we focus on Hayes' 'planning' process we see that the linguistic processes involved in speech are required (e.g. composing the linguistic structure of each sentence) as well as the goal-related nature of writing (e.g. composing a 'story' with a beginning, middle and resolution). All of this draws on long-term memory knowledge of narrative conventions and linguistic rules, thus requiring working memory to access and process this knowledge as we plan. All these processes occur recursively within a short time-frame whilst writing. That is, we are often simultaneously planning what to write next, while currently writing or typing (translation) and also casting a glance back over what has been written (reviewing). The more we practise doing these things the less attention and effort we need to spend while doing them, which is known as 'automisation'. The more automised a process becomes the fewer resources it requires from our working memory. Handwriting and spelling will tend to be more automatised in older children and adults, therefore allowing for working memory resources to be directed towards generating more linguistically complex ideas. Thus, as a consequence of being less mature, both in terms of working memory processes and experience, a young child's approach to writing will be not just be quantitatively different (e.g. write less, include less a diverse vocabulary, shorter words and sentences) but also qualitatively different.

These qualitative differences between younger and older writers are highlighted by Bereiter *et al.* (1988), who devised two models to explain them. The knowledge-telling model proposes that younger children are only able to generate a coherent narrative when they can use information on a familiar topic and in a genre that has been well-practised. By contrast adults are able to generate narratives that involve the transfer of knowledge into a novel genre and/or subject area (the knowledge-transforming model). To do this, the knowledge may need to be reconstructed, which may require additional cognitive resources to support that. Thus, when young children are required to compose a story involving unfamiliar elements there will be marked differences in the cohesiveness of their story compared to an adult writer. Over time, we would expect younger novice writers to grow and develop into more experienced writers, but this development does not occur at the same pace for all children. Bourke and Adams (2003) found that, as children mature, those who first show the ability to move beyond describing action sequences to include episodic narrative components within their writing are more likely to have better central executive resources. An example of this can be seen below in the reconstruction of children's writing samples displayed in Figure 4.1.

Here we can see variation in writing between three children aged 7 years, all of whom are in the same school year (Year 2, end of KS1) and have been receiving formal education instruction in literacy for the same amount of time (about 3 years). As such, the differences we see between the three children in terms of the use of episodic narrative is likely to be a result of differences in central executive resources. It is worth noting that the link between central executive resources and self-regulation does not apply to spoken language, where it is the phonological loop which appears to be crucial in explaining differences between children (Gathercole and Baddeley, 1993).

Encouraging young writers

Young writers should be encouraged to engage in a wider range of strategies than simply 'talk for writing' and there are several methods we can use to support the development of the skills

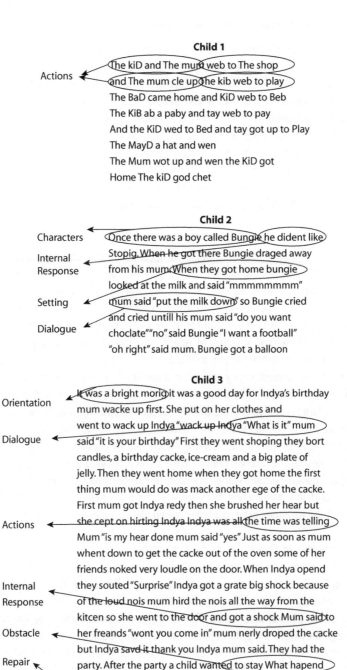

Child 1

Actions

The kiD and The mum web to The shop
and The mum cle up the kib web to play
The BaD came home and KiD web to Beb
The KiB ab a paby and tay web to pay
And the KiD wed to Bed and tay got up to Play
The MayD a hat and wen
The Mum wot up and wen the KiD got
Home The kiD god chet

Child 2

Characters

Internal
Response

Setting

Dialogue

Once there was a boy called Bungie he dident like
Stopig. When he got there Bungie draged away
from his mum. When they got home bungie
looked at the milk and said "mmmmmmmm"
mum said "put the milk down" so Bungie cried
and cried untill his mum said "do you want
choclate""no" said Bungie "I want a football"
"oh right" said mum. Bungie got a balloon

Child 3

Orientation

Dialogue

Actions

Internal
Response

Obstacle

Repair

It was a bright morig it was a good day for Indya's birthday
mum wacke up first. She put on her clothes and
went to wack up Indya "wack up Indya "What is it" mum
said "it is your birthday" First they went shoping they bort
candles, a birthday cacke, ice-cream and a big plate of
jelly. Then they went home when they got home the first
thing mum would do was mack another ege of the cacke.
First mum got Indya redy then she brushed her hear but
she cept on hirting Indya Indya was all the time was telling
Mum "is my hear done mum said "yes" Just as soon as mum
whent down to get the cacke out of the oven some of her
friends noked very loudle on the door. When Indya opend
they souted "Surprise" Indya got a grate big shock because
of the loud nois mum hird the nois all the way from the
kitcen so she went to the door and got a shock Mum said to
her freands "wont you come in" mum nerly droped the cacke
but Indya saved it thank you Indya mum said. They had the
party. After the party a child wanted to stay What hapend
Next

Figure 4.1 Variation in three children's writing aged 7 years

necessary to do this. One such method is to provide narrative frames (or schemes) to act as retrieval aids. An example of this would be when prompts are provided within a genre of writing, including sentence starters: 'Jack enjoyed playing football because ...' and narrative outlines – introduce the story, describe the setting and people, talk about what happened, what emotions were involved, how the problem in the story was resolved, what happened in the end. Narrative frames can lessen the demands on working memory associated with the task by allowing the writer to externalise some of the information required outside of working memory. Another method we can use, and a focus common to many education systems, is to encourage the automatisation of transcription (e.g. handwriting and spelling) in younger writers (DfEE, 2001). This approach is well justified as it will have similar benefits in reducing the cognitive load on working memory.

In addition to these aids to working memory, it is important that all children are provided with the right environment (e.g. adequate timetabled opportunities) to practise simultaneously mana-ging (i.e. juggling) a number of the sub-processes of writing described by Hayes (1996). The ability to move back and forth between keeping in mind the story they want to convey, choosing appro-priate words, constructing relevant sentences and transcribing them onto the page in a meaningful manner needs to be practised if we wish them to be able to write qualitatively good stories (Bourke and Adams, 2003). Therefore, systems of education aimed at promoting good writing need to provide both the time and space for this to occur.

One further way of understanding individual differences in the development of writing is to undertake a qualitative analysis of the errors children make in their writing. Children's attempts at the spellings of unfamiliar words provide a visible opportunity to interpret the way in which they are making sense of the phoneme–grapheme relationships in words (i.e. the way a word sounds compared to how it is written) (Read, 1975). Awareness of phoneme–grapheme relationships is thought to co-occur with the development of inner speech outlined earlier (Vygotsky, 1976), which is to say that in younger writers words are said to oneself before writing them down. There is evidence to support this assumption from spelling mistakes made in writing that are consistent with the idea that the mistakes are sometimes based almost entirely on knowledge of word sounds (Read, 1975).

The writing samples in Figure 4.2 come from three children whose writing was assessed at several different ages as part of a longitudinal study (Bourke and Adams, 2003; 2010). If we look at the errors in the first sample of writing in Figure 4.2, this 5-year-old child is applying a rudi-mentary visual strategy (Ehri, 1980). They understand that graphemes relate to writing, but do not mark the boundaries of individual words. The writing is not decipherable by the reader (you can see the message they were trying to communicate in italics beside it) and so in that sense fails to meet the communication goal of writing which is a requirement of ELG10 (Standards and Testing Agency, 2016). The second sample of writing in Figure 4.2, from a different child, includes spelling errors that are typical of a non-phonological visual strategy (e.g. 'pikr' for *park*, 'thea' *they*, 'clamd' *climbed*, 'triy' *tree*). The third sample of writing in Figure 4.2 contains spellings which are phonically plausible (e.g. 'stirs' for *stairs*) because they can be read by the application of regular phonics rules (DfE, 2013). Therefore, when children move more concretely into an alphabetic strategy (i.e. observed through phonological errors demonstrating phonological coding, as we see in the third child) it will have positive impact on their ability to read and write (Adams *et al.*, 2011; Palmer, 2000). The associations between inner speech and writing suggest that phonological memory is

(1) tiWiNOMOMM　　　　*I play with my friends.*
MMeMRRVOo　　　　　*I open the door.*
enincMvMPbM　　　　　*I played out.*
WKVMOOIIIMe　　　　　*I played hopscotch.*
EiBNROOCnm　　　　　*I played with my friends.*

(2) The boyand The cat　　*The boy and the cat*
Went to the PiKR　　　　*went to the park*
And Thea clamd up　　　*and they climbed up*
The triy　　　　　　　　*the tree.*

(3) I Took my cat for a walk it was good wen we
got home my cat Ran up the stlrs I
Ran afta her Then I whent in to
the graden I and my cat whent on
Swing I whent up in the sky
So DID my cat Mum shotD At the cat

Figure 4.2 Three different children, different strategies, same age (5 years)

an important mediator in the skills associated with this complex, cognitively demanding task. We return to the same three children at age 7 as we consider the samples in Figure 4.3 below.

As we can see from the first sample, the visual strategy which was evident in the writing of the first child from the age 5 years group is evident again in their writing sample from when they are 7 years of age. There is a letter reversal for 'Dad' *Dab*. 'Pit' could be an attempt at a phonological representation of *picked*, if said with an approximate dialectical pronunciation. However, it does not meet the demands of a phonological representation that can be read by legal and permissible rules of language (orthographically). The second sample includes phonologically plausible words, such as 'wated' *waited* and so that child is demonstrating a developmental progression from what was a predominantly visual strategy for them at age 5 years. Interestingly, with the third sample of writing in Figure 4.3, in spelling the word *stethoscope*, the gaps (pauses) perfectly encapsulate the cognitive effort (working memory overload) they are making in sounding out the word despite evidence of a high level of mastery of phonics conventions. Analysing written texts in this way

(1) I went to the docd wen a was 5.
I went to the hobe. I got pit up Pon
My Mum and Dab a went to the docd.
I wnet to the docd. I went to home

(2) Once apon a time there lived a little girl
called Sofy. She Was Very ill so her mum
took her to the dockdas and she Wated a
long time. And She was also upto somethig
els. They were old wiman and she was
pushing them of the cher. Vinly the dockder
called Sofy. The dockder said come here
but he wadont so the dockder don it on his
mum. then Wile the dockder don it on his mum.
　The girl hid be hinde the dockdas
desk and Finly the dockder got her in a
flash She was don then She Went home.

(3) A Visit to the docters
One day Chelsey had to go to the
Docters with her Mum. "Oh Mum do
I have to go to the docters" "Yes
Sweatheart it is for your own good" "Doh"
replied Chelsey. Chelsey walked past two
people. One had hurt her arm. And the
man got plaster on his leg. Then
Chelsey wanted to sit down, they walked
past a chair. "mummy, mummy look
a chair please can I sit on it"? "No
Some body's sitting on it". "Chelsey Knox"
called the docter. "Right sit up here
we'll try the ste th is chope on you".
But there was nothing wrong with Chelsey
so they put something on her back
to check him out. "NO definitely nothing
wrong". So the docter gave Chelsey
a lollipop and Chelsey went home back
in the snow.

Figure 4.3 The same three children, still with different strategies, at a later age (7 years)

provides an objective method of understanding the developmental progression children are making towards effectively processing the sound structures of words (phonological awareness and coding), a key education goal in the early years of writing instruction.

In summary, we can see that a study of the relationship between memory and language can tell us a lot about the causes of many individual differences in language development, and can even suggest methods for promoting language development as well. Indeed, throughout this chapter when we have reviewed the main debates regarding the interrelationship between language skills and literacy, we've seen how the findings of these debates can be applied to both typical literacy development and instruction in education. However, recognising the processes and challenges faced in typical literacy development also provides a potential avenue to explore the difficulties in cognition faced by children diagnosed with dyslexia.

Phonological processing and dyslexia

Definitions of dyslexia are contested (e.g. DfES, 2004) leaving many educators unsure as to its nature and instructional requirements. Possession of only a rudimentary understanding of the condition and a lack of awareness of the variability in the severity of diagnoses can lead some educators to question the usefulness of support methods such as phonics training, provision of laptops or additional time given to dyslexic students. The lack of consensus on how dyslexia should be defined or what diagnostic criteria should be used is surprising considering the amount of research that has been conducted. It has led to a number of debates, including on whether dyslexia exists (as distinct from simply being a poor reader), what causes it, how the diagnosis informs supporting someone with dyslexia to read better, and the implications regarding different approaches. What we will see in this section are some of the main perspectives in explaining what dyslexia is, including its link with phonological processing deficits (phonological awareness and coding).

> Dyslexia is evident when accurate and fluent word reading and/or spelling develops very incompletely or with great difficulty. This focuses on literacy learning at the 'word' level and implies that the problem is severe and persistent despite appropriate learning opportunities.
>
> (BPS, 1999: 64)

The BPS definition of dyslexia shown above demonstrates that psychologists no longer consider the original IQ discrepancy method (at one time widely advocated by psychologists) to be a valid method for establishing whether someone has dyslexia. Under that previous system, an individual who was suspected of having dyslexia would be assessed on the Wechsler Intelligence Scale for Children (WISC-V, Wechsler, 2014) along with single word reading and spelling tests (e.g. Wide Range Achievement Test [WRAT 4], Robertson and Wilkinson, 2006). The assumption was that a mismatch between a child's mental age and chronological age as measured by the Wechsler IQ tests and then matched with difficulties with the reading tests demonstrated a reading difficulty such as dyslexia rather than general cognitive difficulty. One of the weaknesses of the IQ discrepancy method was that it could exclude from the diagnosis, and therefore exclude from appropriate assistance, poor readers with general learning difficulties who may be demonstrating the characteristics associated with dyslexia (Frederickson and Reason, 1995).

Controversy in our definitions of dyslexia have, in part, been driven by developments in our understanding of its causes. They include biological, cognitive and behavioural factors. One widely cited explanation for dyslexia for many years was the cerebellar deficit hypothesis (Frank and Levison, 1973). This is a *biological* model for dyslexia, proposing that the cerebellum (neural level explanation) was responsible, in part, for the motor control difficulties (e.g. a manifestation in speech articulation) that can contribute to the phonological processing deficits in reading which in turn were thought to cause dyslexia. Based on this model, Reynolds and Nicolson (2007) reported on an exercise-based intervention programme, Dyslexia, Dyspraxia, Attention Treatment (DDAT) that aimed to improve motor coordination, eye and hand tracking movements, and dual-task skills through conducting a variety of methods for 5 to 10 minutes, twice daily every day. This resulted in significant benefits in central and peripheral vision, motor skill and cognitive level abilities in speech/language fluency, phonology and working memory for both dyslexic and non-dyslexic low achieving readers over a sustained period of time. However, critics of the DDAT contradicted the evidence to support the effectiveness of the programme in improving literacy skills (Rack *et al.*, 2007). Instead, Rack and colleagues proposed the Phonological Processing Deficit (PPD) hypothesis as an alternative model for explaining dyslexia. Today, the PPD model is the dominant explanation and attempts to recognise the *cognitive* difficulties people have with reading and writing by examining the relationship between phonological awareness, phonological working memory and left hemisphere (language) (neural basis) processing. They suggest that it is difficulties in detecting and discriminating between phonemes in speech sounds and written forms (e.g. decoding of nonsense words) that accounts for the primary difficulties associated with dyslexia. Therefore, instructional programmes related to this perspective are closely aligned to the phonics approaches described previously.

Alongside changes in the definition of dyslexia and explanations for its origins, the other factor which makes dyslexia difficult for many educators to understand are the differences in diagnoses of dyslexia. Sometimes these differences are due to the variability in severity of the condition or the specific features of reading or memory that are affected (e.g. working memory, phonological awareness, verbal fluency, reading and spelling). Furthermore, challenges to literacy development can co-occur with other diagnoses (e.g. Irlen Syndrome, dyspraxia, attention deficit disorder). Irlen Syndrome can also be known as visual stress and the reaction to some wavelengths of light might mean that some people wear glasses with tinted lenses and/or use coloured overlay sheets similar to some dyslexics (Robinson and Conway, 1990). With all of these potential permutations out there, treating dyslexia appropriately is likely to be a complex process, even so far as to first identify which form of the condition the individual has. Therefore, it is unlikely that a single approach to assisting people with dyslexia will provide the answer to all forms of the condition. In addition, any approach to treating dyslexia needs to take into account that alongside any associated biological, cognitive and behavioural outcomes there are emotional factors related to their academic self-concept (e.g. self-esteem, self-efficacy) that need to be considered as well.

The assessments used to indicate dyslexia tend to focus on issues with word level skills (reading and spelling). However, it is important to acknowledge that someone with dyslexia often needs to direct considerable cognitive effort and processing resources (e.g. working memory) towards accurately representing the phonology of language (e.g. in spelling). This can come at the expense of monitoring and regulating handwriting fluency, grammatical constructions, punctuation, and the overall structure and coherence of texts, therefore adding to the complexity of the difficulties people with dyslexia are presenting with. As previously outlined, one approach to assisting students with organising their work is to provide an outline (narrative scheme) of the overall goals of the task to be completed. In particular, emphasising the sequence in which to place ideas, words and sentences. For example, young children might be encouraged to develop a mind map, with the main idea at the centre and then the supporting details around this. It would allow them to visualise the central idea together with their associated thoughts. Audio-recording ideas without thinking about the legibility of writing would enable them to capture their linguistic expression without the challenge of the slowness associated with their hand-writing. Considering positive and imaginative ways to encourage writing in people with dyslexia will complement the supplementary phonics instruction that they will undoubtedly be engaging in once they have been diagnosed.

Research focus: diagnosing dyslexia

This is typically represented in a three-part process. Initially, a dyslexia checklist is likely to be completed. The checklist usually comprises questions and/or statements that relate to ideas about the traits and behaviours someone might have if they are suspected of being dyslexic. It is fairly quick to work through but covers a wide range of factors (e.g. general areas of functioning, visual processes, reading, spelling, hearing, speech, writing, motor skills, maths, time management, memory, cognition, behaviour, health, development and personality). Examples can be easily found on an internet search. At the next stage a standardised 'at risk' profile is established using, for example, the Dyslexia Screening Test (DST-J) (Fawcett and Nicholson, 2004). This takes about 30 minutes to administer. It's worth noting that one of the authors of this test contributed to the debate on dyslexia outlined earlier. The assessments include: bead threading, postural stability, backward digit span, rapid naming, verbal fluency, phonological awareness, reading, spelling, writing and vocabulary.

The diagnosis of dyslexia can be conducted by a number of professionals, including educational and clinical psychologists. The practitioner should be registered with the Health and Care Professions Council (HCPC) and the British Psychological Society. Further information can be gained through agencies such as Dyslexia Action (www.dyslexia.action.org.uk) and local education authorities. The diagnosis should take 2–3 hours and can be undertaken over a number of separate sessions. There may be a focus on social and emotional factors as well.

Reflections

Think about the differences between the checklist, screener and diagnosis. Depending on which one(s) inform a child's assessment for dyslexia, what implications does this have for treatments and interventions?

Conclusion

A young reader or writer, with or without a diagnosis of dyslexia, faces a number of challenges in becoming fluent in their literacy skills. In this chapter we have explored how that fluency is related to a number of key factors, including self-talk (sub-vocalisation), vocabulary, self-esteem and memory. Ultimately, I hope to have demonstrated that an integrated perspective which understands how those processes develop in relation to each another in the context of instruction programmes is vitally important to delivering effective and motivational literacy education.

Key points

- Reading and writing are complex cognitive activities.
- Children within the same class progress at different rates.
- Understanding some of the neuropsychological and cognitive processes that underpin reading and writing will assist in providing appropriately targeted and adapted instruction programmes.
- Literacy is fundamental to the contribution we can make to society. Therefore, it is important to safeguard children on issues related to self-esteem, self-efficacy and motivation.
- Talking, reading and writing are fun, socially interactive and knowledge transforming accomplishments.

Recommended readings

Siegel, L. (2013) *Understanding dyslexia and other learning disabilities.* British Columbia: Pacific Educational Press
Snowling, M.J. and Hulme, C. (2005) *The science of reading: A handbook.* London: Wiley Blackwell.

References

Adams, A.-M., Simmons, F.R., Willis, C.S. and Porter, S. (2011) The impact of the development of verbal recoding on children's early writing skills. *British Journal of Educational Psychology,* **83**(1), pp. 76–97.
Baddeley, A.D. (1986) *Working memory.* Oxford: Oxford University Press.
Baddeley, A.D. (2000) The episodic buffer: A new component of working memory? *Trends in Cognitive Science,* **4**(11), pp. 417–423.
Behrend, D.A., Rosengren, K. and Perlmutter, M. (1989). A new look at children's private speech: The effects of age, task difficulty, and parent absence. *International Journal of Behavioural Development,* **12**(3), pp. 305–320.
Bereiter, C., Burtis, P. and Scardamalia, M. (1988) Cognitive operations in constructing main points in written composition. *Journal of Memory and Language,* **27**, pp. 261–278.
Bourke, L. and Adams, A.-M. (2003) The relationship between working memory and early writing assessed at the word, sentence and text level. *Educational and Child Psychology,* **20**(3), pp. 19–36.
Bourke, L. and Adams, A.-M. (2010) Cognitive constraints and the early learning goals in writing. *Journal of Research in Reading,* **33**(1), pp. 94–110.
Bourke, L. and Adams, A.-M. (2012) Is it differences in language skills and working memory that account for girls being better at writing than boys? *Journal of Writing Research,* **3**(3), pp. 249–277.
Bourke, L., Davies, S.J., Sumner, E. and Green, C. (2014) Individual differences in the development of early writing skills: Testing the unique contribution of visuo-spatial working memory. *Reading and Writing,* **27**(2), pp. 315–335.
British Psychological Society (BPS) (1999) *Dyslexia, literacy and psychological assessment.* Leicester: British Psychological Society.

Bryant, P., Maclean, M. and Bradley, L. (1990) Rhyme, language, and children's reading. *Applied Psycho-linguistics*, **11**, pp. 237–252.

Cowan, N. (2010) Multiple concurrent thoughts: The meaning and developmental neuropsychology of working memory. *Developmental Neuropsychology*, **35**(5), pp. 447–474.

Currie, J. and Thomas, D. (1995) Does Head Start make a difference? *American Economic Review*, **80**, pp. 341–364.

DfE (2013) The national curriculum in England: Key stages 1 and 2 framework document. www.gov.uk/gov ernment. Accessed 27 February 2017.

DfE (2014a) Statistical first release: Provision for children under 5 years of age in England. London: Department for Education.

DfE (2014b) Statutory framework for the early years foundation stage: Setting the standards for learning, development and care for children from birth to five. London: Department for Education.

DfE (2016) *Early years foundation stage profile results: 2015–2016*. www.gov.uk/government/statistics/ea rly-years-foundation-stage-profile-results-2015-to-2016. Accessed 23 February 2016.

DfEE (1999) *The National Literacy Strategy: Progression in phonics*. London: Department for Education and Employment.

DfEE (2001) *The National Literacy Strategy: Developing early writing*. London: Department for Education and Employment.

DfES (2001) *The National Literacy Strategy: Framework for teaching*. Nottingham: Department for Education and Skills.

DfES (2004) *A framework for understanding dyslexia*. Leicester: Department for Education and Skills.

Dickinson, D.K., McCabe, A., Anastasopoulos, L., Peisner-Feinberg, E.S. and Poe, M.D. (2003) The comprehensive language approach to early literacy: The interrelationships among vocabulary, phonological sensitivity, and print knowledge among preschool-aged children. *Journal of Educational Psychology*, **9**(3), pp. 465–481.

Ebbinghaus, H. (1885) Über das Gedächtnis [Memory: A contribution to experimental psychology]. Translated by Henry A. Ruger and Clara E. Bussenius (1913). New York: Teachers College, Columbia University.

Ehri, L.C. (1980) The development of orthographic images. In U. Frith (ed.) *Cognitive processes in spelling*. London: Academic Press.

Fawcett, A. and Nicholson, R. (2004) *Dyslexia screening test –Junior (DST-J)*. London: Pearson.

Fernald, A. Marchman, V.A. and Weisleder, A. (2013) SES differences in language processing skill and vocabulary are evident at 18 months. *Developmental Science*, **16**(2), pp. 234–248.

Frank, J. and Levison, H. (1973) Dysmetric dyslexia and dyspraxia: Hypothesis and study. *Journal of American Academy of Child Psychiatry*, **12**(4), pp. 690–701.

Frederickson, N. and Reason, R. (1995) Discrepancy definitions of specific learning difficulties. *Educational Psychology in Practice*, **10**, pp. 195–205.

Gathercole, S.E. and Baddeley, A.D. (1993) Phonological working memory: A critical building block for reading development and vocabulary acquisition? *European Journal of Psychology of Education*, **8**(3), pp. 259–272.

Hayes, J.R. (1996) A new framework for understanding cognition and affect in writing. In C.M. Levy and S. Ransdell (eds) *The science of writing: Theories, methods, individual differences, and applications*. Hillsdale: Erlbaum.

Hemphill, L. and Tivnan, T. (2008) The importance of early vocabulary for literacy achievement in high poverty schools. *Journal of Education for Students Placed at Risk*, **13**(4), pp. 426–451.

Henry, L.A. (1991) The effects of word length and phonemic similarity in young children's short-term memory. *The Quarterly Journal of Experimental Psychology Section A. Human Experimental Psychology*, **43**(1), pp. 35–52.

Hepplewhite, D. (2016) *No nonsense phonics skills box set*. London: Raintree.

Hitch, G.J., Halliday, S., Schaafstal, A.M. and Scraagen, J.M.C. (1988) Visual working memory in children. *Memory and Cognition*, **16**(2), pp. 120–132.

Johnston, R.S., McGeown, S. and Watson, J.E. (2012) Long-term effects of synthetic versus analytic phonics teaching on reading and spelling ability of 10 year old boys and girls. *Reading and Writing*, **25**(6), pp. 1365–1384.

Kellogg, R.T. (1996) A model of working memory in writing. In C.M. Levy and S. Ransdell (eds) *The science of writing: Theories, methods, individual differences, and applications*. Hillsdale: Erlbaum.

McNeil, A.M. and Johnson, R. (2004) Word length, phonemic and visual similarity effects in poor and normal readers. *Memory and Cognition*, **32**(5), pp. 687–695.

National Evaluation of Sure Start (NESS) (2010) *The impact of Sure Start local programmes on five year olds and their families*. London: Department for Education.

Palmer, S. (2000) Working memory: A developmental study of phonological recoding. *Memory*, **8**(3), pp. 179–193.

Peterson, C. and Roberts, C. (2003) Like mother, like daughter: Similarities in narrative style. *Developmental Psychology*, **39**, pp. 551–562.

Rack, J.P., Snowling, M.J., Hulme, C. and Gibbs, S. (2007) No evidence that an exercise-based treatment programme (DDAT) has specific benefits for children with reading difficulties. *Dyslexia*, **13**(2), pp. 97–104.

Read, C. (1975) *Children's categorization of speech sounds in English*. Urbana: National Council of Teachers of English.

Reynolds, D. and Nicolson, R. (2007) Follow-up of an exercise-based treatment for children with reading difficulties. *Dyslexia*, **13**(2), pp. 78–96.

Robertson, G.J. and Wilkinson, G.S. (2006) *Wide range achievement test*. 4th edition. London: Pearson.

Robinson, G.L. and Conway, R.N.F. (1990) The effects of Irlen colored lenses on specific reading skills and perception ability: A twelve-month validity study. *Journal of Learning Disabilities*, **23**, pp. 588–597.

Rose, J. (2006) *Independent review of the teaching of early reading*. London: Department for Education and Skills.

SCAA (1996) *Nursery education: Desirable outcomes for children's learning on entering compulsory education*. London: SCAA and Department for Education and Employment.

Standards and Testing Agency (2016) *Early years foundation stage profile 2017 handbook*. London: Department for Education. www.gov.uk/government/publications. Accessed 13 March 2017.

Sweetman, J. (1996) *Parents' guide to primary schools and the National Curriculum*. London: Letts Educational.

The Telegraph (2012, 17 June) Sir Jim Rose criticises children's authors in phonics row (Julie Henry, education correspondent). www.telegraph.co.uk/education/educationnews/9335860/Sir-Jim-Rose-criticises-childrens-authors-in-phonics-row.html. Accessed 14 February 2017.

Torgesen, J.K. and Burgess, S.R. (1998) Consistency of reading-related phonological processes throughout early childhood: Evidence from longitudinal-correlational and instructional studies. In J. Metsala and L. Ehri (eds) *Word recognition in beginning reading*. Hillsdale: Erlbaum.

Vygotsky, L.S. (1976) Play and its role in the mental development of the child. *Soviet Psychology*, **5**, pp. 6–18.

Wechsler, D. (2014) *Wechsler Intelligence Scale for Children*. 5th edition. London: Pearson.

Part II

Identities: examining the role of the mind and identity in learning

5 Bodies of education
How brain, body, and environment are entangled in thinking and learning

Marek McGann

Introduction

The body matters for thinking, more than you might realize. The manner in which a person's body enables and constrains their perception of, and interaction with, the environment around them, plays a central role in their thinking. This viewpoint challenges what is perhaps the most common way of understanding cognitive processes – as computational processes. In this chapter I will briefly review how this dominant computational (or information processing) view arose, and touch on how it influences (often implicitly) our practices in education. I will then explore some of the research on embodiment that challenges this computational view, research which indicates that the messy specifics of bodily and physical reality play a significant role in cognition. Embodiment may not completely overturn the computational model of cognition (the jury is out on that big question), but it is increasingly clear that we will at least have to refine our conceptions of how the mind works.

Your brain is a computer, cognition is information processing

The idea that the brain is a computer is one that has worked its way into the core of psychological science, as well as into our common-sense everyday notions of how the mind works. The notion that thinking is, in essence, a form of computation underlies basic ideas about how memory and perception work on the one hand, and helps us to understand what was going on with all of those people plugged into the Matrix in the movies, on the other.

In psychology, the rise of this way of thinking about how the mind works is sometimes called the 'Cognitive Revolution' (Gardner, 1985), so completely did it dominate mainstream psychology in the middle decades of the twentieth century. Most histories of psychology depict the first half of the twentieth century as dominated by behaviouristic approaches. According to behaviourism, achieving a true picture of people's experiences, what they thought of what was going on around them, was impossible and so their experiences were not included in the study of how they learned. Instead behaviourists paid attention to the stimuli presented to their subjects (more often rats, mice, and pigeons than people), and the observable behaviours that were produced in response. No reference was made to what the stimuli might *mean* to the subjects. This perspective is sometimes lampooned as a 'black box' approach to psychology. The person was treated as a closed vessel, and behaviourists were only interested in what went into the box (observable stimuli, or reinforcements of various kinds), and what came out of it (observable, physical behaviours). Nothing could or should be said about what happened inside it.

The shift from a behaviourist-dominated paradigm to a cognitive/computational-dominated one can be attributed to a number of different strands of research. In the section that follows I will outline some of the most commonly cited studies in this area, including the work of researchers such as Bruner and Chomsky, who will be well known to many educators. Much like behaviourism before it, the computational model may now have passed its peak of influence, and is facing criticism from many researchers within the field. Like so many facets of life, science frequently involves a process of interest, enthusiasm, exuberance, overindulgence and then a correction toward moderation. Over the past three decades of work in psychology, and in the interdisciplinary field of cognitive science (which draws from psychology, computer science, and philosophy, amongst many others), the pendulum has begun to swing away from the overly computational or information-focused description of psychological processes. In researching cognition, more attention is now being paid to the grounded, perhaps mundane, reality of physical, bodily movements and coping with the messy, meaty details of a person interacting with the world around them.

In what follows, I will outline the rise of cognitive psychology and its appeal as a model for understanding what people are doing when they are attending, learning, remembering, and solving problems. We will then explore some of the reasons why recent research has questioned this way of thinking about thinking, and what the implications might be for how we do the science of psychology, and the practice of professional work such as teaching and education.

The 'New Look' – not all stimuli are made equal

Some of the earliest work credited with the rise of cognitive psychology was conducted by a name well known to educators: Jerome Bruner. Classic experiments conducted by Bruner, along with Cecile Goodman (Bruner and Goodman, 1947) and Leo Postman (Bruner and Postman, 1949), showed that people don't respond to 'bare' experience. Rather, their interpretations, their values, and understanding of the stimuli they encounter, affect the way they respond to, think about, and remember those stimuli. For example, children tend to overestimate the size of coins, as opposed to valueless discs of the same size, and this effect is exaggerated for children from lower socio-economic brackets (Bruner and Goodman, 1947). This has commonly been interpreted as indicating that how much something matters to you can affect your perceptions of it. Conversely, people presented with stimuli that are incongruent with their expectations (e.g. playing cards with black hearts or red spades) will frequently not notice, or mis-remember those stimuli (Bruner and Postman, 1949).

These New Look experiments did not introduce the notion of computation itself, but made it clear that something about people's reactions to events needed to be explained beyond their encountering of a bare stimulus. This recognition underpinned the constructivist philosophy of Bruner's approach to education and challenged the 'hard-edged' highly structured teaching associated with the behaviouristic views on education at the time. If Bruner and his colleagues were right, then we could not understand a person's responses to their environment without considering how their perspective, habits, and skills shaped their interpretation of that environment. (See Chapter 9 for more on the behaviourist model of learning and the issues surrounding the inclusion of any mental concepts in that model.)

These findings caused significant difficulties for a behaviourist-dominated paradigm in psychology, but if that paradigm was to fall, what should replace it? It was during this period that the first digital computers were being designed and built. Before long, the theories of computation that drove those machines were being used to explain and influence the world outside of the computer as much as inside it. With experiments like the New Look studies making waves in psychological literature, the stage was set for parallel developments occurring in computer science, neuroscience, engineering, and linguistics.

The information processing approach

The event most frequently cited as the origin of the Cognitive Revolution is a symposium at MIT on 11th September 1956. This one symposium involved the presentation of several seminal papers, crammed into one busy day. In a presentation showing how information processing theories could account for aspects of the structure of language in a manner entirely unavailable to behaviourism, Noam Chomsky attacked the dominant model of psychological science of the time, laid the groundwork for nearly all of the discipline of linguistics ever since, and helped drive the shift in thinking that led to psychologists considering the mind to be a computational system.

A substantial part of Chomsky's criticism of Skinner is now known as the 'poverty of the stimulus' argument (Chomsky, 1959; 1981). If the behaviourist model of language acquisition was right, then language would have to be learned by children through observation of the language spoken around them. Through processes of reinforcement and shaping, they would eventually learn to follow the rules of grammar of their native tongue. Chomsky argued that the amount and quality of language that a child experiences during the first few years of life is simply not enough to account for the linguistic capability that children display (Chomsky, 1981; see also Pinker, 1995, for an entertaining and much more readable introduction). Not only do parents and others in a child's life frequently use poorly structured, fragmented sentences or messy articulations, they also directly reinforce or correct only a tiny percentage of the utterances that infants and toddlers make (and children typically ignore such correction). This 'poverty of the stimulus' argument claims that there just isn't enough information or support available in the linguistic experiences of a young child to explain how they become so adept at speaking their native language at such a young age.

What Chomsky articulated within the domain of language learning, the notion that people do not just respond to 'bare' experience, was exactly the point that Bruner and others were making about learning in general. We don't just react to stimuli, there is a complex structure to people's minds that prepares them to engage with, form interpretations of, and process the stimuli that they encounter. This inner complexity had a bigger role to play in the way we described our interactions with the environment than behaviourism would acknowledge. For Chomsky, people must be pre-loaded with an innate capacity for certain kinds of interpretation and processing. He proposed that we are all born with a set of general language rules that can be refined and made specific based on the immediate linguistic setting in which children find themselves. This was his famous Universal Grammar theory, which underpins what Chomsky called a Language Acquisition Device and enables children to become native speakers of the language around them (Chomsky, 1965).

Although Chomsky's specific claims about language acquisition have come under increasing critical scrutiny in recent years (see, for example, Stemmer, 1990; Tomasello, 2003), the specifics of his theories are not as important as the underlying principles when it comes to understanding how his work helped us get to a computational world view. What he showed us was that the challenges faced by behaviouristic theories could be overcome by proposing a psychological system capable of representing, manipulating, and interpreting stimuli. It was clear that the information-processing model developed from the study of computation was potentially just such a system.

What Chomsky showed in principle, Newell and Simon helped to show in practice. It was in 1955 that Alan Newell, Herbert Simon, and J. Cliff Shaw began writing 'Logic Theorist', a computer program explicitly designed to operate in a manner akin to human thinking (Newell *et al.*, 1958; Newell and Simon, 1956). Newell and Simon appreciated very early on that the kinds of 'number crunching' done by the earliest digital computers could be used to process more than just numbers, so long as there was a way to encode the ideas and relationships properly. They examined the ways in which such encodings could be achieved, and developed what can be considered the first computational model of cognitive processing – in this case, the proving of logical theorems. Simon famously told his students 'Over Christmas Allen Newell and I invented a thinking machine' (quoted in McCorduck, 1979: 116). It's interesting to note that one place where they presented their work was at the same symposium where Chomsky presented his work on information theory and syntax.

Not only was the program capable of proving logical theorems put forward by some of the best-known names in philosophy such as Russell and Whitehead (1910), but in some cases produced proofs that were novel, and more elegant than those previously known. Newell and Simon followed up their success with the General Problem Solver (Newell and Simon, 1972), which used rules of thumb (a.k.a. heuristics), similar to those used by actual people, to solve a wider range of problems. These striking demonstrations illustrated the power of imagining cognitive processes as information processes. If you could determine how the world might be encoded into representations that could be used by digital computers, the kinds of cognitive work that could be carried out by a computer armed with those representations would be immense.

In the following years, a mass of research put the theories of information processing at the forefront of key developments in psychological research (Gardner's 1985 history is authoritative here). These developments recast psychology as a computational phenomenon, and so the purpose of psychology became essentially an attempt to reverse engineer the particular kind of 'biological computer' which has evolved in the form of the human brain (Pinker, 1997).

For a great many researchers inspired by Chomsky, Newell, and Simon, and others, the study of psychology became the search for ever more accurate explanations of how human beings process information. Perception, understanding, reasoning, and behaviour are all processes by which information is brought into the psychological system (often considered simply in terms of information being brought into the *brain* in some way), manipulated according to the needs and aims of the person, and then used to select and coordinate the appropriate behaviours.

In her work, the philosopher Susan Hurley (1998) describes these intuitive associations that people tend to make between 'perception' and 'input into a computer' on the one hand, and between 'behaviour' and 'output from a computer' on the other. She terms this the 'input-output picture', and notes that its intuitiveness is seductive. It just makes sense. Information comes in from the world (perception), it gets processed in some way by the central cognitive system (which is also the central nervous system), and on the basis of that information processing, some commands are output to the body and limbs (behaviour).

We can fit our understanding of our physiology easily within this intuitive model. We know that the outside of our bodies are constantly bombarded by many different kinds of energy (e.g. light, sound, heat). Different parts of our bodies are particularly affected by some of this energy, for instance the cells of the retinae react strongly to electromagnetic waves of various kinds, the eardrums and cochlea react to pressure, and so on. These reactions we call sensations, and they set off a chain of events in the peripheral, and then the central nervous system, that we usually describe as 'transmitting' information about the world from the sensory organ to the brain. In the brain, the sensation is 'interpreted' by various brain areas (often illustrated these days with pictures of sections of brains 'lighting up' while a person is doing something cognitive in an MRI scanner). This process of drawing in information and interpreting it we label as 'perception', and the end result of this process is a set of models or representations of the world in our heads where we can analyse, manipulate, and even rehearse a couple of different ways of responding to it. On the basis of that processing which we label as 'cognition', we then select a next best action to take. That action is programmed up in the motor areas of the brain, and the instructions sent out via the motor nervous system to the limbs and trunk, so that we do whatever we are supposed to do next (this is 'behaviour' or 'action').

Interacting with the world around us, in this admittedly simplified view, is a bit like a game of message passing. The world does something, we receive the message, decide on a reply, and send our message back out into the world, usually causing some kind of change out there which we get informed about thanks to new incoming information ... and round and round we go. All of the psychology, the mind and cognition bit, happens inside the body, specifically inside the brain. Thinking is presented as something that 'starts' in response to updates received from the senses via perception, and the thinking has to 'finish' in some way before the response or action can start. This presents a model of cognitive processes that exist in 'discrete units': perception, cognition, and action are all distinct from one another.

The computational view of cognition also plays a substantial, but often implicit, role in the way various aspects of education and teaching are understood. Everywhere we see educational practices which are based on notions of 'encoding' or 'decoding', of 'information storage', 'retrieval', 'representations', 'processing', 'cognitive load', or even 'schemas'. Literacy education, for example, frequently makes mention of the 'activation of prior knowledge' (Keene and Zimmermann, 2007), which is typically taken to imply a stored representation of information becoming 'switched on' in some fashion. The 'universal design for learning' movement advocates that information be presented to students in a wide variety of forms in order to address individual differences in the ways in which those students process that information (Courey et al., 2013). Underlying all of these practices and the psychological concepts that inspire them is the central idea that thinking is a form of information processing which is analogous to computation.

Reflections

What do you think the mind is? Are there phrases or idioms that you use (e.g. 'I can't process that' or 'I have stored that memory somewhere') that implicitly use computational or information processing metaphors and ideas?

Are there ways in which your thinking about teaching, education, or learning, assumes that we are basically computers, and that normal psychological activity involves the processing of information in the brain? If you have them, have you ever considered where these metaphors come from?

A focus on information processing brings certain things to the fore, and pushes others to the background. Consider cognitive load, and the limited capacity of working memory, for instance. (See Chapter 2 for a more detailed exploration of the capacities and structure of working memory.) If cognition is seen as a limited computational system, then as educators we become greatly concerned whether a child has a capacity to take in all of the information presented in their environment, and use that information effectively to construct representations or knowledge about objects, or relations in the world. In order to make sure they can take it all in, we might adopt specific aspects of information management in our teaching, such as Mayer's widely cited notions of multimedia learning (Mayer, 1997; 2008; Moreno and Mayer, 1999) or organize our classes and lesson plans around avoiding distraction and overload (Gathercole *et al.*, 2006).

At present these are evidence-based examples of best practice guidelines, but developments within the field of cognitive science have raised the question as to whether they are overly focused on too narrow a range of capacities appropriate to a conception of brain-based information processing. Consequently, these approaches could be overlooking the possibility that people's cognitive abilities may in fact involve a larger system, including not only the brain, but also the body, and the environment it's interacting with. The suggestion that the body might be a more active factor in our thinking (as opposed to a passive channel for information) than we have acknowledged to date, is encapsulated in the term 'embodied cognition'.

Habeas corpus: bringing the body to mind

For the past few decades, the computational approach to psychology has been a major success. It has produced mountains of experimental data and a plethora of theories across the full range of behavioural and psychological phenomena. In addition, it has played a role in the way we interpret everything from developmental changes in ability (Case, 1992; Case *et al.*, 1988; Pascual-Leone *et al.*, 1978) through psychological disorders (Beck and Clark, 1997; Cornblatt *et al.*, 1985; Frith, 1979; Ingram, 1984), to social interactions (Fiske and Taylor, 2013; Wyer Jr and Srull, 2014). Since the early 1990s, however, dissatisfaction with the computational approach has grown amongst many researchers both within psychology and within the broader discipline of 'cognitive science' (which includes such related domains such as robotics, philosophy, linguistics, and anthropology). A chief concern among the majority of these critics is that the computational approach is seen as disregarding the impact of the body on cognition. Instead, recent research suggests that the body is not peripheral, but integral, to basic cognitive processes – the mind is 'embodied'.

All of our interactions with the world, from experiencing the world around us to taking action in it, involve our body. If we look at psychology through the lens of the computational approach, the body quickly recedes into the background. It is something that passes information into the cognitive system and back out again after cognition is complete, but its role is passive, playing no direct role in cognition. Similarly, the importance of the environment is downplayed because our experience of that environment is entirely a product of our perceptions of it. Thus, through the use of interpretation, perceptual strategies, and other cognitive processes, new meanings or values can be attributed to that environment in an almost arbitrary fashion (e.g. even if it's raining I can decide that it's a 'lovely day').

Increasingly, however, research has shown that the body is not simply a conduit for information being channelled to or from the environment, but is used to perform what would usually be considered 'central' cognitive processes on that information. If you classify 'behaviour' as 'actions taken by the body' then in a surprising array of situations, our 'behaviour' is not so much the outcome of a set of discrete and distinct cognitive processes, but instead seems to be an intrinsic part of those cognitive processes. In a sense, we seem to 'think' as much with the body as with the mind. What is more, our cognition and behaviour both adapt to take advantage of 'happy coincidences' in the physical world. There appear to be numerous structures or physical processes in the world that help us to get things done in such a way that we can avoid a lot of effortful cognitive processing, and instead get the world to 'do a lot of our thinking' for us.

Therefore, in the context of psychology 'embodiment' refers to a general principle that the body plays an active role in psychological phenomena. It is not a peripheral to the cognitive system, not simply a channel for getting information into and out of the central nervous system. A debate currently rages in the research literature as to whether this means that we should change the way we define computation as it applies to the mind; talk about computation not just as something that brain does, but as something the whole person does. More radical options are also on the table, which suggest that the computational model for thinking needs to be done away with altogether, and alternative ways of thinking about thinking adopted. Either one of these outcomes could have substantial implications for how we approach learning, causing us to change our methods, emphases, and expectations. What is quite clear is that when it comes to thinking and learning, we need to pay much more attention to the body than we have done in the past. In view of this, let us first consider the impact that the body can have on our thinking.

Embodied cognition

In this section, we will review a number of research findings that illustrate how the body plays a role in cognitive processes. This includes situations where our actions (normally considered 'output') can play a role in perception (which is normally considered 'input'). We will also explore the ways in which the physical stuff of ourselves and our environments can both constrain and guide cognitive processes, suggesting that some cognitive functioning actually happens outside of the brain.

Visceral decision making

Some of the seminal neuropsychological research on embodiment can be found in the work of neuroscientist Antonio Damasio and his colleagues. In his 1994 book *Descartes' Error*, Damasio describes the case of a patient of his, Eliot, who had suffered damage to a region of his frontal lobes known as the orbito-prefrontal cortex (that's at the very front of the brain, just behind the eyes) during an operation to remove a tumour there. Though Eliot showed no deficits on any of the typical tests of frontal lobe functioning, and scored well above average on intelligence tests, his life following the operation was a catalogue of problems and mistakes that led to him being dependent on his brother.

Having worked through a battery of tests and been unable to identify what Eliot's problem was, Damasio's colleague Antoine Bechara developed a test now known as the Iowa Gambling Task

(Bechara *et al.*, 2005; Bechara *et al.*, 1994; Damasio, 1994). In this test, participants have four decks of cards to choose from and an amount of realistic looking 'play' money to start with. The person playing the game freely picks a card from one of the four decks, with each card telling them they have either won or lost a certain amount of money (or sometimes both). Unbeknownst to the player, two decks are 'good' decks, comprised mostly of cards that show modest gains or a few cards that show losses that are even more modest. The other two decks are 'bad' decks that involve more losses, some of which are substantial. Players play for one hundred draws of the cards (though they don't know this in advance). Neurotypical players (i.e. people without any brain damage) tend to start veering away from the bad decks after 20 or 30 draws of the cards, but people with orbito-prefrontal damage don't seem to be able to steer clear of the bad decks; they don't learn very well from their mistakes.

Investigating further, Damasio found that people with such frontal lobe damage did not seem to be sensitive to the visceral, bodily, emotional responses that happen when we are punished (such as with a loss from the decks). Damasio described neurotypical players in the later stages of the task having *pre-emptive* bodily responses while reaching for a bad deck; their skin conductance spiked as they reached. Damasio suggested that this 'feedback' from our bodily reactions is part of what guides us away from the wrong choices. He argued that the bodily feelings associated with emotions are vital to learning even in high-level cognitive domains such as reasoning or decision making. In a sense, for the neurotypical players, as they reached for the 'bad' deck their body was reacting as though something was going wrong.

Evidence that the body sets the general tone for decision making is not limited to decisions made in the lab. Danzinger *et al.* (2011) found that judges in parole board hearings became more negative (were less likely to grant parole), simply as they became more hungry. At the beginning of a day of hearings, granting of parole typically starts at around 65 per cent, but drops off over the course of the day, resetting to approximately 65 per cent again after food breaks. This slide toward harsher judgement associated with hunger might be something for educators to consider if they are marking a larger number of assignments over the course of a day, or indeed if they are engaged in a series of tests such as a set of oral language examinations.

From a computational perspective, the mind (i.e. cognition) and the body are distinct things, utterly separate. What the research by Damasio and others on the role of emotion and visceral processes in cognition suggests is that our bodies have a much more important role in guiding cognition than the computational approach gave them credit for.

Paying attention with your hands

Our bodies' influence on our ability to perform various cognitive tasks is not always so subtle, however. An example of this is the work of Yu *et al.* (2009) examining visual attention and word learning in toddlers. If you've ever met a toddler, you will not be surprised by the observation that they are easily distracted. Children face challenges in paying attention, but one exception to this rule is the attention needed to associate the name for something with the visual object itself. This should be a very tricky task; object names are briefly occurring events, spoken in fractions of a second, often within a stream of other words that don't name the object in question. Furthermore, in complex environments, keeping a toddler's attention on one object at a time can be difficult. Thus, associating the right name with the right object is a demanding visual attention and association task, but you would never know this from the rate at which children pick up new vocabulary (on average a word every two hours or so, as estimated by Miller and Gildea, 1987). Given toddlers' immature visual attention, what's going on here? According to Yu *et al.* (2009) children partly solve this visual attention problem through a combination of sensible parents and short arms.

Yu *et al.* brought children with their caregivers into a laboratory and mounted a tiny camera on the child's head, giving them a clear indication of the child's visual field. They then had the children and their caregivers play with some new toys. The playroom lab had a number of new objects, all of them visually appealing and potentially distracting, but they found a pattern in the child and caregiver's behaviour. Caregivers were much more likely to speak the name of an object while the child was holding that object, and because toddlers have short arms, objects they were holding were relatively close to their face, and thus likely to be dominating their visual field at the time. While the environment is complicated, and the visual attention task of associating a spoken sound with a particular object is a difficult task when described abstractly, in the concrete, specific case of a small human being, the bodily details simplify the task substantially. This allows a toddler's short arms to support their immature capacity for attention, an example of embodiment supporting developing cognitive abilities. Or, to put it another way, what looks like a very challenging cognitive task becomes a lot simpler when the specifics of the body, the environment, and the actual actions involved are all considered.

Changing our minds with actions

Running counter to the idea that actions are a result of cognitive processing (i.e. an *output* from a problem solving system) is Kirsch and Maglio's (1994) notion of an 'epistemic action'. Epistemic action is a kind of action that is done not to achieve a particular change in the environment, but primarily to change our knowledge of the environment, or our relationship with it. In order to better understand epistemic actions Kirsch and Maglio studied the behaviour of expert players of the computer game Tetris.

In Tetris, the aim is to rotate new blocks that are falling from the top of the screen so that they fit into the pattern of older blocks that builds up from the bottom of the screen. Kirsch and Maglio argued that the speed requirements of Tetris would require a strategy which minimized the number of moves a person would make – that is, the number of times they would rotate the falling pieces before dropping them into place in the pile at the bottom of the screen. What they found, however, was that expert players would frequently rotate the pieces in order to allow a simpler visual assessment about whether it would fit the array of gaps in the pile beneath, rather than mentally rotating the object to predict the fit. This appears to show that people used the objects in the environment as a means to figure out a fit or, in other words, a solution to a problem, rather than computing that solution for themselves. This showed that the simple version of the input-output picture doesn't apply here; since the players rotated the blocks in their environment to facilitate their decision making about placing those blocks, the distinction between inputs, outputs, and manipulations of the cognitive system gets pretty blurry.

We can see everyday examples of this same phenomenon in education, such as the way we use intermediate stages of note keeping during a long division, or the way in which many students seem to think more clearly with a pen in their hand, allowing their notes or diagrams to play an active role in their thinking. The fact that engaging with something *perceptually* can be a means by which we also engage with it *conceptually* provides us with just one example of how our bodies and the environment interact with our thinking and learning.

Embodied learning

To apply the principles of embodiment to education is to suggest that when we wish to understand and promote student cognition within educational settings, the physicality of the body and perceptual aspects of the environment must be taken into account. In this section, we will review a number of examples of these principles, ranging from the suggestion that learning to read could be facilitated using visual 'props', to the idea that abstract thought could depend on perception. However, we will start with another good example of embodied learning in the study of hand gestures and problem solving.

Learning with your hands

The gestures we make with our hands while speaking are typically seen to be a kind of behavioural 'froth', something that accompanies what a person is saying or doing, but generally has little role to play in the content or essence of things. And yet, a number of research studies (e.g. Church and Goldin-Meadow, 1986; Garber *et al.*, 1998) have shown that such gestures are not simply decorative hand-waving, but play an important supporting role in perceptually structuring, and perhaps representing, the concepts being worked with. In this way, the gestures that students make as they learn might influence how well they respond to instruction, and the gestures that teachers make might help structure abstract concepts for their students.

For instance, building on substantial previous work Broaders *et al.* (2007) gave children several maths tasks and asked them to gesture when explaining their solutions. If the children were told to use their hands when explaining how they reached a conclusion these gestures appeared to interact in some manner with the children's thinking about the problems. In cases where a child's gestures weren't fully congruent with their spoken explanations, those children adapted their problem solving and responded better to instruction than those who were not told to gesture. This suggests that the children's own bodily actions affected their awareness and understanding of the mathematical processes they were engaged with – their bodily movements helped to change their relationship to, or understanding of, the maths.

Research focus: on the one hand ...

Cook *et al.* (2008) found that children who gestured during learning were more likely to remember the material for longer. They suggest that gesture helps scaffold or structure cognition, or might even help to represent concepts directly. For example, imagine a situation in which you face a choice between two options. Without realizing it, you can end up assigning particular volumes of space in front of you to the two different options that you are comparing or contrasting. In such cases, you might have one hand associated with the benefits of one option, while the benefits about the alternative option are 'placed' on the other hand. If you are not consistent as to which hand is associated with which option, then things will get confusing very quickly both for the people listening and for yourself. Thus, if the benefits of one option are far more numerous than the benefits of the other option, the hand that is 'holding' those benefits needs to sink lower as if carrying something heavier than the other hand. In that way, your hands and the volume of space in front of you are playing a part in the thinking of yourself and the people with whom you are speaking. (See Chapter 10 for further discussion of the idea that thinking may exist between people in a social context rather than within each person individually.)

Reviewing the literature on gesture and learning, Goldin-Meadow (2016) makes three recommendations for using this awareness of movement in the classroom. First, teachers can take care to be cognizant of their own gestures, to ensure that those gestures are congruent with what they are discussing, and not misleading students or otherwise confusing what they are saying. Second, students can be encouraged to use gesture themselves when explaining a problem, or their approach to a solution, which may help structure their own thinking on the matter. Finally, students can be encouraged to gesture as they address a problem directly, to improve the likelihood that they take advantage of implicit knowledge about the situation that may help their more explicit thinking.

One of the key recurring lessons of the embodied cognition literature is to respect the value of mundane behaviour and experience. There can be deep value in the kinds of things that people take for granted, such as gesturing with our hands when we speak. Recognizing the impact of the concrete, physical aspects of what we do when engaged in conceptual, ostensibly knowledge-focused, activities can lead to some eye-opening implications. Rather than seeing the physical reality of an activity as something to get away from when striving for intellectual development, it can be seen as something to be built upon, or exploited even, as part of such abstract skills as reading, mathematics, and science.

Reading the real world

Arthur Glenberg and his colleagues have examined the ways in which children's learning to read can be scaffolded using physical objects and movements. Reading is typically considered an abstract task, one which is almost defined by the fact that it is divorced from the physical world. It is part of the power of reading that it need not involve physical re-enactment of the ideas and facts being read, and that it can even explore and describe events that are impossible in the real world.

Despite this fact, though, reading should not be seen as existing in a universe that is entirely separate from the real world. For one thing, the effects of reading, through changes in people's behaviour, can have a significant impact on reality. Think, for instance, of how the physical world, such as your classroom practice, or your conversations with other people, might be changed on the basis of reading this chapter (whether or not you agree with the conclusions suggested). Intriguingly, there are some who suggest that the interaction between reading and the physical world takes place while we read as much as afterwards. Furthermore, it may be that this interaction between physical and mental in the case of reading could be harnessed to help those who are learning to read.

With this in mind, Glenberg and others argue that learning to read might be best supported by a form of scaffolding which would enable children to make a connection between the written word and events in the physical world (Glenberg *et al.*, 2004; Marley *et al.*, 2007). The idea here is to present the narrative of the book, not as something abstract, but a series of events that can really occur, and can be physically represented in the real world. Thus, by allowing children to physically manipulate objects so as to mirror relationships and events described in written text, we can substantially improve their grasp of the narrative they are trying to read. Marley *et al.* (2010) showed that when allowed to either manipulate toys to enact the narrative in a text, or when they observe someone else doing this, the children showed a substantial improvement in their memory for the story, as well as their understanding of new words. By scaffolding the children's activity to enable them to explore the parallels between the structures of sentences, paragraphs, or stories, and the structure of events in the world, the skill of reading is embodied, and supported through its early development.

Reflections

What role does physical activity play in the classroom? What physical movements, and arrangements of materials or objects, are involved in some classroom practices? How might the orientation of furniture, the closeness or distance between illustrations, or the ways in which physical components get moved, affect students' perceptions of what is important, or how concepts are related to one another?

In the cases of reading and problem solving, we have studied how cognition extends into the physical world via our hands. Such physical manipulation represents only one of many forms of potential interface between the physical and conceptual. Thus, when we wish to understand the impact of embodiment on scientific thinking for, example, we find that perceptual engagement with the phenomena in question, not just manual engagement, can be a powerful thing, and that our perception of abstract things may not itself be very abstract.

Seeing is part of thinking

Part of the appeal of the computational approach is its abstraction; you can process all kinds of information, essentially in the same way. This means that the computational framework provides us with the optimistic viewpoint that if we can teach people to process information about their world, they can apply those lessons to a very wide variety of settings. Abstraction enables generalization. If the embodied cognition theorists are correct, however, we need to be much more wary of abstraction. From the embodied learning perspective, learning is likely to be more successful when based on interaction with things in our environment. This would make the case for experience with concrete specifics being more useful than the learning of abstract generalities.

Goldstone and colleagues have found precisely this advantage of learning through experience with physical examples and simulations over abstract principles. However, it's worth noting that their research found that generalizability of the principles learned was still high, even when the learning activity was based on specific examples, so long as those examples were well chosen. Goldstone *et al.* (2010) offered a group of higher education students the chance to play around with computational simulations that illustrate certain principles in science. They found that the students who learned the principles via this method came to appreciate those principles better, and were more likely to be able to apply them in new situations compared to students who learned about those principles as formal rules to be memorized. It seems, therefore, that seeing the principles in action was an important factor in facilitating the students' thoughts and learning concerning those principles.

What is more, Landy and Goldstone (2007) have shown that our learning of even very formal mathematical processes may also be affected by perceptual factors. For example, our natural tendency to group together things that are perceptually close to one another can affect the way that students complete mathematical tasks. For example, having learned the rule that multiplication precedes addition in a complex equation, students could recite the rule and demonstrate its use. However, when given problems akin to the one below ...

$$R \quad \times \quad E+L \quad \times \quad W \quad = \quad L \quad \times \quad W+R \quad \times \quad E$$

... participants were six times more likely to make a mistake in applying that rule. Simple perceptual differences seem to change the way a person thinks about the problem; the perceptual can trump the conceptual. In other words, the details of the world in front us can substantially affect how we think about it.

The implication of all this is that the specifics of how we present problems and tasks to students will affect how well they cope with them and learn from them, even in abstract domains such as maths or science. While there is a clear argument for the use of concrete examples and physical materials to promote students' learning in maths and elsewhere, it is not the case that just using any old physical materials associated with the problem will do. The material or example we draw on needs to illustrate something important regarding the relationships, actions, or patterns in both the task in hand and the principles it seeks to demonstrate (see Brown *et al.*, 2009, and the special issue they introduce).

Research focus: what embodied cognition is not

Like all new approaches in science that have created buzz and energy within their respective communities, a large and very diverse group of people have adopted the notion of 'embodiment', using the term in a variety of ways. There are a number of popular programmes and educational interventions that may seem related to embodied psychological approaches. It is worth bearing in mind that while the existing science on embodiment certainly suggests benefits to certain kinds of bodily engagement with school tasks and learning, we must be careful to distinguish evidence-based approaches from those without any empirical backing.

Two related interventions that have enjoyed substantial popularity in educational circles in recent times are 'movement-based learning', and Brain Gym®. As it stands, neither of these approaches enjoys a sound evidence base (Hyatt, 2007; Spaulding *et al.*, 2010; Stephenson, 2009; Watson and Kelso, 2014), and they are not supported by embodied cognitive science. Implications of embodied cognition research for educational practice are still being worked out (see the rest of the chapter for some examples beginning to show real evidence-based promise). What appears to be emerging from research on these applications is that value comes not just from movement in-and-of itself. The movement and bodily interaction with the world will only support and strengthen learning when designed to be specific to the tasks and activities in question and not an attempt to devise a universal set of 'learning-' or 'focus-'encouraging motions.

Conclusion

The debate over the importance of embodiment, the degree to which cognition interacts with the physical realities of our body and the world around us rather than abstractly *understanding* the world around us, is still being played out in ongoing research. In that body of research we have seen that learning activities are more effective when there is a resonance between behaviour and thought, because the structures we need to guide our thoughts are often present in our behaviour. We have also seen that concrete activity rather than abstract information processing is a more effective means by which we can plan and implement lessons in both science and maths. However, we've further seen that concreteness *for its own sake* is not enough – parallels and appropriate resonances between the abstract concepts and physical resources or activities matter (Brown *et al.*, 2009).

In the final analysis, by challenging the 'certainties' of the computational model, embodiment can leave us feeling less clear as to the nature and extent of the mind or the exact role that our body plays in our psychology. What *is* clear is that we cannot ignore the body, or treat the movements, behaviours, and particulars of our physical interaction with the world as irrelevant when it comes to understanding how we think and how we learn.

Key points

- Much of psychology, and educational practice, operates within a 'computational paradigm' considering the mind as a computer, and considering thinking as computation.
- Embodied cognition research suggests that the body, and the physical environment, play a more active role in cognitive processing that commonly realized.
- Actions are often not the 'outcome' of cognitive processes, but instead play a central role in those processes.
- Apparently 'perceptual' phenomena often play a direct role in 'conceptual' processes.
- Embodied cognition has implications for how we consider the physical aspects of learning situations, such as hand gestures during teaching and learning, the movement of objects to represent events in stories, or physical arrangement of materials presented as problems or tasks to students.

Recommended readings

Barrett, L. (2011) *Beyond the brain: How body and environment shape animal and human minds.* Princeton: Princeton University Press.

Clark, A. (2008) *Supersizing the mind: Embodiment, action, and cognitive extension.* Oxford: Oxford University Press.

Glenberg, A.M. (2008) Embodiment for education. In P. Calvo and A. Gomila (eds) *Handbook of cognitive science: An embodied approach*. New York: Elsevier.

Goldin-Meadow, S. (2016) Using our hands to change our minds. *WIREs Cognitive Science*. doi: 10.1002/wcs.1368.

Wilson, A.D. and Golonka, S. (2013) Embodied cognition is not what you think it is. *Frontiers in Cognitive Science*, **4**, p. 58.

References

Bechara, A., Damasio, A.R., Damasio, H. and Anderson, S.W. (1994) Insensitivity to future consequences following damage to human prefrontal cortex. *Cognition*, **50**(1–3), pp. 7–15.

Bechara, A., Damasio, H., Tranel, D. and Damasio, A.R. (2005) The Iowa Gambling Task and the somatic marker hypothesis: Some questions and answers. *Trends in Cognitive Sciences*, **9**(4), pp. 159–162.

Beck, A.T. and Clark, D.A. (1997) An information processing model of anxiety: Automatic and strategic processes. *Behaviour Research and Therapy*, **35**(1), pp. 49–58.

Broaders, S.C., Cook, S.W., Mitchell, Z. and Goldin-Meadow, S. (2007) Making children gesture brings out implicit knowledge and leads to learning. *Journal of Experimental Psychology: General*, **136**(4), p. 539.

Brown, M.C., McNeil, N.M. and Glenberg, A.M. (2009) Using concreteness in education: Real problems, potential solutions. *Child Development Perspectives*, **3**(3), pp. 160–164.

Bruner, J.S. and Goodman, C.C. (1947) Value and need as organizing factors in perception. *The Journal of Abnormal and Social Psychology*, **42**(1), p. 33.

Bruner, J.S. and Postman, L. (1949) On the perception of incongruity: A paradigm. *Journal of Personality*, **18**(2), pp. 206–223.

Case, R. (1992) Neo-Piagetian theories of child development. In R.J. Sternberg and C.A. Berg (eds) *Intellectual development*. Cambridge: Cambridge University Press.

Case, R., Hayward, S., Lewis, M. and Hurst, P. (1988) Toward a neo-Piagetian theory of cognitive and emotional development. *Developmental Review*, **8**(1), pp. 1–51.

Chomsky, N. (1959) A review of B.F. Skinner's *Verbal Behavior*. *Language*, **35**(1), pp. 26–58.

Chomsky, N. (1965) *Aspects of the theory of syntax*. Cambridge, MA: MIT Press.

Chomsky, N. (1981) *Rules and representations*. New York: Columbia University Press.

Church, R.B. and Goldin-Meadow, S. (1986) The mismatch between gesture and speech as an index of transitional knowledge. *Cognition*, **23**(1), pp. 43–71.

Cook, S.W., Mitchell, Z. and Goldin-Meadow, S. (2008) Gesturing makes learning last. *Cognition*, **106**(2), pp. 1047–1058.

Cornblatt, B.A., Lenzenweger, M.F., Dworkin, R.H. and Erlenmeyer-Kimling, L. (1985) Positive and negative schizophrenic symptoms, attention, and information processing. *Schizophrenia Bulletin*, **11**(3), p. 397.

Courey, S.J., Tappe, P., Siker, J. and LePage, P. (2013) Improved lesson planning with universal design for learning (UDL). *Teacher Education and Special Education*, **36**(1), pp. 7–27.

Damasio, A.R. (1994) *Descartes' error*. New York: Papermac.

Danziger, S., Levav, J. and Avnaim-Pesso, L. (2011) Extraneous factors in judicial decisions. *Proceedings of the National Academy of Sciences*, **108**(17), pp. 6889–6892.

Fiske, S.T. and Taylor, S.E. (2013) *Social cognition: From brains to culture*. London: Sage.

Frith, C.D. (1979) Consciousness, information processing and schizophrenia. *British Journal of Psychiatry*, **134**(3), pp. 225–235.

Garber, P., Alibali, M.W. and Goldin-Meadow, S. (1998) Knowledge conveyed in gesture is not tied to the hands. *Child Development*, **69**(1), pp. 75–84.

Gardner, H. (1985) *The mind's new science*. Boston: Basic Books.

Gathercole, S.E., Lamont, E. and Alloway, T.P. (2006) Working memory in the classroom. In S. Pickering (ed.) *Working memory and education*. London: Academic Press.

Glenberg, A.M., Gutierrez, T., Levin, J.R., Japuntich, S. and Kaschak, M.P. (2004) Activity and imagined activity can enhance young children's reading comprehension. *Journal of Educational Psychology*, **96**(3), p. 424.

Goldin-Meadow, S. (2016) Using our hands to change our minds. *WIREs Cognitive Science*. doi: 10.1002/wcs.1368.

Goldstone, R.L., Landy, D.H. and Son, J.Y. (2010). The education of perception. *Topics in Cognitive Science*, **2**(2), pp. 265–284.

Hurley, S.L. (1998) *Consciousness in action*. Cambridge, MA: Harvard University Press.

Hyatt, K.J. (2007) Brain Gym®: Building stronger brains or wishful thinking? *Remedial and Special Education*, **28**(2), pp. 117–124.

Ingram, R.E. (1984) Toward an information-processing analysis of depression. *Cognitive Therapy and Research*, **8**(5), pp. 443–477.

Keene, E.O. and Zimmermann, S. (2007) *Mosaic of thought: The power of comprehension strategy instruction*. 2nd edn. Portsmouth, NH: Heinemann Educational Books.

Kirsch, D. and Maglio, P. (1994) On distinguishing epistemic from pragmatic action. *Cognitive Science*, **18**, pp. 513–549.

Landy, D. and Goldstone, R.L. (2007) The alignment of ordering and space in arithmetic computation. In *Proceedings of the twenty-ninth annual meeting of the Cognitive Science Society*. Available at: https://pdfs.semanticscholar.org/f9bc/8bef87d7d05f96f1f96939ce58b8e7f3c514.pdf (Accessed 17 January 2017).

Marley, S.C., Levin, J.R. and Glenberg, A.M. (2007) Improving Native American children's listening comprehension through concrete representations. *Contemporary Educational Psychology*, **32**(3), pp. 537–550.

Marley, S.C., Levin, J.R. and Glenberg, A.M. (2010) What cognitive benefits does an activity-based reading strategy afford young Native American readers? *Journal of Experimental Education*, **78**(3), pp. 395–417.

Mayer, R.E. (1997) Multimedia learning: Are we asking the right questions? *Educational Psychologist*, **32**(1), pp. 1–19.

Mayer, R.E. (2008) Applying the science of learning: Evidence-based principles for the design of multimedia instruction. *American Psychologist*, **63**(8), pp. 760–769.

McCorduck, P. (1979) *Machines who think*. New York: W.H. Freeman.

Miller, G.A. and Gildea, P.M. (1987) How children learn words. *Scientific American*, **257**(3), pp. 94–99.

Moreno, R. and Mayer, R.E. (1999) Cognitive principles of multimedia learning: The role of modality and contiguity. *Journal of Educational Psychology*, **91**(2), pp. 358–368.

Newell, A., Shaw, J.C. and Simon, H.A. (1958) Elements of a theory of human problem solving. *Psychological Review*, **65**(3), p. 151.

Newell, A. and Simon, H. (1956) The logic theory machine: A complex information processing system. *IRE Transactions on Information Theory*, **2**(3), pp. 61–79.

Newell, A. and Simon, H.A. (1972) *Human problem solving*. Englewood Cliffs: Prentice Hall.

Pascual-Leone, J., Goodman, D., Ammon, P. and Subelman, I. (1978). Piagetian theory and neo-Piagetian analysis as psychological guides in education. In J. McCarthy Gallagher and J.A. Easley (eds) *Knowledge and development*. London: Plenum Press.

Pinker, S. (1995) *The language instinct: The new science of language and mind*. London: Penguin.

Pinker, S. (1997) *How the mind works*. London: Allen Lane.

Russell, B. and Whitehead, A.N. (1910) *Principia mathematica*. Vol. I. Cambridge: Cambridge University Press.

Spaulding, L.S., Mostert, M.P. and Beam, A.P. (2010) Is Brain Gym® an effective educational intervention? *Exceptionality*, **18**(1), pp. 18–30.

Stemmer, N. (1990) Skinner's *Verbal Behavior*, Chomsky's review, and mentalism. *Journal of the Experimental Analysis of Behavior*, **54**(3), pp. 307–315.

Stephenson, J. (2009) Best practice? Advice provided to teachers about the use of Brain Gym® in Australian schools. *Australian Journal of Education*, **53**(2), pp. 109–124.

Tomasello, M. (2003) *Constructing a language: A usage-based theory of language acquisition*. Cambridge, MA: Harvard University Press.

Watson, A. and Kelso, G.L. (2014) The effect of Brain Gym® on academic engagement for children with developmental disabilities. *International Journal of Special Education*, **29**(2), pp. 75–83.

Wyer Jr, R.S. and Srull, T.K. (2014) *Handbook of social cognition: Volume 2: Applications.* Hove: Psychology Press.

Yu, C., Smith, L.B., Shen, H., Pereira, A.F. and Smith, T. (2009) Active information selection: Visual attention through the hands. *Autonomous Mental Development, IEEE Transactions,* **1**(2), pp. 141–151.

6 Learning to relate

How social understanding helps children to make sense of their social worlds

Jim Stack

Introduction

Being able to form and maintain relationships with others is an important predictor of the quality of children's personal and social experiences and academic success. In order to achieve this important goal, the measure of which can be seen in levels of peer acceptance and the development of friendships, each child must possess some understanding of their social environment.

One only has to pause for a moment to consider the multitude of social situations that a child needs to make sense of in any given day. For example, they may witness another child becoming upset or in difficulty and therefore may offer support, comfort or help. They may be bullied or victimised by a second child, due to some perceived weakness or difference. A friend of theirs may play a practical joke or use sarcasm or irony as a way of communicating with them. In each of these situations the child needs to make sense of the behaviour of others in order to help them decide on an appropriate response. Was the teacher being fair or mean-spirited when they set the child a difficult task such as solving a tricky maths problem? Did the school bus driver see them as he drove away in the pouring rain? The list of examples that could be used here is endless. The key points here are (1) that the social context permeates our experiences within educational settings, and (2) our ability to understand the actions and behaviours of others shapes the quality of our social experience. Such an understanding involves the ability to put ourselves in the shoes of others, at times suspending our own thoughts and feelings, and instead make sense of what other people are thinking and feeling (Wellman *et al.*, 2001).

In this chapter we will explore this process, first by posing a series of questions and then using relevant research in the area of children's social understanding in order to provide a critical review of our current understanding of these questions. These questions include: How do children make sense of the behaviour of others in such situations? Does this ability to understand our social environment influence the development and maintenance of social relationships, or do social relationships provide the social contexts for children to practise and refine their social understanding? Do children learn how to make sense of the behaviours of others through the richness of communication with others at home (e.g. conversations with parents and siblings about mental states and emotions)? Do social experiences with peers and friends during time spent at school have an important role to play here? Can social understanding be applied in both a positive and negative manner during interactions with others? And finally, can teachers and practitioners working with children influence the development of social understanding? These questions will be considered starting with the first, and potentially most challenging question, concerning the nature of social understanding.

What is social understanding?

Understanding other people within our everyday interactions is the key mechanism that allows us to engage with others in the wonderfully complex ways that we do. In many respects, understanding others is the glue that binds people together within human social experience, fosters meaningful human interactions and provides a basis for culture and shared values within communities (Tomasello, 1999). It allows us to move beyond mere behavioural explanations of the actions of others and instead attempt to make sense of others in terms of the mental and emotional processes that underscore actions and motivate behaviour (Wellman, 2014).

Various forms of social understanding, or what has been termed 'theory of mind' (Carpendale and Lewis, 2006), have been the subject of extensive research over the last 35 years (Wimmer and Perner, 1983; Wellman *et al.*, 2001). This period has seen the rapid growth of empirical studies and theoretical accounts with the common focus on how children make sense of their social worlds, and the factors responsible for the development of such understanding, and how children use such forms of understanding in their interactions with others (see Wellman, 2014, and Carpendale and Lewis, 2006, for excellent reviews). Key developments during this period have revolved around the question of how infants and young children begin to move away from an egocentric view of the world and learn to make accurate inferences within their increasing complex social worlds.

One product of the many decades of research is that we now have a clearer grasp of the way in which the concept of social understanding breaks down into various components. While these different aspects of social understanding have largely been studied separately we must keep in mind that our social worlds are incredibly complex, and therefore within any given social situation we may employ various forms of social understanding in order to make sense of others' actions. In the following section a more detailed overview of these different aspects of social understanding will be outlined.

The components of social understanding

Understanding other people's mental and emotional states, known by some as 'theory of mind' (ToM), is a concept that has been used interchangeably with other labels such as folk psychology, mentalising, mind reading, or more recently, social understanding (Carpendale and Lewis, 2006). According to Wellman *et al.* (2001: 655) 'the phrase ... emphasizes that everyday psychology involves seeing oneself and others in terms of mental states, the desires, emotions, beliefs, intentions, and other inner experiences that result in and are manifested in human action'.

For most of the twentieth century our theoretical understanding of children's mental capacities was dominated by conceptualisations such as the 'tabula rasa' (blank slate) or the pre-operational child and sensori-motor infant. While both models, which are drawn from behavioural and Piagetian accounts of child development respectively, differ radically in their underlying assumptions; they equally underestimate infants' and young children's abilities to make sense of their social worlds. (See Chapter 9 for a more detailed discussion of behavioural model of learning, and Chapter 8 for a discussion on Piaget.) In short, both models underestimate how much children understand what other people are doing and why they are doing it. This ability to 'make sense' of others' actions is applicable not only to adults and young children, but also has also been recently demonstrated empirically by infants within their first 18 months of life and has become quite sophisticated by the time young children enter school (Wellman and Liu, 2004).

Table 6.1 Aspects of social understanding

The broad framework	The narrow framework
Goals	False belief
Understanding that other people perform actions in order to achieve certain goals	Understanding that other people may not have witnessed an event and therefore have an out-dated or false belief about the current state of affairs
Intentions Understanding that other people's actions have both intended and unintended consequences	
Desires Understanding that other people may have desires that differ from our own	
Visual perspectives Understanding that other people may see an event differently from ourselves	
Emotions and emotional perspectives Recognising emotional displays and understanding that other people may have emotional states that may differ from how we feel	
Knowledge/True belief and ignorance Understanding that other people may be either knowledgeable or ignorant of things that we know	

For conceptual reasons, researchers in this area have divided the different processes within social understanding into two categories, known as the 'broad' and narrow' frameworks respectively (see Table 6.1 above). In the present chapter, the processes covered in the broad framework consist of our understanding of the goals, intentions, perceptions, knowledge and emotions of others, while the narrow framework consists of our understanding of others' false beliefs (Call and Tomasello, 2008). However, in our complex everyday social interactions we effortlessly employ both broad and narrow frameworks, allowing us to see the world in the unique and sophisticated ways that we do.

In order to make sense of these different components of social understanding and how these may affect our social relationships in educational settings, we will now review the components in turn through a series of hypothetical case studies.

The broad framework

Goals and intentions

Two children (Peter and Paul) are working side-by-side painting pictures for their parents. Peter leans over the glass of water that contains brushes being used and accidentally knocks it over, spilling the water and spoiling Paul's painting. The key question here is whether Paul is able to understand that this outcome was a result of an accidental action by Peter. Research suggests that this rudimentary understanding of the goals and intentions of others is evident in children from the second half of their first year of life (Behne *et al.*, 2005).

Desire-state reasoning

Peter and Paul are now waiting in line to be served lunch. They arrive at the serving counter and are told that while there are several portions of chocolate cake still available there is only one portion of rhubarb and crumble left. The child first in line (Peter) likes rhubarb and crumble, but also likes chocolate cake and knows that crumble is Paul's favourite dessert. The key question here is whether Peter will be able to move beyond his own desires, 'put himself in the shoes' of Paul, and comprehend that Paul's desire for the crumble is greater than his own. Evidence suggests that a rudimentary understanding of the desires of others is evident from around 18 months of age (Repacholi and Gopnik, 1997).

Visual perspectives

Peter and Paul are sitting face-to-face at a table. Paul has drawn a picture that he wants to show to Peter. Paul realises that in order for Peter to be able to make sense of the drawing he will need to turn the picture around to face Peter. If he does this, Paul is demonstrating that he is able to realise that Peter's visual perspective (what Peter can see from where he is sitting) is different from his own. Research has demonstrated that young children (Hughes, 1975) and, under more simplified conditions, even infants (Moll and Tomasello, 2004) can understand the visual perspectives of others.

Recognising emotions and emotional perspective taking

Peter and Paul have put their names on the class list to visit the local forest school. On the day of the visit the teacher announces that only half of the children will be able to attend this week, with the second half attending next week. The teacher reads children's names from the first half of her register and says that these children will be attending this week. She calls out Peter's name but not Paul's. The question here is whether Peter can recognise that Paul looks upset (emotional recognition) and understand that this means Paul is feeling very sad (emotional perspective-taking). Evidence demonstrates that emotional recognition is evident within early infancy (Haviland and Lelwica, 1987) but that due to the linguistic demands of tests that assess it, emotional perspective taking can only be reliably demonstrated from around 3 years of age (Eisenberg *et al.*, 2006).

Knowledge/True belief and ignorance

Peter and Paul are now in class. Peter decides he would like to play a trick on Paul by taking his favourite pencil and hiding it in his coat pocket. Peter realises that if he acts while Paul is present then Paul will know what has happened and therefore have a 'true belief' about where his pen currently is; so he waits for Paul to either turn his back or leave the room before hiding Paul's favourite pencil in his coat. In this instance Paul is now currently 'ignorant' about its current location. By doing this, Peter is demonstrating that he is able to make accurate inferences about Paul's current and future levels of knowledge and manipulate the environment accordingly. Evidence suggests that a rudimentary understanding of the knowledge-states of others is evident during infancy (Moll and Tomasello, 2007).

The narrow framework

False belief

In the previous example there were only two possible outcomes: either Paul knew (a true belief) or he didn't know (ignorance). But there is another side to the story. If he doesn't know it's been moved, when Paul returns where will he look for his pencil? If asked this question most of us would, without any real effort, state that he will look for it in his own schoolbag, even though we know it has been moved in Paul's absence. Paul's continued belief that his pencil is where he left it is known as a 'false belief' and our awareness that he will have this false belief is a demonstration of our mastery of this element of social understanding.

This awareness of false beliefs has, for the last 35 years, been considered the 'acid test' for mature social understanding (Wellman *et al.*, 2001). Such awareness is thought to demonstrate that we can (a) suspend our own egocentric view of reality (e.g. 'I' know that the pencil has been moved), (b) mentally represent another person's view on reality (e.g. Paul still thinks the pencil is located in his bag), and (c) subsequently use this mental representation to understand why Paul will, at first, search for his pencil in his schoolbag.

This everyday example echoes the procedure pioneered in Wimmer and Perner's (1983) now classic 'false-belief unexpected transfer task', which is the typical scenario within the English version of this task (Baron-Cohen *et al.*, 1985). The findings from Wimmer and Perner's (1983) study demonstrate that over 90 per cent of 6–9 year-olds and nearly 60 per cent of 4–5 year-olds were able to predict correctly where Sally would look for the marble. This is contrasted with a zero per cent success rate for 3-year-olds. These findings have been replicated by numerous subsequent studies, leading most theorists to argue that the ability to attribute false beliefs typically emerges in children at around 4 years of age (Wellman *et al.*, 2001).

In summary, this review of the components of social understanding shows us two things. The first conclusion is that social understanding needs to be understood not as a single ability but rather as a collection of abilities. However, while these have been largely studied independently by researchers we must be aware that children will be using such understanding in a much more fluid manner in attempting to make sense of the vast array of information within their social environments (Wellman *et al.*, 2001). The second conclusion, which follows on from the first, is that the development of these abilities in any individual is not guaranteed to be uniform and, as will be argued below, can be influenced by the quality of social experience and interactions with others within the home and educational environments.

Early developments in social understanding: social understanding and autism

The components of social understanding may initially seem abstract or even trivial to the reader, but consider what the world would be like if you judged others on their actions alone without any consideration of their underlying mental or emotional states. Remarkably, this deficit of social understanding exists; Baron-Cohen identified what he later termed 'mindblindness', with most evidence suggesting a lack of awareness of others' false beliefs, in children with autism (Baron-Cohen *et al.*, 1985). There is now a substantial body of research which both supports and extends this early finding (Happe, 1994; 1995).

Moving beyond the study of false beliefs alone, we see that autistic children are also compromised on other measures related to social understanding. For example, such children perform less well on social understanding tasks where the child is required to articulate the understanding that 'seeing leads to knowing' (Baron-Cohen and Goodhart, 1994), monitoring another's intentions (Phillips *et al.*, 1998) or recognising basic emotional expressions (Uljarevic and Hamilton, 2012). There is also mixed evidence to suggest that autistic children have difficulty following the gaze-direction of others (Leekam *et al.*, 2000).

At a more applied social level, early research demonstrated that autistic children perform less well on tasks that require an understanding of deception (Sodian and Frith, 1992). However, later studies suggested that autistic children have some levels of competence in terms of telling antisocial lies (to conceal a transgression) or white lies (related to being polite) but struggle to maintain this deception when further questioned about it. In a similar vein it has also been demonstrated that autistic children have difficulties understanding more advanced forms of social understanding such as sarcasm and irony (Happe, 1994). Finally, autistic children infrequently use mental state terms (e.g. think, know, pretend, believe, etc.) even while participating in activities that promote such usage in non-autistic children (Baron-Cohen *et al.*, 1986).

Importantly, naturalistic observations of conversations between mothers and autistic children demonstrate that their dialogue tends to be characterised by a lack of reference to internal mental states (Tager-Flusberg, 2003). This is noteworthy because, as we will see in the next section, there is an abundance of research demonstrating the beneficial effects that conversations about mental states within the family setting can have on children's emerging social understanding.

In summary, in this section we have reviewed various components of social understanding and considered how autistic children have difficulty in making sense of their social worlds. However, children do not learn in a social vacuum. Rather, it could be said that the development of social understanding 'begins at home' and so, as we will see in the next section, the factors that facilitate or inhibit the emergence of such understanding are rooted in the family, in family relationships and interactions.

Further developments in the research on social understanding: the role of families

As was mentioned earlier in this chapter, social understanding is evident from infancy (Behne *et al.*, 2005; Moll and Tomasello, 2007) and becomes more advanced during the pre-school years and beyond (Wellman *et al.*, 2001; Wellman and Liu, 2004). Researchers are increasingly interested in understanding how the development of social understanding is facilitated within both educational and non-educational contexts. There is now a wealth of evidence from researchers adopting a social interactionist stance (Carpendale and Lewis, 2006), which endorses the view that families play a significant role in supporting children's emerging social understanding.

As we will see, the impact of family is an important factor affecting children's ability to use social understanding in educational contexts. The argument presented here is based on the perspective that early experiences within the home environment provide both the social contexts and the supportive conditions that help to shape a child's emerging social understanding and will therefore influence how they engage with, and make sense of, others in non-family settings such as school. In this section we will first consider the role of parental influences on children's emerging social understanding, followed by a consideration of sibling and peer influences.

Parental influences on social understanding

Parental influences on children's social understanding have been studied extensively over the last 30 years. These studies have highlighted a number of important aspects of parental behaviour which appear to have a significant influence on the development of social understanding in their children. Key behaviours include parental responsiveness and sensitivity to their child (Meins *et al.*, 2001), parenting styles and disciplinary approaches (Ruffman *et al.*, 1999) and the extent of parent–child conversations which incorporate mental-state and emotion-state themes (Bartsch and Wellman, 1995; Dunn *et al.*, 1991).

A key series of studies in this area is the highly influential work on maternal sensitivity and social understanding by Liz Meins and colleagues (Meins *et al.*, 1998; 2001; 2002). Meins' 'mind-mindedness' model suggests that the development of social understanding rests, in part, on the mother's ability to make correct inferences of her child's mental state from the child's behaviour and respond appropriately. For example, development is not promoted if a mother incorrectly interprets her infant's behaviour and responds with mental-state language which does not correspond with the infant's actual mental state (e.g. by saying 'Are you bored?' when the child is merely distracted and has only temporarily turned away from an object). By contrast, development will be promoted if mother and child engage in behaviours that are more in tune with the infant's mental state, thus allowing the mother to provide behaviours and language that facilitate these social exchanges. In these situations it also helps if the mother uses language in a manner that makes verbal inferences about the infant's current mental state (e.g. I *know* what you *want*).

Research focus: maternal speech patterns with infants influence social understanding in early childhood

In order to evaluate the impact of maternal language use on the development of social understanding in children, Meins *et al.* (2002) conducted a longitudinal study with two assessments, the first at 6 months and the second at 48 months. In the first assessment mothers were asked to engage with their 6-month-olds in a period of play with objects. During this interaction the researchers coded the amount of mental state language used by mothers. The researchers were interested in finding out what the impact would be if bouts of joint play were infused with language that tapped into various components of social awareness such as perceptual awareness, intentions, desires, knowledge and ignorance and beliefs. In the follow-up assessment at 48 months the same children were tested for their social understanding skills using a standard false belief task. The key findings from this study showed a positive correlation between early exposure to mother's use of mental state language at 6 months and more advanced social understanding, or theory of mind, for children at 48 months.

The key issues here are that the mother is not only 'in tune' with her infant but is treating her child as an intentional goal-directed agent (i.e. a separate individual with their own intentions and goals) who has the capacity to make sense of their social world. In this instance, it can be argued that the mother's sensitivity to her infant and her ability to draw on her own levels of social understanding provides a means of supporting her infant's emerging social understanding during bouts of interaction. Mein's 'mind-mindedness' model has been supported by numerous earlier studies, such as Dunn et al. (1991) who investigated the causes of individual differences in the development of social understanding among toddlers. Dunn carried out longitudinal observations within family settings and found a significant relationship between children's conversations with their mother about feelings at age 3 and the ability of those same children to recognise emotions of others at age 6. Collectively, the findings of Mein, Dunn and others demonstrate that the quality and richness of mental-state conversations is related to the development of social understanding in early and middle childhood. It's worth noting that in addition to looking at conversations with the mother, Dunn and colleagues also considered the impact of conversations about emotions with siblings, and this is a topic we will look at in more detail in the next section.

Sibling influences on social understanding

The quality of relationships with their siblings is another factor which has been linked with the development of social understanding in young children. Early work on this topic supported the view that membership of a larger family has a positive influence on pre-schoolers' understanding of false beliefs (Lewis et al., 1996; Perner et al., 1994). Sibling interactions also offer the opportunity for young children to engage in more 'child-oriented' forms of communication (Dunn and Brophy, 2005) and pretend play (Youngblade and Dunn, 1995). Such relationships also allow a greater opportunity for young children to engage in 'other-oriented' forms of communication which not only contribute to their emerging understanding of others' perspectives (Ruffman et al., 1999) but also their ability to more appropriately manage any conflict or disputes that arise during interactions with their siblings (Randell and Peterson, 2009).

Following on from Perner et al. (1994), numerous studies have emerged that shine further light on the nature of this 'sibling effect' (i.e. the beneficial effect of siblings) on the development of social understanding. For example, Ruffman et al. (1998) suggested that it was not the number of siblings per se which was is the key influence here, rather that interaction with older siblings was responsible for enhancing the development of social understanding in the younger siblings. An explanation for this effect can be found in a similar study by Lewis et al. (1996) conducted on Greek and Cypriot pre-schoolers. Lewis and colleagues proposed an 'apprenticeship model' within which younger children develop a better understanding of their social worlds through meaningful interactions with more knowledgeable members of their social environment (e.g. their older siblings).

McAlister and Peterson (2006) provided further detail here by demonstrating that young children's social understanding was positively influenced by having a sibling of similar age when compared with children from families with a large age-gap between children. Furthermore, Jenkins and Astington (1996) also demonstrated the positive effects of family size on children's social understanding. However, their study found that the 'sibling effect' was more beneficial for children who were less verbally competent. This finding suggests that meaningful interactions with siblings can provide a compensatory influence on the development of social understanding in children who may be delayed in their language development. While this is an encouraging finding, a number of studies demonstrate that the positive effects of having siblings on children's social understanding is not evident in lower-income British families (Cole and Mitchell, 2000; Cutting and Dunn, 1999; Hughes and Ensor, 2005). Potential explanations for this can be related the mother's level of education, levels of maternal sensitivity and quality of the home environment (Cutting and Dunn, 1999). If true, this may put children from lower-income families at a double disadvantage, not just in terms of having a less well developed social understanding but, as we will see in the next section, potentially fewer of the social and educational benefits that are related to more advanced forms of social understanding. This issue in turn supports the need for a greater emphasis on training programmes which provide additional non-familial encouragement to pre-schoolers' emerging social understanding.

The relationship between social understanding and social and educational outcomes

The previous sections provide an overview of what is meant by the term 'social understanding' as well as some of the key developments of this concept over the last 35 years. All of this begs the question as to what impact, if any, does social understanding have on those children's social relationships within educational settings? Furthermore, do social experiences, such as their acceptance or rejection by other children, further influence children's social understanding of others? It is the last of these questions that we will consider first as we look into the connections between social understanding and friendships during childhood.

Children's friendships

A review of the wider literature shows that social understanding, as measured through false-belief tasks, appears to be positively related to levels of engagement in pretend-play with friends. This is found both in terms of quantity (e.g. Hughes and Dunn, 1997) and quality (e.g. Astington and Jenkins, 1995) of engagement. Similar findings show links between false-belief understanding and levels of 'mental-state talk' during informal conversations (Hughes and Dunn, 1998) as well as the levels of connectedness during communications between friends (Slomkowski and Dunn, 1996).

Research focus: social understanding and school readiness in pre-schoolers

According to Lecce et al. (2011: 314), 'The term school readiness encompasses the cognitive and socioemotional skills that children need when they enter school'. There are numerous studies linking social understanding to various social and academic outcomes which demonstrate clearly the critical role that social understanding abilities will play in determining the school readiness of any child.

With regard to the social and emotional aspects emphasised in the school readiness definition, research has found a link between pre-schoolers' social understanding and positive relationships with peers or friends (Hughes and Dunn, 1997; 1998) and teachers (Garner and Waajid, 2008). Children who score well on measures of social understanding typically show higher levels of maturity (Peterson *et al.*, 2007) and less evidence of problem behaviours (Hughes and Ensor, 2005).

With regard to cognitive aspects of the school readiness definition, research indicates that pre-schoolers' abilities on the emotional perspectives component of social understanding are related to their performance on literacy tasks (Bierman *et al.*, 2008) and later levels of academic achievement (Izard *et al.*, 2001). Similar findings for pre-schoolers have been found when assessing false-belief understanding, such that Blair and Razza (2007) found a relationship between false-belief performance and pre-schoolers' knowledge of letters.

Some researchers have suggested that advanced levels of social understanding come at the cost of greater sensitivity to criticism (Cutting and Dunn, 2002). However, research by Lecce and colleagues studying the relationship between levels of social understanding, sensitivity to criticism (age 6) and academic achievement (ages 7 and 10) has challenged this view (Lecce *et al.*, 2011; Lecce *et al.*, 2014). Instead, they support a 'benefit' model arguing that advanced levels of social understanding earlier in development enable children to better account for and reflect on criticism received and utilise such information to promote later academic achievement.

As well as showing how social understanding may allow for smoother and more sophisticated forms of play in early childhood, a second question that can be asked is whether social understanding is related to the development and maintenance of mutual friendships during and beyond this period. Peterson and Siegal (2002) provide some clues here. Using a cross-sectional design, their research showed that for most children better performance on measures of social understanding was related to having a greater number of mutual friendships. In a 2-year longitudinal follow-up to this study Fink *et al.* (2015) reassessed these same variables in a sample of 5–7-year-olds. The researchers argued that this age represents an important milestone in the child's emerging social world as it accounts for the period where young children are acclimatising to the demands of a more formal experience of education. It is also a period where first friendships appear to be made. Two key findings emerge from their study. First, among the 5-year-olds there was a significant relationship again between possession of a mutual friend and performance on measures of false-belief reasoning. Second, when longitudinally assessing this connection between the two variables it was found that children who were chronically friendless at age 7 had been characterised by their exceptionally poor performance on measures of social understanding 2 years earlier at age 5.

Peer relationships

Mutual friendships are only one form of peer relationship and so it may be worth widening our scope and considering the connection between social understanding and peer relationships in general to get the full picture on this issue. Peer relationships, or rather peer acceptance or rejection, is a common feature of children's experiences during school. Peer rejection (i.e. being overtly disliked or excluded from peer activities) affects around 15–20 per cent of children in school (Badenes *et al.*, 2000) and has been linked with children's levels of social understanding

(Caputi *et al.*, 2012). As we will see, such outcomes have both short- and long-term impacts on the quality of children's social relationships.

One of the key studies in this area by Slaughter *et al.* (2002) explored this question by asking children aged 4–6 years to provide peer nominations for those children in their class they would invite to a hypothetical party. Repeated for the entire class, this provides a measure of each child's level of general popularity as well as evidence of mutual friendships. These nominations were then classified into five status groups (popular, controversial, average, neglected or rejected). Each child was then asked to complete a number of tasks that measured their levels of social understanding. The main findings from this study showed that children who were popular among their peers scored significantly higher on the social understanding tasks when compared to children who had been rejected by their peers.

Slaughter *et al.* (2002) make two important observations from these findings. First, that children with more advanced levels of social understanding may, through being able to see the world through the eyes of their friend, have greater opportunity to become more popular and likeable. Second, by being popular such children may, in turn, have greater opportunity to use these social interactions as a basis to further develop their existing levels of social understanding. It is also worth considering the 'rejected' children here. Based on this model, children who do not possess the same levels of social understanding, and are therefore more likely to be rejected from the peer group, have reduced opportunities to engage with peers and therefore fewer chances to develop their social understanding.

These findings raise a number of potential implications for teachers to consider. If we assume that the link between social understanding and peer acceptance is causal then it may be helpful for children who are socially isolated to be encouraged and supported to practise perspective-taking skills within classroom and non-classroom settings. Furthermore, since prevention is better than cure, it may be prudent to consider how activities at earlier periods of development could provide children with more advanced levels of social understanding prior to entering school. For example, recent research has sought to assess the potential impact of teaching mental- and emotional-state understanding through story-telling and conversations within nursery and school environments (Grazzani *et al.*, 2016; Ornaghi *et al.*, 2011). These ways in which an educator might promote the development of social understanding will be considered in more detail later in this chapter. Before that, we will first consider how social understanding can be used in a prosocial and antisocial manner.

Prosocial behaviours

Prosocial behaviour involves engaging in acts that both benefit and express concern for the well-being of others. Such behaviour includes helping, sharing, empathy or comforting, and cooperating (Caputi *et al.*, 2012). A view that has persisted within the literature in this area argues that children's demonstration of prosocial behaviours is based on their ability to use social understanding. The rationale here is that once children are able to make sense of how others think and feel, they can then use such awareness as a basis to engage in a range of prosocial behaviours (Eisenberg and Mussen, 1989).

This perspective appears to be consistent with the findings of the majority of empirical studies in the field. For example, research with older infants demonstrates that children will monitor the actions of others (e.g. noticing that someone has both hands full and is trying, but failing, to open a cupboard door) and intervene (by opening the door) when they see that the goals of others are not being met (Warneken and Tomasello, 2006). At a similar age children will also show signs of distress and attempt to comfort others when they perceive them to be in distress (Zahn-Waxler *et al.*, 1992). Starting at around age 3–4 years, children also engage in more equitable forms of sharing with others (e.g. Moore, 2009). Such behaviours appear to be related to levels of cooperation and teamwork with other children (Hamann *et al.*, 2011) as well as being linked to the child's performance on measures of social understanding (Takagishi *et al.*, 2010).

Research focus: social understanding and prosocial behaviours in school

A number studies have explored the link between social understanding and prosocial behaviour in a school setting. For example, prosocial behaviours have been linked with more cooperative bouts of joint play with other pre-school children (Cutting and Dunn, 1999) and quality of friend-ships beyond the transition to primary school (Dunn *et al.*, 2002).

Caputi *et al.* (2012) provide a related assessment focusing on how social understanding and prosocial behaviours influence peer acceptance or rejection between 5 and 7 years of age. The findings from this study show important links between levels of social under-standing and prosocial behaviour, and show that the presence or absence of these rela-tionships influences whether children will be accepted or rejected by peers.

Antisocial behaviours

Deception and lying

The relationship between social understanding and deception and lying has been studied exten-sively. Sodian and Frith (1992) argue that deception is characterised by the ability to intentionally manipulate other people's beliefs. It is worth noting that such skills are evident in early develop-ment, with Chandler *et al.* (1989) finding that even 2½-year-olds possess the ability to deceive others.

In an attempt to better understand the relationship between deception and social understanding, Polak and Harris (1999) presented 3–5-year-olds with a situation where they had an opportunity to break the rules and then lie about it. In this study the researcher left the children alone in a room with a mysterious box but asked children not to look in the box. Despite this instruction (or because of it, perhaps) the majority of children tested in this study looked inside. However, having looked inside many children denied doing this. Furthermore, a minority of these children also feigned ignorance of the contents of the box. In exploring links between these actions and social understanding the researchers found that the children's performance on false-belief tasks (a component of social understanding) did predict their ability to deceive. However, there was no link found between false-belief performance and the ability to feign ignorance. These findings suggest that there may be different forms of deception which draw on different components of social understanding and emerge at different developmental periods.

Bullying

Despite bullying being a common problem that persists both within and outside of schooling it is only in the last 20 years or so that we see any systematic form of research in the area of bullying (e.g. Olweus, 1994). The definition of bullying which has gradually come to be accepted by most researchers and practitioners involves three criteria. Bullying is (1) intentional negative behaviour that (2) typically occurs with some repetitiveness and is (3) directed against a person who has difficulty defending himself or herself (Olweus, 2011). Bullying behaviour can be organised into three categories: direct bullying, involving physical aggression; verbal bullying, involving relational or indirect aggression (e.g. spreading rumours); and, more recently, cyber-bullying (e.g. through social media) (van Rensburg and Raubenheimer, 2015).

Early conceptualisations of the relationship between social abilities and bullying can generally be summed up by the social skills deficit model (Crick and Dodge, 1994). These theorists argue that children who engage in bullying behaviour do so as a result of prior experiences with aggression which have adversely influenced the child's ability to interpret and respond appropriately to social situations. In contrast, the social understanding model of bullying (Sutton et al., 1999) argues that bullies typically possess superior levels of social understanding when compared to other children. Such children can therefore (1) more readily identify perceived weakness in others and (2) assess and predict how their actions will be experienced by a victim (Gasser and Keller, 2009). Importantly, recent longitudinal research also supports the view that less advanced levels of social understanding in early childhood are related to both greater exposure to bullying and both being the victim and the perpetrator of bullying episodes in early adolescence (Shakhoor et al., 2012).

The mixed profile here shows that bullying can be related to both advanced and under-developed social understanding. Such variation supports an earlier argument by Sutton et al. (1999) who observe that in order for school-based anti-bullying strategies to be effective there is first a requirement for educators to have an accurate understanding of the factors underlying this behaviour. When considering victims of bullying it would appear valid to encourage the development of social understanding within earlier periods of development (some examples of such school-based interventions are discussed in the next section).

The role of educators and practitioners: training studies, school readiness and social understanding

Thus far in this chapter we have seen that social understanding can be both influenced by, and in turn influence, the quality of a child's social relationships with adults and other children. We have also seen that social understanding provides a basis for both prosocial and, in some instances, antisocial behaviour. It is also worth considering here that children's levels of social understanding have been linked with a number of social and academic outcomes important for cognitive growth and school readiness. With these issues in mind, the final section of this chapter will consider a number of methods for promoting social understanding within school settings.

There is an emerging and growing body of evidence which demonstrates that social understanding can be advanced through appropriate training approaches (Grazzani et al., 2016). These approaches fall within the wider social interactionist model (Carpendale and Lewis, 2006) and thus are based on the assumption that environmental factors, in this instance teachers' use of storytelling and conversational techniques within a school setting, provide a richness of experience that will allow children to engage with, converse about, and reflect on the mental states and behaviour of others.

For example, Ornaghi *et al.* (2011) devised a two-month training programme wherein 3- and 4-year-olds were read stories that were rich in mental-state language. For the experimental group this was followed by conversations and language games designed to promote children's use of that mental-state language. The control group did not engage in any language-based activities. The findings from this study show advances by the experimental group in their use of mental-state language for both the 3- and 4-year-old age groups. The 3-year-olds also showed advances in emotional understanding while the 4-year-olds also showed advances in false-belief understanding.

Ornaghi and colleagues extend this line of research by focusing on conversations that related to emotional understanding with pre-schoolers and older children. Focusing on older children and over the course of a 2-month intervention period, Ornaghi *et al.* (2014) had 7-year-olds read different emotional scenarios followed by children either engaging in conversations that were rich in emotional understanding (the experimental group) or drawing a picture about the story (the control group). The findings from this study showed greater advances in the conversational group in the areas of emotional understanding, empathy and theory of mind.

An important consideration for the story-telling and conversational approaches described here is their potential use in tackling the below-average levels of social understanding typically found among children from lower-income backgrounds. The arguments presented in this chapter demonstrate that there are children with a variety of life circumstances (e.g. autism, low-income family) which appear to influence their levels of social understanding and their ability to adjust to and engage with others in educational settings. Therefore, the approaches outlined in this section are particularly useful in that not only do they provide evidence of clear advances in key areas of research on children's social development, but they also offer affordable and accessible school-based interventions for enhancing social understanding. This makes them ideal for being utilised in communities and educational environments where resources are limited and there are large numbers of children from low-income families who would benefit greatly from exactly this kind of intervention.

Conclusion

Through the models and findings presented in the chapter we have come to see that social understanding is a multifaceted construct that encompasses comprehension of a range of mental and emotional states. Children's understanding of the mental and emotional states of others emerges gradually across their early years of development and is influenced by the opportunities afforded to them to engage in various rich, socially embedded forms of communication with adults and other children. Importantly, these processes take place within both family and school environments. We also saw that children can use social understanding in both a prosocial and an antisocial manner, and that it is likely to have a significant impact on both their social and academic outcomes during their time in education and beyond. Finally, we saw evidence from training studies with pre-schoolers and young children which showed us that social understanding is both malleable and can be enhanced through appropriate forms of social interaction, such as story-telling, conversations and opportunities to further reflect on these experiences. All of this supports the view that social understanding is a concept which should be familiar to any educator both as a factor affecting their students and as something they have a duty to enhance by providing educational experiences embedded in a socially rich and relevant discourse.

Key points

- Social understanding involves our ability to attribute mental and emotional states to self and others.
- This ability to 'make sense' of other people's actions is a fundamental skill that children use in their interactions with others.
- Social understanding emerges early and becomes more sophisticated as children progress through preschool and into early childhood.
- Children's home environment and their levels of social interaction with parents and siblings all have a significant effect on the child's emerging understanding of their social world.
- Social understanding has been linked to the quality of children's social relationships with friends and peers and can be used in either prosocial or antisocial ways.
- Social understanding is not a fixed ability; it can be facilitated within early years settings through story-telling and conversational activities.

Recommended readings

Bartsch, K. and Wellman, H.M. (1995) *Children talk about the mind.* New York: Oxford University Press.

Carpendale, J.I.M. and Lewis, C. (2006) *How children develop social understanding.* Oxford: Blackwell.

Ornaghi, V., Brookmeyer, J. and Grazzani Gavazzi, I. (2011) The role of language games in children's understanding of mental states: A training study. *Journal of Cognition and Development,* **12**, pp. 239–259.

Sutton, J., Smith, P.K. and Swettenham, J. (1999) Bullying and 'theory of mind': A critique of the 'social skills deficit' view of anti-social behaviour. *Social Development,* **8**(1), pp. 117–134.

References

Astington, J.W. and Jenkins, J.M. (1995) Theory of mind development and social understanding. *Cognition and Emotion,* **9**, pp. 151–165.

Badenes, L., Estevan, R. and Bacete, F. (2000) Theory of mind and peer rejection at school. *Social Development,* **9**(3), 271–283.

Baron-Cohen, S. and Goodhart, F. (1994) The 'seeing-leads-to-knowing' deficit in autism: The Pratt and Bryant probe. *British Journal of Developmental Psychology,* **12**, pp. 397–401.

Baron-Cohen, S., Leslie, A.M. and Frith, U. (1985) Does the autistic child have a 'theory of mind?' *Cognition,* **21**, pp. 37–46.

Baron-Cohen, S., Leslie, A.M. and Frith, U. (1986) Mechanical, behavioural and intentional understanding of picture stories in autistic children. *British Journal of Developmental Psychology,* **4**, pp. 113–125.

Bartsch, K. and Wellman, H.M. (1995) *Children talk about the mind.* New York: Oxford University Press.

Behne, T., Carpenter, M., Call, J. and Tomasello, M. (2005) Unwilling versus unable: Infants' understanding of intentional action. *Developmental Psychology,* **41**, pp. 328–337.

Bierman, K.L., Domitrovich, C.E., Nix, R.L., Gest, S.D., Welsh, J.A. and Greenberg, M.T. (2008) Promoting academic and social-emotional school readiness: The Head Start REDI program. *Child Development,* **79**, pp. 1802–1817.

Blair, C. and Razza, R.P. (2007) Relating effortful control, executive function, and false belief understanding to emerging math and literacy ability in kindergarten. *Child Development,* **78**, pp. 647–663.

Call, J. and Tomasello, M. (2008) Does the chimpanzee have a theory of mind? 30 years later. *Trends in Cognitive Sciences,* **12**, pp. 187–192.

Caputi, M., Lecce, S., Pagnin, A. and Banerjee, R. (2012) Longitudinal effects of theory of mind on later peer relations: The role of prosocial behavior. *Developmental Psychology,* **48**(1), pp. 257–270.

Carpendale, J.I.M. and Lewis, C. (2006) *How children develop social understanding*. Oxford: Blackwell.

Chandler, M., Fritz, A.S. and Hala, S. (1989) Small scale deceit: Deception as a marker of 2-, 3-, and 4-year-olds' early theories of mind. *Child Development*, **60**, pp. 1263–1277.

Cole, K. and Mitchell, P. (2000) Siblings in development of executive control and a theory of mind. *British Journal of Developmental Psychology*, **18**, pp. 279–295.

Crick, N.R. and Dodge, K.A. (1994) A review and reformulation of social information-processing mechanisms in children's social adjustment. *Psychological Bulletin*, **115**, pp. 74–101.

Cutting, A.L. and Dunn, J. (1999) Theory of mind, emotion understanding, language, and family background: Individual differences and interrelations. *Child Development*, **70**(4), pp. 853–865.

Cutting, A.L. and Dunn, J. (2002) The cost of understanding other people: Social cognition predicts young children's sensitivity to criticism. *Journal of Child Psychology and Psychiatry*, **43**, pp. 849–860.

Dunn, J. and Brophy, M. (2005) Communication, relationships and individual differences in children's understanding of mind. In J.W. Astington and J.A. Baird (eds) *Why language matters for theory of mind*. Oxford: Oxford University Press.

Dunn, J., Brown, J., Slomkowski, C., Tesla, C. and Youngblade, L. (1991) Young children's understanding of other people's feelings and beliefs: Individual differences and their antecedents. *Child Development*, **62**, pp. 1352–1366.

Dunn, J., Cutting, A.L. and Fisher, N. (2002) Old friends, new friends: Predictors of children's perspective on their friends at school. *Child Development*, **73**(2), pp. 621–635.

Eisenberg, N. and Mussen, P. (1989) *The roots of prosocial behavior in children*. Cambridge: Cambridge University Press.

Eisenberg, N., Spinrad, T.L. and Sadovsky, A. (2006) Empathy-related responding in children. In M. Killen and J. G. Smetana (eds) *Handbook of moral development*. Mahwah: Erlbaum.

Fink, E., Begeer, S., Peterson, C.C., Slaughter, V. and Rosnay, M. (2015) Friendlessness and theory of mind: A prospective longitudinal study. *British Journal of Developmental Psychology*, **33**, pp. 1–17.

Garner, P.W. and Waajid, B. (2008) The associations of emotion knowledge and teacher–child relationships to preschool children's school-related developmental competence. *Journal of Applied Developmental Psychology*, **29**, pp. 89–100.

Gasser, L. and Keller, M. (2009) Are the competent the morally good? Perspective taking and moral motivation of children involved in bullying. *Social Development*, **18**, pp. 798–816.

Grazzani, I., Ornaghi, V., Agliati, A. and Brazzelli, E. (2016) How to foster toddlers' mental-state talk, emotion understanding and prosocial behavior: A conversation-based intervention at nursery school. *Infancy*, **21**(2), pp. 199–227.

Hamann, K., Warneken, F., Greenberg, J.R. and Tomasello, M. (2011) Collaboration encourages equal sharing in children but not in chimpanzees. *Nature*, **476**(7360), pp. 328–331.

Happe, F.G.E. (1994) An advanced test of theory of mind: Understanding of story characters' thoughts and feelings by able autistic, mentally handicapped, and normal children and adults. *Journal of Autism and Developmental Disorders*, **24**(2), pp. 129–154.

Happe, F. (1995) The role of age and verbal ability in the Theory of Mind task performance of subjects with autism. *Child Development*, **66**, pp. 843–855.

Haviland, J.M. and Lelwica, M. (1987) The induced affect response: 10-week-old infants' responses to three emotion expressions. *Developmental Psychology*, **23**, pp. 97–104.

Hughes, C. and Dunn, J. (1997) 'Pretend you didn't know': Preschoolers' talk about mental states in pretend play. *Cognitive Development*, **12**, pp. 381–403.

Hughes, C. and Dunn, J. (1998) Understanding mind and emotion: Longitudinal associations with mental-state talk between young friends. *Developmental Psychology*, **34**, pp. 1026–1037.

Hughes, C. and Ensor, R. (2005) Theory of mind and executive function in two-year-olds: A family affair? *Developmental Neuropsychology*, **28**, pp. 645–668.

Hughes, M. (1975) Egocentrism in preschool children. Unpublished doctoral dissertation, University of Edinburgh.

Izard, C., Fine, S., Schultz, D., Mostow, A., Ackerman, B. and Youngstrom, E. (2001) Emotion knowledge as a predictor of social behavior and academic competence in children at risk. *Psychological Science*, **12**(1), pp. 18–23.

Jenkins, J.M. and Astington, J.W. (1996) Cognitive factors and family structure associated with theory of mind development in young children. *Developmental Psychology*, **32**, pp. 70–78.

Lecce, S., Caputi, M. and Hughes, C. (2011) Does sensitivity to criticism mediate the relationship between theory of mind and academic achievement? *Journal of Experimental Child Psychology*, **110**, pp. 313–331.

Lecce, S., Caputi, M. and Pagnin, A. (2014) Long-term effect of theory of mind on school achievement: The role of sensitivity to criticism. *European Journal of Developmental Psychology*, **11**, pp. 305–318.

Leekam, S.R., Lopez, B. and Moore, C. (2000) Attention and joint attention in preschool children with autism. *Developmental Psychology*, **36**(2), pp. 261–273.

Lewis, C., Freeman, N.H., Kyriakidou, C., Maridaki-Kassotaki, K. and Berridge, D.M. (1996) Social influences on false belief access: Specific sibling influences or general apprenticeship? *Child Development*, **67**(6), pp. 2930–2947.

McAlister, A. and Peterson, C.C. (2006) Mental playmate: Siblings, executive functioning and theory of mind. *Journal of British Psychological Society*, **24**, pp. 733–751.

Meins, E., Fernyhough, C., Fradley, E. and Tuckey, M. (2001) Rethinking maternal sensitivity: Mother's comments on infants' mental processes predict security of attachment at 12 months. *Journal of Child Psychology and Psychiatry*, **42**(5), pp. 637–648.

Meins, E., Fernyhough, C., Russell, J. and Clark-Carter, D. (1998) Security of attachment as a predictor of symbolic and mentalising abilities: A longitudinal study. *Social Development*, **7**(1), pp. 1–24.

Meins, E., Fernyhough, C., Wainwright, R., Das Gupta, M., Fradley, E. and Tuckey, M. (2002) Maternal mind-mindedness and attachment security as predictors of theory of mind understanding. *Child Development*, **73**(6), pp. 1715–1726.

Moll, H. and Tomasello, M. (2004) 12- and 18-month-olds follow gaze behind barriers. *Developmental Science*, **7**, pp. F1–F9.

Moll, H. and Tomasello, M. (2007) How 14- and 18-month-olds know what others have experienced. *Developmental Psychology*, **43**, pp. 309–317.

Moore, C. (2009) Fairness in children's resource allocation depends on the recipient. *Psychological Science*, **20**, pp. 944–948.

Olweus, D. (1994) Bullying at School: Basic Facts and Effects of a School Based Intervention Program. *Journal of Child Psychology and Psychiatry*, **35**(7), pp. 1171–1190.

Olweus, D. (2011) Bullying at school and later criminality: Findings from three Swedish community samples of males. *Criminal Behavior and Mental Health*, **21**(2), pp. 151–156.

Ornaghi, V., Brockmeier, J. and Grazzani Gavazzi, I. (2011) The role of language games in children's understanding of mental states: A training study. *Journal of Cognition and Development*, **12**, pp. 239–259.

Ornaghi, V., Brockmeier, J. and Grazzani, I. (2014) Enhancing social cognition by training children in emotion understanding: A primary school study. *Journal of Experimental Child Psychology*, **119**, pp. 26–39.

Perner, J., Ruffman, T. and Leekam, S. (1994) Theory of mind is contagious: You catch it from your sibs. *Child Development*, **65**, pp. 1228–1238.

Peterson, C.C. and Siegal, M. (2002) Mindreading and moral awareness in popular and rejected preschoolers. *British Journal of Developmental Psychology*, **20**, pp. 205–224.

Peterson, C.C., Slaughter, V.P. and Paynter, J. (2007) Social maturity and theory of mind in typically developing children and those on the autism spectrum. *Journal of Child Psychology and Psychiatry*, **48**(12), pp. 1243–1250.

Phillips, W., Baron-Cohen, S. and Rutter, M. (1998) Understanding intention in normal development and in autism. *British Journal of Developmental Psychology*, **16**, pp. 337–348.

Polak, A. and Harris, P.L. (1999) Deception by young children following noncompliance. *Developmental Psychology*, **35**, pp. 561–568.

Randell, A.C. and Peterson, C.C. (2009) Affective qualities of sibling disputes, mothers' conflict attitudes, and children's theory of mind development. *Social Development*, **18**(4), pp. 857–874.

Repacholi, B.M. and Gopnik, A. (1997) Early reasoning about desires: Evidence from 14- and 18-month-olds. *Developmental Psychology*, **33**(1), pp. 12–21.

Ruffman, T., Perner, J., Naito, M., Parkin, L. and Clements, W.A. (1998) Older (but not younger) siblings facilitate false belief understanding. *Developmental Psychology*, **34**, pp. 161–174.

Ruffman, T., Perner, J. and Parkin, L. (1999) How parenting style affects false belief understanding. *Social Development*, **8**, pp. 395–411.

Shakoor, S., Jaffee, S.R., Bowes, L., Ouellet-Morin, I., Andreou, P., Happe, F., Moffitt, T.E. and Arseneault, L. (2012) A prospective longitudinal study of children's theory of mind and adolescent involvement in bullying. *Journal of Child Psychology and Psychiatry*, **53**, pp. 254–261.

Slaughter, V., Dennis, M.J. and Pritchard, M. (2002) Theory of mind and peer acceptance in preschool children. *British Journal of Psychology*, **20**, pp. 545–564.

Slomkowski, C. and Dunn, J. (1996) Young children's understanding of other people's beliefs and feelings and their connected communication with friends. *Developmental Psychology*, **32**, pp. 442–447.

Sodian, B. and Frith, U. (1992) Deception and sabotage in autistic, retarded and normal children. *Journal of Child Psychology and Psychiatry*, **33**, pp. 591–605.

Sutton, J., Smith, P.K. and Swettenham, J. (1999) Bullying and 'theory of mind': A critique of the 'social skills deficit' view of anti-social behaviour. *Social Development*, **8**(1), pp. 117–134.

Tager-Flusberg, H. (2003) Exploring the relationship between theory of mind and social communicative functioning in children with autism. In B. Repacholi and V. Slaughter (eds) *Individual differences in theory of mind: Implications for typical and atypical development.* New York: Psychology Press.

Takagishi, H., Kameshima, S., Schug, J., Koizumi, M. and Yamagishi, T. (2010) Theory of mind enhances preference for fairness. *Journal of Experimental Child Psychology*, **105**, pp. 130–137.

Tomasello, M. (1999) *The cultural origins of human cognition.* Cambridge, MA: Harvard University Press.

Uljarevic, M. and Hamilton, A. (2012) Recognition of emotions in autism: A formal meta-analysis. *Journal of Autism and Developmental Disorders*, **43**, pp. 1–10.

van Rensburg, E.J. and Raubenheimer, J. (2015) Does forgiveness mediate the impact of school bullying on adolescent mental health? *Journal of Child and Adolescent Mental Health*, **27**(1), pp. 25–39.

Warneken, F. and Tomasello, M. (2006) Altruistic helping in human infants and young chimpanzees. *Science*, **311**, pp. 1301–1303.

Wellman, H.M. (2014) *Making minds: How theory of mind develops.* New York: Oxford University Press.

Wellman, H.M., Cross, D. and Watson, J. (2001) Meta-analysis of theory-of-mind development: The truth about false belief. *Child Development*, **72**, pp. 655–684.

Wellman, H.M. and Liu, D. (2004) Scaling of theory-of-mind tasks. *Child Development*, **75**, pp. 523–541.

Wimmer, H. and Perner, J. (1983) Beliefs about beliefs: Representation and constraining function of wrong beliefs in young children's understanding of deception. *Cognition*, **13**, pp. 103–128.

Youngblade, L.M. and Dunn, J. (1995) Individual differences in young children's pretend play with mother and sibling: Links to relationships and understanding of other people's feelings and beliefs. *Child Development*, **66**, pp. 1472–1492.

Zahn-Waxler, C., Radke-Yarrow, M., Wagner, E. and Chapman, M. (1992) Development of concern for others. *Developmental Psychology*, **28**, pp. 126–136.

7 Boys do maths, girls do English
Tracing the origins of gender identity and its impact in education

Cathal Ó Siochrú

Introduction

The belief that there are fundamental differences between the two genders in terms of abilities, personality and behaviour is well established in the minds of the public. This belief extends into the realm of education where there are different expectations of the two genders in terms of their learning behaviours and the subjects at which they will excel. Males are expected to have superior visuospatial skills and outperform females in technical subjects like science and mathematics. Females are expected to have greater verbal abilities and outperform males in literary subjects. The impact of these assumptions on our education system and the men and women in it is considerable, but are these differences real? If they are real, what causes the two genders to differ in these ways? Are the differences innate or learnt, and if they are learnt where and when do we learn them?

The first part of this chapter will draw on key studies and reviews of the research on the origins of gender differences. In the second part we will explore the relationship between education and gender. Ultimately we will see how our gender identity is a much more fluid and socially defined concept than we might have expected and that it is our expectations about each gender and the way those expectations are connected to certain subjects that has the greatest impact on educational outcomes.

Reflections

Which gender do you think each of the following adjectives refers to? Affectionate, Analytical, Forceful, Loyal, Sympathetic, Individualistic, Ambitious, Compassionate and Cheerful. Why is it possible to divide these adjectives in this way?

What this activity reveals is that we divide much of our world into male and female. There are typically masculine behaviours, typically feminine occupations. We will try and answer two very important questions about the gendered world around us: how did this happen and what does it mean in relation to education? But before we can start with either of those questions we first need to have a little chat about sex.

Sex and gender

An important thing to clarify at the start is the difference between the terms 'sex' and 'gender'. In both common usage and in research the two terms are often used interchangeably. However, they refer to very different things.

Sex refers to biological differences which can be used to divide humans into two main categories, male and female. This is usually determined by chromosomes as well as internal and external genitalia. This will typically allow you to identify someone as a member of one of the two sexes, although other sub-categories such as hermaphrodites and those whose chromosomes or external genitalia are inconsistent with their sex also exist.

Gender on the other hand refers to an identity which is usually a result of a combination of biological, personal and social factors. As such, a person's sex is a part of their gender identity but not the only part. Gender can also be used to divide humans into two main categories, masculine and feminine, although other sub-categories such as androgynous also exist.

On the surface it's easy to see why sex and gender are seen as being interchangeable but there are some critical differences. To begin with, sex is much more of a 'binary' concept than gender. Outside of the very rare biological conditions I've just mentioned the quality of 'maleness', biologically speaking, does not vary among members of the male sex. If you have any one of the qualities of maleness you almost always have all the others too and the qualities that constitute 'maleness' or 'femaleness' are very well defined. But with gender both masculinity and femininity are much more variable and much less well defined. Someone who is masculine can have more or less of the qualities of masculinity than another person who is also masculine. Also, although sex and gender typically co-vary it's been argued that a member of either sex may have elements of both masculinity and femininity in their gender identity. As such, equating sex and gender is a very problematic thing to do.

There are a few ways that equating sex and gender can cause problems in terms of our understanding of gender development and gender in education. To begin with, the fact that our sex is biologically determined means that when most people are seeking to explain a difference in behaviour between the sexes they tend to seek a biological explanation. However, if the difference in question was presented as a difference between the 'genders' rather than the 'sexes' then we see that the root of the difference may be biological but it could also be social. As a result, the equating of sex with gender can cause people to over-estimate the impact of biology and under-estimate the impact of socialisation on gender differences.

To even use the term 'gender differences' is to fall into another trap, thinking of gender as being divided into two discrete groups which can be compared to see if they are similar or different. By only focusing on the difference between the two groups we can end up over-looking potential variation within in each group. A large number of studies on gender make this mistake by limiting themselves to a comparison between males and females. Consequently, they miss out on all the variation that exists among males in terms of their levels of masculinity and among females in terms of their femininity. They also ignore the possibility that there may be elements of masculinity in females and femininity in males which are affecting the results.

Mind the gap: popular obsession with gender 'gaps' in education

Concern over reports of a gender 'gap' in some aspect of the education system is a recurrent theme in our society's general worries about education. One serious problem with many of these reports is the lack of validity for the 'gap' being reported because, often as not, the supposed gap between the genders is actually an illusion. What is not commonly known is that when we look at the average scores of any two groups on any educational issue, finding a difference is a very likely outcome. Most of these differences will be meaningless, the product of random fluctuations rather than the impact of gender or any other variable. It's for this very reason that statisticians have specific tests to analyse these differences and find the 'significant' ones, the differences that are a result of something other than random chance and normal fluctuations. Many of these reports on gender 'gaps' fail to include any statistical tests, possibly because those doing the reporting have no training in statistics or they fear their audience will not understand. Instead they treat all differences they find as meaningful differences and attribute their cause to gender effects. This creates what statisticians call 'false positives', results which create the illusion of a gender difference on some educational issue. The harm this can cause is shown by Elmore and Oyserman (2012) who showed that portraying success in education as being associated with one gender more than the other led to differences in motivation and aspiration between the two genders. This could result in a self-fulfilling prophecy. We will see later on in this chapter how we could instead approach reports of gender 'gaps' in education with a more sceptical eye and so avoid falling into the trap of accepting an unhealthy gender gap narrative.

Therefore, for the purposes of this chapter when we talk about gender and education we will be talking about the impact that someone's gender identity has on their education and related abilities. Your gender identity includes your biological sex but also society's expectations for gender and your own conceptions of gender. With gender identity it is still possible to talk about males and females as the two main categories, but we should see them as two halves of a single continuum rather than two separate groups. For example, your biological sex might place you on the female end of the continuum; but exactly where you lie inside that female end, closer to the androgynous middle or further out towards the highly feminine extreme, is determined by a combination all the elements of your gender identity.

What this means is that when we talk about how 'gender impacts on education' you can still think of how men and women differ as your starting point, but you shouldn't leave it there. You should also consider what biological and social factors within each gender are the cause of any gender effect and how those factors may differ amongst women and amongst men as well as between the genders. We should also be thinking about how those factors might vary not just between males and females but across all students.

Gender development

As with all forms of development, the roots of gender development have been traced to a number of factors, some of which are biological factors (Nature) and others of which are social factors (Nurture). There are a number of different theories, each of which focuses on one or more of these factors and attempts to explain the impact of that factor on your gender identity. These theories can be grouped into three categories: Biological theories, Learning theories and Cognitive Development theories.

These shouldn't be seen as competing theories. None of them claims to have the one and only answer to the question of how our gender identity is formed. Instead, they should be seen as a team of cooperating theories, each one bringing something different to the table and helping us to understand how a different element of our gender identity has developed.

Biological theories of gender development

The biological theories of gender development suggest that major influences on our gender identity can be found in a variety of different biological features including our anatomy, our brain structure and our hormones. We will start with the first and certainly the most obvious indicator of our gender, our anatomy.

Anatomical gender

The primary anatomical attribute which is linked to our gender is our genitalia. Genitalia can be divided into internal genitalia (also known as the gonads) and external genitalia. There is no evidence that our genitalia directly influence our behaviour in any way. Most of those influences attributed to the genitals are linked to hormones, and we will consider those separately in the next section. The real impact of our genitals on our gender identity is as the major signifier of our sex. The importance of this role for genitals, as gender signifiers, is not to be under-estimated.

The development of your genitals will assign typically you to one of two main categories of gender, and everything else described in this chapter follows from that first step. However, it is worth noting that there is an increasing awareness in society and in psychology of transgender individuals; those who believe their gender identity is opposite to that indicated by their anatomical gender. Although small in number they represent an important challenge to the view that gender identity is determined by anatomy.

Hormonal gender

Hormones act as chemical messengers in the body. They are created by the endocrine glands, which are located in numerous areas of the body including the gonads. Hormones serve a variety of purposes, helping to regulate everything from hunger to reproduction. Certain hormones are associated with specific genders; testosterone with males and oestrogen and progesterone with females. There is a biological basis for these associations. Although all three hormones are present in both genders, levels of testosterone are typically higher in males and levels of oestrogen are typically higher in females.

There is a popular perception that gender-related hormones can influence behaviour. As such, behaviours that are believed to be associated with testosterone (e.g. anger, sexual arousal) are seen as more likely to occur in males while behaviours associated with oestrogen (e.g. irritability, absent-mindedness or distress) are seen as more likely to occur in females. However, there is very little reliable evidence for any of these direct links between hormone levels and behaviour in either gender.

For example, in order to explore the potential relationship between testosterone and aggression, studies have been conducted looking at testosterone levels in violent offenders (Banks and

Dabbs, 1996; Brooks and Reddon, 1996). Results appear to show that the majority of those who commit violent crimes have significantly higher levels of testosterone compared to non-violent offenders. And yet, the link between testosterone and aggression is a correlational one, which means researchers cannot be sure that testosterone is the cause of the aggression. There is always the chance the causality runs in the other direction (high testosterone as a result of being aggressive) or an unknown 'third factor' which is causing changes in both aggression and testosterone levels. To establish causality, we would need to control testosterone levels artificially to see what impact this would have. This has been done as part of studying the effects of hormone therapies on men. A review of such studies by O'Connor (2007) found that it was only when testosterone was administered in doses much higher than ever naturally found in the body that it produced aggressive-style behaviour, and even then it was more like mania than anger. Otherwise, men taking therapeutic doses of testosterone at naturally occurring levels showed no link between their hormone levels and their own levels of aggression, either self-reported or reported by their partners. These findings would throw doubt on any attempt to present testosterone as a causal factor for aggression.

This is just one example, but it shows a pattern which is repeated in many other studies which have attempted to link these gender-related hormones with gendered behaviour or indeed any kind of behaviour. Time and again the only behaviour which seems to be consistently linked with hormones is reproductive behaviour (Bancroft, 1988), but even then their effects are mediated by other factors and filtered through a level of conscious decision-making. It may be that our expectations regarding hormones and behaviour are the real culprits here. As we will see later in this chapter, our expectations arising from gender roles and schemas could more readily explain all those behaviours that many people currently attribute to hormones.

Research focus: the menstrual cycle and student learning

There is a widespread assumption among both men and women that women experience some impairment to their intellectual functioning during the premenstrual and menstrual phases of the menstrual cycle. Many women report difficulties in studying and other academic activities during certain phases of their cycle. One of the most common problems reported is a difficulty in concentrating. The exact mechanism by which the menstrual cycle is supposed to produce these effects is unclear. Most theories point to hormone levels as the likely culprit, most probably because hormones are one of the few things known to vary considerably during the cycle (Dalton, 1955).

However, a review of the research evidence in this area by Richardson (1991) found that there was little or no reliable evidence of variation in academic performance during the menstrual cycle. Zimmerman and Parlee (1973) concluded that women's subjective reports of variations in their own performance were heavily influenced by stereotypes concerning menstruation as opposed to their own experience of any variations. Supporting this view was the finding that complaints of poor concentration were more frequent among women who regarded menstruation as a debilitating occurrence compared to those women who saw it as something that should have little effect upon their behaviour (Brooks-Gunn and Ruble, 1980). This shows us is that what appears to be a clear case of a biological gender impacting on education is in actuality a result of our gender-related expectations. It's a very good example of how a belief regarding gender and education can be powerful enough by itself to produce an effect on the academic abilities of female students all over the world.

Of course one of the biggest impacts that hormones have on our gender development takes place before we are even born. It's believed that levels of testosterone present in the womb during the first trimester are the factor which determines the gender of the foetus. Once gender is determined, most of the resulting gender differences in anatomical development are self-evident, with one exception. An area where there is some debate regarding the extent of gender differences in anatomical development is the brain. There is evidence to suggest the brains of males and females may develop differently – but what is the extent of those differences and how they might affect our gender identity?

Neuroanatomical gender

When we compare male and female brains the one difference that is universally accepted is that on average male brains are larger. But before any males reading this start to feel too smug, there is no clear advantage to a larger brain in terms of intelligence. The reason for this may be that although men have more neurons (grey matter), and hence the larger brain, women have more connections (white matter) and thus both genders achieve similar levels of performance through different means (Haier *et al.*, 2005; Rabinowicz *et al.*, 1999). The only impact these differences might have is a gender difference in vulnerability to certain illnesses and injuries that are linked cognitive deficits (de Courten-Myers, 1999). In short, the abundance of grey matter makes men more vulnerable to some illnesses but less vulnerable to others, and the same is true for women and white matter.

When it comes to the major brain structures though, there are no significant differences between the two genders. However, in terms of brain function there may be some evidence of gender difference in terms of a greater degree of lateralisation in male brains compared to female brains (Kolb and Whishaw, 1996; McGlone, 1980). For example, Vogel *et al.* (2003) found that processing of spatial information was more left-lateralised in males than in females. It's not clear what difference, if any, lateralisation makes to the gender identity or behaviour of either gender. Like the grey matter/white matter difference, lateralisation may just be another example of male and female brains achieving the same outcome in different ways. A good example of this is Asano *et al.* (2014), who looked at brain activation in both genders during a visual processing activity. Asano found a gender difference as to which brain areas were activated during the task but no gender difference in performance levels on the task. According to Asano *et al.* this shows that there may be a gender difference as to which visual processing strategy is employed by the brain on a given task but that these different strategies are simply different methods of achieving the same end.

All in all, these studies on gender and brain anatomy show us that while there are few anatomical differences between the brains of men and women; areas of commonality are considerably more numerous than areas of difference. Furthermore, where there are physical differences between male and female brains this does not always equate to a psychological or behavioural difference.

In conclusion, I would suggest that biological factors play a critical role in the development of our gender identity but that the relative impact compared to social factors is small. However, rather than view biological factors as simply less important than social factors, it may be better to see them as having a high level of impact but in a very limited time period or on a very limited scope of behaviour.

Thus, the best way to view the impact of biology on gender identity is through a biosocial approach such as that proposed by Money and Ehrhardt (1972). From the biosocial viewpoint biological factors have a critical early influence on gender development which sets the scene for the later social factors to react to and accentuate the initial gender identities formed by the biological factors. In this way the impact of biological factors can be small but critical nonetheless. Having reviewed those biological factors, it's now time to consider the social side of the equation.

Social theories of gender development

The social theories of gender development suggest gender identity is a socially defined concept which is influenced by a number of key social concepts and processes including gender roles, learning theories and gender schemas. We will start with the way in which the two main categories of gender identity are socially defined through gender roles.

Gender roles

To understand the nature of gender roles you first need to understand the dynamics of social groups. Social groups can range from formal groups (e.g. your nationality) to informal groups (e.g. your school friends) but all groups have certain characteristics in common. All groups have boundaries, interdependence, core values and identities within the group known as 'roles' (Hogg et al., 1995). A role typically assigns certain things to the person who occupies that role. Sometimes a role comes with benefits and responsibilities (e.g. the group's leader) and sometimes it comes with specific duties (e.g. the 'peacemaker' of the group).

Within society there are two gender-related roles: masculine and feminine. Your gender role is typically assigned to you automatically at birth based on your sex. Each role is associated with certain behaviours and qualities, expectations that we are expected to fulfil (Simon, 1992). These expectations influence our behaviour through a form of social influence known as 'conformity'. Conformity describes the social pressure we feel to follow a group norm. All groups have norms, written and unwritten rules which represent the group's core values. Some norms apply to the whole group in the same way (e.g. thou shalt not kill) but other norms are specific to certain roles within the group (i.e. mum knows best, big boys don't cry). We are more likely to follow norms when we don't know what to do or when we want to fit in with the group (Deutsch and Gerard, 1955).

If you break the norms connected to your gender role you risk disapproval of the other group members, a reduction in your status in the group, and even expulsion from the group. Consequently, the perception that you are failing to fulfil your role, whether that evaluation comes from others or from yourself, tends to lower self-esteem and cause distress (Callero, 1985). Conversely, the more you embrace your role and uphold the norms of the group the more you will gain approval and status in the group as well as enhancing your self-esteem.

Research focus: tackling gender stereotypes in the classroom

If a teacher wishes to tackle gender stereotypes found in standard materials, there are a number of options. One option is to ask the students to take the perspective of the stereotyped group (Galinsky and Moskowitz, 2000). For example, if all princesses are trapped in towers awaiting rescue by the prince ask the students what they would do if they were the princess; why she doesn't rescue herself or should she have to marry the prince who rescues her?

We should also make students aware of the existence of stereotypes and encourage them to try to overcome them. Promoting the norms for fairness and equality that exist in most societies is another way a teacher can help their students combat stereotyping. Duguid and Thomas-Hunt (2015) found that telling people that society expects them to work hard to overcome stereotypical views rather than accept them as inevitable caused them to show less gender bias in their behaviour. In other words, if you make it the norm not to be stereotypical then people will work harder to conform to that norm and stereotyping will be reduced.

It is because of the rewards and penalties associated with gender norms that so many of us find ourselves falling in line with our gender roles, whether we feel they are a good fit or not. Similarly, it can explain why people react so negatively when they encounter someone acting in a way that ignores or even goes directly against the norms of their gender role. A woman who tries to be dominant or a man who tries to be nurturing could find themselves the focus of disapproval, stereotypical discrimination or even outright hostility from other group members. By rejecting the group's norms, you are challenging the group's core values. Since many group members will have internalised those values they can react to an attack on the group's values as a challenge to them personally. Thus, we quickly learn that following gender roles and related norms is the secret to a quiet life and social approval. We also learn to avoid or hide any behaviours which are inconsistent with our gender role and so might offend others and invite social disapproval (Asch, 1951). This process, by which we are gradually shaped and pushed into adopting a gender identity which matches our gender role, is known as 'gender-role socialisation' or 'sex-role socialisation'.

Gender roles, gender norms and conformity provide us with an effective explanation of how our gender identity develops so that it remains largely in line with the gender roles of society. However, conformity on its own is not enough to explain the process by which we learn to adopt a gender identity in the first place. Long before we understand about wanting to fit into society or public approval we have already begun to develop our gender identity. As such, we need to turn to another set of theories, known as Learning Theories, to explain how the development of our gender identity is guided on its first faltering steps.

Behaviourist learning theories and social learning theories

Behaviourist learning theories originate from the work of Watson, Skinner and others who sought to explain the development of all behaviours (i.e. learning) via the processes of association and reinforcement. A more complete review of the behaviourist model of learning can be found in

Chapter 9, and so in this chapter will focus on using learning theories to explain the development of gender identities.

Consider this: What is the first question we ask when we hear someone has had a baby? For most of us the first question is some variation on 'Is it a boy or girl?' For the parents it may have started even earlier, with many parents wishing to know the gender of their child before it's even born. Why do they need to know this in advance? Because there are preparations to make which depend on the gender; rooms and clothes need to be the right colour, for example. From birth, children are bombarded with gender related messages and lessons. In their games and stories males are presented in roles such as cowboys, knights, soldiers and leaders; females occupy roles such as mothers, nurses, cooks and princesses. Children receive approval (i.e. a reward) from their parents, teachers and friends in reaction to their gender appropriate behaviour and disapproval in reaction to gender inappropriate behaviour (Fauls and Smith, 1956). Not all of this is intentional indoctrination. Gelman *et al.* (2004) found that even those parents who were very egalitarian in their views on gender ended up endorsing implicit gender stereotypes when reading a story and did not correct the children when they made stereotypical comments about gender. All in all, learning theorists would say that the end product of all this association and reinforcement is long-term conditioning toward gender-appropriate behaviour.

Research focus: parental support for study and career plans in STEM

The American National Center for Science and Engineering Statistics (2013) reported that the number of women in engineering and computing careers in the United States had remained below 30 per cent for the previous 20 years. One reason offered to explain this under-representation of women in STEM is that female students receive less encouragement in STEM subjects (Calabrese Barton *et al.*, 2013). According to Crisp *et al.* (2009) parents and teachers are the most important sources of encouragement in terms of influencing student achievement and career choices. Unfortunately, Ceci and Williams (2010) found that many parents end up reinforcing gender stereotypes or assumptions about female abilities, interests and career options, thus steering them away from STEM.

If we wish to see more females in STEM subjects then helping parents to see past such stereotypes is essential, but this alone may not be enough. Research by Ing (2013) found that parental encouragement on its own was not enough to help female students overcome a wider lack of encouragement for women in STEM. Parental support needs to be echoed by other important role models such as teachers. Unfortunately, a review of the research on teacher beliefs in mathematics by Li (1999) found that most teachers stereotyped mathematics as a male domain, which led them to have higher expectations of male students in mathematics. Thus, teachers and parents both need to address their own gender stereotypings and preconceptions in this area if we wish to see a change.

Bandura *et al.*'s (1961) social learning theory expanded the behaviourist model of learning by showing us how we can learn though observing the consequences of the behaviour of others. Bandura suggested we are more likely to learn from the experiences of certain individuals, known as role models. As parents are often the most influential role models, the gendered behaviour of parents and its consequences are absorbed by their children. According to Leaper (2002) the primary care-giver, typically the mother, is a key source of learning on gender-related beliefs. However, we should remember that the parents are not the only potential role models. Friedman *et al.* (2007) looked at the relationship between the attitudes of mothers and their children in relation to gender and found a strong relationship in the pre-school group but not in those of school age. Thus we see that peers and teachers can also become an important a source of learning on gender. For example, Martin *et al.* (1995) found that children in a nursery context showed a preference for a toy that was liked by children of the same gender over toys liked by children of the opposite gender.

While learning theories fill in several of the gaps in our understanding of the development of gender identities, some gaps remain. We are not passive in our response to the social influences or learning experiences that we are subjected to. In the case of both norms and reinforcements, we actively interpret the experience and react in a way that is influenced by our perceptions of what is happening, coloured by our beliefs and past experiences as well as our knowledge of the wider world and our gender. To get a more complete picture of these cognitive processes, how we process our gender-related experiences and relate them to our gender-related knowledge, we need to turn to another set of theories which explain how we represent gender to ourselves: our gender schemas.

Gender schemas

We've seen how our gender identity is shaped by society's gender roles as well as reinforcements from our parents and others. Over time these experiences lead to the formation of our own personal conception of each gender role, described by Bem (1981) as our gender schemas. A schema is a hypothetical mental construct; a collection of everything we have learned in relation to the thing, person, place or concept that is the focus of the schema. (See Chapter 8 for a more detailed discussion of the schema concept and how schemas evolve.)

Our schemas for the concepts of 'masculine' and 'feminine' contain our personal beliefs regarding everything from likely abilities and interests, right down to appropriate behaviour and dress. Some would argue that our gender schema divides into two components, our gender self-concept (how we see ourselves) and our gender attitudes (how we see others) (Bigler, 1997; Katz and Ksansnak, 1994). Our gender self-concept serves as a guide to our behaviour; our gender attitudes help us anticipate and evaluate the behaviour of those around us. There is some debate about whether our gender beliefs about ourselves and others will always be in agreement. For most people they are the same but some have argued that it's possible we apply one set of gender beliefs to ourselves while applying a slightly different set of beliefs to everyone else.

Our gender schemas develop as a result of our personal experiences and the influences of significant others such as our parents. In a meta-analysis of research on the relationship between parents' gender schemas and the gender schemas of their children, Tenenbaum and Leaper (2002) found that most of the research supported a small but significant relationship between the two. However, the researchers were keen to point out that their review only highlights a relationship between parents' schemas and their children's gender schemas and this does not prove that one is causing the other. There are potential third factors which might explain gender schemas of both parents and children. One such potential common factor is education, as children tend to have similar levels of education to their parents and higher levels of education are associated with holding less traditional gender schemas (Leaper and Valin, 1996).

The difference between gender schemas and the gender roles that we saw earlier is that a schema is a personal concept whereas a role is a group concept. Each group you belong to may have its own gender roles with associated norms. If you wish to fit in with the group, you will be expected to conform to the gender norms but you will filter those expectations through your gender schema. If you value the group membership but your gender schemas are not in alignment with the group's gender roles you may well find that your gender schemas change over time to bring them more in line with the group's roles through a process known as 'cognitive dissonance' (Festinger, 1957). That being said, some groups (e.g. the Suffragettes) seek to run the process in reverse and strive to change the gender roles of the group to bring them more in line with their gender schemas. Moscovici and Faucheux (1972) describe this process as 'minority influence' and it can be used to challenge group norms on gender, race, religion or indeed anything else that forms the basis of a group norm.

As we grow older our gender schemas can change, a reaction to a combination of factors including being exposed to new or evolving gender roles, reinforcement and modelling and our own reflections and learning on the topic of gender. Education can serve an important function in that process, although we need to keep in mind that along with the gender schemas of those being educated there are the schemas of the educators to consider as well.

In conclusion, what we can see now having reviewed these social theories are some of the important ways in which our gender identities are formed and maintained as a result of social forces. This means that, as a social construct, gender identity can be changed through learning, whether that is reinforcement, social learning or merely expanding the knowledge contained in our gender schemas.

All of this places education at the very centre of the development of our gender identity. Indeed, the relationship between gender and education may well be reciprocal, with education affecting our gender identity but also gender identities affecting our education. In the next section we will see how our educational experiences can be influenced by our gender identity and by the expectations of both educators and students regarding the impact of gender on education.

Gender and education

Gender differences in learning

We saw earlier that there are regular moral panics regarding supposed gender 'gaps' in education. Even if we disregard these there still remains a fairly constant thread of research which appears to show some relationship between gender and various aspects of education. The bulk of these studies still approach the issue of gender in education in terms of gender 'difference', insisting on dividing the genders into two distinct groups and comparing the groups on one or more educational outcomes. We will see later how this approach represents something of a weakness in the field of research on gender and education. However, if we were to overlook this limitation and consider these studies on their own merits there is a credible body of research on gender differences in education. In this section we will review some of the more widely cited research on gender differences in education. But before we conduct this review we need to consider the reasons for reviewing it.

To simply catalogue a list of published gender differences would serve little purpose; we need to dig a bit deeper than that. In studies that show a gender difference in education, it's likely that gender identity is influencing some variable, such as self-efficacy or motivation, which in turn is influencing education. In this way studies of gender difference can help us to find those mediating factors which lie between gender and educational outcomes. If we then wish to affect those educational outcomes we can disregard gender and instead target the mediating factor in any student irrespective of their gender. In this way the study of gender differences can be used to help everyone and not just help one gender or the other to 'close the gap'.

Let us begin by considering two areas of education which are widely believed to be the domain of one gender more than the other: mathematics and linguistic ability.

Gender differences in mathematics

One area where men are believed to have an advantage academically is mathematics (Halpern, 2004). It is possible that the male advantage here is a result of mathematics being seen as a masculine subject. As a result of this there is a good chance that the teacher in the mathematics class will unconsciously favour male students, something we will consider later in this chapter. This combination of teacher encouragement and being in the gender majority in mathematics is likely to result in male students being more motivated to learn in a mathematics class and have greater self-efficacy in relation to mathematics when compared to female students. (See Chapter 9 for a more detailed discussion of the concept of self-efficacy.) A study by Ganley and Vasilyeva (2014) appears to support this by showing that lower self-efficacy and high levels of anxiety experienced by female students during a mathematics exam impaired their memory and thus inhibited performance. This identifies self-efficacy alongside motivation as mediating factors which could explain an apparent gender difference.

In addition, there could be a link between the male advantage in visuospatial ability and their advantage in mathematics. Several studies have found that one area of mathematics where male students do particularly well is spatial reasoning (Gibbs, 2010; Vasilyeva *et al.*, 2009). By contrast, when you look at other areas of mathematics, such as computation, the gender difference disappears or even starts to favour female students. Even this well supported male advantage in visuospatial abilities could be a result of the fact that men are more likely to play sports which promote hand-eye coordination. More time spent practising these skills could well lead to greater development in those areas of the brain related to visuospatial tasks (Draganski *et al.*, 2004; Stumpf, 1995). This would make practice, not gender, the real cause of difference.

Gender differences in linguistic ability

One area where there seems to be an advantage for women is in verbal and literacy tasks. Research in this area shows that on average women outperform men in tasks like these (Halpern, 2004). A wide variety of studies report female students outperforming male students on tests of reading ability (Klecker, 2006), writing tests (Willingham and Cole, 1997) and verbalisation (Bartholomew, 2004). (See Chapter 4 for more on gender differences in reading ability.)

Differences in brain structure between men and women are often cited as a reason for different abilities in this area (Kolb and Whishaw, 1996). The most obvious example of this is the greater level of bilateral distribution of language in women. Even though the differences are well documented it's hard to say why these differences in brain structure produce the differences in language ability that we see. For this reason, it is difficult to be absolutely sure that the neuroanatomical differences are the sole cause or even the main cause.

In contrast to the biological explanation, Barrs and Pidgeon (2002) suggest that the teaching strategies used to teach writing might be less effective in motivating male students. Furthermore, Daly (2003) found that when male students were asked to write much shorter pieces their performance drastically improved. These findings point towards the possibility that this apparent difference in language ability might be mediated by motivational or concentration issues.

Finally, as with mathematics there are also cultural expectations that women will perform better in language subjects such as English Studies (Gleitman *et al.*, 1999). Furthermore, certain activities which are thought to promote linguistic development (e.g. reading and poetry) are seen as more feminine. This makes those activities more appealing to many females. This in turn would produce a practice-effect similar to that discussed when we looked at male superiority in visuospatial tasks.

In conclusion, what these studies on gender difference in education show us is that biological differences between the genders are unlikely to provide us with a convincing explanation of any gender differences in education that we encounter. Even when there is a widely acknowledged gender difference in anatomy, such as the case with lateralisation in language centres, it does not seem to explain the subtler differences such as in language ability that we see. Furthermore, the evidence from studies of biological differences in the case of the visuospatial processing centres suggests that some of these neuroanatomical differences could be the result of practice and are not necessarily innate.

Instead, what we learn from these studies is that the mediating factors such as practice, self-efficacy, motivation and concentration may be the real explanation for many of the supposed gender differences we see in education. These findings have value as they can help us to understand student experiences and issues in education more generally and not just limited to the context of gender.

In addition to these there is also evidence which points towards a further factor in the form of the perception of a subject becoming gendered which may be an important additional element in explaining these gender differences in education. We will consider the evidence for and implications of a subject becoming gendered in more detail in the next section.

Research focus: a more critical approach to gender research

In many published studies the choice of gender as a variable is driven by convenience as much as anything else. Gender is easy to measure and gender comparisons are relatively easy to analyse. As such, much of the research on gender is seriously lacking in a theoretical framework and prone to confirmation bias.

In order to help you sift through this deluge of questionable gender research and find the few genuine gender studies that are worthy of note you should remember the following question when evaluating a piece of gender research: 'Was a gender comparison planned in advance or an afterthought in this study?' A reliable indicator as to the importance of any variable in a study is how prominently it features in the literature review. If the literature review contains little or no previous research that links gender to any of the other key variables then it's almost certain gender was never intended as a serious variable in the current study. With no theoretical foundation from previous studies, any attempt to explain a gender result found in the current study will tend to rely on uncritical assumptions about the natures of men and women, or at worst outright stereotypes of the two gender roles. You should treat any result they report with caution.

Gendered subjects

Some academic subjects have become 'gendered' in the sense that they are associated with one gender more than the other in the mind of the public. Some subjects are seen as being more masculine (business, science, engineering) and others are seen as more feminine (humanities, languages) (Hudson, 1972). The means by which a subject becomes gendered in the first place is hard to trace. However, in this case our interest lies not so much in the cause as in the effect: what effect will the gendered nature of a subject have on those who elect to study it?

The impact of being the minority gender

In gendered subjects the majority of students studying the subject are of the gender associated with that subject. Whether this is a cause or an effect of the subject being gendered is not clear. We saw earlier how conformity influences us all to follow the gender norms and gender roles of society. While it is true to say that we are all influenced by conformity, there are situations where the pressure to conform is higher on some than on others. Sistrunk and McDavid (1971) found that both men and women conformed more when performing tasks that were traditionally associated with the other gender. This is going to result in members of a minority gender being under more pressure to conform to the norms and conventions of the subject, making them less likely to challenge the views of the teacher or their fellow students.

The idea that students in this situation might self-sensor and even silence themselves parallels a concept proposed by Gilligan (1982) which she termed 'loss of voice'. Gilligan saw loss of voice as something affecting all women entering university, not just in subjects where they were the minority gender (Brown and Gilligan, 1992). Nevertheless, the concept is useful in explaining the potential impact of disempowerment experienced by anyone who perceives themselves to be in the minority in their studies. For this reason, loss of voice as a concept has been revised to look beyond gender and instead consider how a perceived lack of social power could predict loss of voice in a variety of groups with lower social status. For example, loss of voice has been found to be common among economically disadvantaged students who are among the first in their family to attend higher education (McVicker Clinchy, 2002).

Being in a minority gender may also affect levels of performance in the subject. McGivern *et al.* (1997) found that women had a better memory than men for 'feminine' objects and vice versa for 'masculine' objects. This difference in memory could be a result of each gender being more interested and attentive to gender appropriate objects and topics, since that would be seen as the norm for their gender (see Chapter 2 for more on the role of attention in memory). Indeed, Elmore and Oyserman (2012) found that both genders were more motivated when they were told that academic success was more likely for one of their gender. What all this suggests is that some of the gender differences in academic performance that we discussed earlier may be a product of these differences in memory and motivation which result from the subject becoming gendered in the eyes of the students.

Of course the student is not the only one who can be influenced by the subject being gendered. Whether it happens consciously or subconsciously, the perceptions and behaviour of the teacher can be influenced by the gendered nature of a subject and their preconceptions linked to the gender of their students.

Gender preconceptions in the classroom

There are very few educators who would be happy with the suggestion that they are in any way prejudiced in their treatment of students. As well as the legal prohibitions against such things, most educators would consider it a sign of their professionalism that they avoid any prejudiced behaviour. And yet, there are several studies which show that a teacher's gender expectations can influence both their perceptions of and their behaviour towards their students. It's worth then considering how this might apply to understanding some of the gender differences in education that we discussed earlier. It's also of interest to consider exactly how and why teacher expectations might translate into differences in their behaviour.

For example, Bell (2001) found that in science classrooms teachers were more likely to direct a question to a male student and they were willing to wait longer for an answer before moving on to another student. Similarly, Li's (1999) review of the research on teachers' beliefs and gender differences in mathematics found that teachers interacted more with male students in the mathematics classroom. One possible explanation for these behaviours is that according to Fennema *et al.* (1990), mathematics teachers took more personal responsibility for failure in male students than female students, seeing failure in a male student as a result of insufficient support from themselves as a teacher. This greater sense of responsibility for ensuring that male students reach their 'true potential' in subjects like mathematics and science could be one explanation for the differences in teacher behaviour such as paying more attention to male students.

In conclusion, having reviewed the impacts that a subject becoming gendered can have on those who study it, we can see that many of the gender differences we observe in education may be influenced as much by this factor as any other. It presents a challenge to us all to break out of this cycle of gendering subjects and rationalising it by seeking gender differences in our students, when the real root of the difference may lie in our expectations.

Conclusion

This brings us to the end of our review of gender and education. We hope to have provided you with food for thought, revealing a more complex and critical perspective on the issues surrounding both the nature of gender and its role in education. Ultimately, while we may face considerable challenges as educators in avoiding or overcoming the dangers of prejudice and preconception in our practice, there are also terrific opportunities to challenge those preconceptions in our students and others. By sharing a more critical perspective on gender we can help students overcome the barriers of gender roles and gendered subjects, unlocking a student's true potential irrespective of their gender.

Key points

- Our gender identity includes our biological sex, but also society's expectations of gender (gender roles) and our own personal conceptions of gender (gender schemas).
- The development of gender identity appears to be more heavily influenced by social factors than biological ones.
- Biological factors have a small but critical early influence on gender development that establishes certain elements of gender identity which later social factors react to and accentuate.
- When we encounter either gender norms or reinforcement/punishment of our gender-related behaviour, we actively interpret the experience and react in a way that is influenced by both our perception of what is happening and our gender schemas.
- The relationship between gender and education may well be reciprocal, with education affecting our gender identity but also our gender identity affecting our education.
- Factors such as practice, self-efficacy motivation and concentration may be the mediating factors which explain many of the supposed gender differences we see in education.
- Gender differences in education are more likely to be a product of gender expectations of students, teachers and parents or the impact of 'gendered' subjects, than any biological differences between the genders.

Recommended readings

Bem, S.L. (1981) Gender schema theory: A cognitive account of sex typing source. *Psychological Review*, **88**, pp. 354–364.

de Courten-Myers G.M. (1999) The human cerebral cortex: Gender differences in structure and function. *Journal of Neuropathology and Experimental Neurology*, **58**(3), pp. 217–226.

Friedman, C.K., Leaper, C. and Bigler, R.S. (2007) Do mothers' gender-related attitudes or comments predict young children's gender beliefs? *Parenting: Science and Practice*, **7**(4), pp. 1–15.

Richardson, J.T.E. (1991) The menstrual cycle and student learning. *The Journal of Higher Education*, **62**(3), pp. 317–340.

References

Asano, K., Taki, Y., Hashizume, H., Sassa, Y., Thyreau, B., Asano, M., Takeuchi, H. and Kawashima, R. (2014) Healthy children show gender differences in correlations between nonverbal cognitive ability and brain activation during visual perception. *Neuroscience Letters*, **577**, pp. 66–71.

Asch, S.E. (1951) Effects of group pressure upon the modification and distortion of judgments. In H. Guetzkow (ed.) *Groups, leadership and men: Research in human relations*. Oxford: Carnegie Press.

Bancroft, J. (1988) Reproductive hormones and male sexual function. In J.M.A. Sitsen (ed.) *Handbook of sexology. The pharmacology and endocrinology of sexual functions*, vol. **6**. Amsterdam: Elsevier.

Bandura, A., Ross, D. and Ross S.A. (1961) Transmission of aggression through imitation of aggressive models. *Journal of Abnormal and Social Psychology*, **63**(3), pp. 575–582.

Banks, T. and Dabbs, J.M. (1996) Salivary testosterone and cortisol in a delinquent and violent urban subculture. *Journal of Social Psychology*, **136**(1), pp. 49–56.

Barrs, M. and Pidgeon, S. (2002) *Boys and writing*. London: Centre for Literacy in Primary Education.

Bartholomew, D.J. (2004) *Measuring intelligence: Facts and fallacies.* Cambridge: Cambridge University Press.

Bell, J.F. (2001) Investigating gender differences in the science performance of 16-year-old pupils in the UK. *International Journal of Science Education,* **23**(5), pp. 469–486.

Bem, S.L. (1981) Gender schema theory: A cognitive account of sex typing source. *Psychological Review,* **88**, p. 354.

Bigler, R.S. (1997) Conceptual and methodological issues in the measurement of children's sex typing. *Psychology of Women Quarterly,* **21**, pp. 53–69.

Brooks, J.H. and Reddon, J.R. (1996) Serum testosterone in violent and nonviolent young offenders. *Journal of Clinical Psychology,* **52**(4), pp. 475–483.

Brooks-Gunn, J. and Ruble, D.N. (1980) Menarche: The interaction of physiological, cultural, and social factors. In A.J. Dan, E.A. Graham and C.P. Beecher (eds) *The menstrual cycle, vol. I: A synthesis of interdisciplinary research.* New York: Springer.

Brown, L.M. and Gilligan, C. (1992) Meeting at the crossroads: Women's psychology and girls' development. *Feminism and Psychology,* **3**(1), pp. 11–35.

Calabrese Barton, A., Kang, H., Tan, E., O'Neill, T.B., Bautista-Guerra, J. and Brecklin, C. (2013) Crafting a future in science: Tracing middle school girls' identity work over time. *American Educational Research Journal,* **50**(1), pp. 37–75.

Callero, P.L. (1985) Role identity salience. *Social Psychology Quarterly,* **48**(3), pp. 203–215.

Ceci, S.J. and Williams, W.M. (2010) Sex differences in math-intensive fields. *Current Directions in Psychological Science,* **19**(5), pp. 275–279.

Crisp, G., Nora, A. and Taggart, A. (2009) Student characteristics, pre-college, college, and environmental factors as predictors of majoring in and earning a STEM degree: An analysis of students attending a Hispanic Serving Institution. *American Educational Research Journal,* **46**(4), pp. 924–942.

Dalton, K. (1955) Discussion on the premenstrual syndrome. *Proceedings of the Royal Society of Medicine,* **48**, pp. 339–347.

Daly, C. (2003) The language debate – what is going on here? In H. Claire (ed.) *Gender in education 3–19: A fresh approach.* London: ATL.

de Courten-Myers G.M. (1999) The human cerebral cortex: Gender differences in structure and function. *Journal of Neuropathology and Experimental Neurology,* **58**(3), pp. 217–226.

Deutsch, M. and Gerard, H.B. (1955) A study of normative and informational social influences upon individual judgment. *The Journal of Abnormal and Social Psychology,* **51**(3), pp. 629–636.

Draganski, B., Gaser, C., Busch, V., Schuierer, G., Bogdahn, U. and May, A. (2004) Neuroplasticity: Changes in grey matter induced by training. *Nature,* **427**, pp. 311–312.

Duguid, M. and Thomas-Hunt, M. (2015) Condoning stereotyping? How awareness of stereotyping prevalence impacts expression of stereotypes. *Journal of Applied Psychology,* **100**(2), pp. 343–359.

Elmore, K.C. and Oyserman, D. (2012) If 'we' can succeed, 'I' can too: Identity-based motivation and gender in the classroom. *Contemporary Educational Psychology,* **37**, pp. 176–185.

Fauls, L.B. and Smith, W.D. (1956) Sex-role learning of five-year olds. *Journal of Genetic Psychology,* **89**, pp. 105–117.

Fennema, E., Peterson, P.L., Carpenter, T.P. and Lubinski, C.A. (1990) Teachers' attributions and beliefs about girls, boys, and mathematics. *Educational Studies in Mathematics,* **21**, pp. 55–69.

Festinger, L. (1957) *A theory of cognitive dissonance.* Stanford: Stanford University Press.

Friedman, C.K., Leaper, C. and Bigler, R.S. (2007) Do mothers' gender-related attitudes or comments predict young children's gender beliefs? *Parenting: Science and Practice,* **7**(4), pp. 1–15.

Galinsky, A.D. and Moskowitz, G.B. (2000) Perspective-taking: Decreasing stereotype expression, stereotype accessibility, and in-group favoritism. *Journal of Personality and Social Psychology,* **78**(4), pp. 708–724.

Ganley, C.M. and Vasilyeva, M. (2014) The role of anxiety and working memory in gender differences in mathematics. *Journal of Educational Psychology,* **106**(1), pp. 105–120.

Gelman, S., Taylor, M. and Nguyen, S.P. (2004) Mother–child conversations about gender. *Monographs of the Society for Research in Child Development,* **69**(1), pp. 1–42.

Gibbs, B.G. (2010) Reversing fortunes or content change? Gender gaps in math-related skill throughout childhood. *Social Science Research,* **39**, pp. 540–569.

Gilligan, C. (1982) *In a different voice: Psychological theory and women's development.* 1st edn. Cambridge, MA: Harvard University Press.

Gleitman, H., Fridlund, A.J. and Reisberg, D. (1999) *Psychology.* 8th edn. London: W.W. Norton and Company.

Haier, R.J., Jung, R.E., Yeo, R.A., Head, K. and Alkire, M.T. (2005) The neuroanatomy of general intelligence: sex matters. *Neuroimage*, **25**(1), pp. 320–327.

Halpern, D.F. (2004) A cognitive-process taxonomy for sex differences in cognitive abilities. *Current Directions in Psychological Science*, **13**, pp. 135–139.

Hogg, M.A., Terry, D.J. and White, K.M. (1995) A tale of two theories: A critical comparison of identity theory with social identity theory. *Social Psychology Quarterly*, **58**(4), pp. 255–269.

Hudson, L. (1972) *The cult of the fact.* London: Cape.

Ing, M. (2013) Gender differences in the influence of early perceived parental support on student mathematics and science achievement and stem career attainment. *International Journal of Science and Mathematics Education*, **12**, pp. 1221–1239.

Katz, P.A. and Ksansnak, K.R. (1994) Developmental aspects of gender role flexibility and traditionality in middle childhood and adolescence. *Developmental Psychology*, **30**, pp. 272–282.

Klecker, B.M. (2006) The gender gap in NAEP fourth-, eighth-, and twelfth-grade reading scores across years. *Reading Improvement*, **43**(1), pp. 50–56.

Kolb, B. and Whishaw, I.Q. (1996) *Fundamentals of human neuropsychology.* New York: W.H. Freeman.

Leaper, C. (2002) Parenting girls and boys. In M.H. Bornstein (ed.) *Handbook of parenting: Children and parenting.* 2nd edn, vol. **1**. Mahwah: Erlbaum.

Leaper, C. and Valin, D. (1996) Predictors of Mexican American mothers' and fathers' attitudes toward gender equality. *Hispanic Journal of Behavioral Sciences*, **18**, pp. 343–355.

Li, Q. (1999) Teachers' beliefs and gender differences in mathematics: A review. *Educational Research*, **41**(1), pp. 63–76.

Martin, C.L., Eisenbud, L. and Rose, H. (1995) Children's gender-based reasoning about toys. *Child Development*, **66**(5), pp. 1453–1471.

McGivern, R.F., Huston, J.P., Byrd, D., King, T., Siegle, G.J. and Reilly, J. (1997) Sex differences in visual recognition memory: Support for a sex-related difference in attention in adults and children. *Brain and Cognition*, **34**(3), pp. 323–336.

McGlone, J. (1980) Sex differences in human brain asymmetry: A critical survey. *Behavioral and Brain Sciences*, **3**(2), pp. 215–263.

McVicker Clinchy, B. (2002) Revisiting women's ways of knowing. In B. Hofer and P. Pintrich (eds) *Personal epistemology: The psychology of beliefs about knowledge and knowing.* Mahwah: Lawrence Erlbaum Associates.

Money, J. and Ehrhardt, A.A. (1972) *Man and woman, boy and girl: Differentiation and dimorphism of gender identity from conception to maturity.* Baltimore: Johns Hopkins University Press.

Moscovici, S. and Faucheux, C. (1972) Social influence, conforming bias, and the study of active minorities. In L. Berkowitz (ed.) *Advances in experimental social psychology.* Vol. **6**. New York: Academic Press.

National Science Foundation, National Center for Science and Engineering Statistics (2013) *Women, minorities, and persons with disabilities in science and engineering: 2013.* Arlington: National Science Foundation.

O'Connor, D.B. (2007) Effects of testosterone on aggression, anger and mood in men. In E.I. Clausen (ed.) *Psychology of anger.* New York: Nova Science.

Rabinowicz, D.E., Petetot, J.M. and de Courten-Myers G.M. (1999) Gender differences in the human cerebral cortex: More neurons in males; more processes in females. *Journal of Child Neurology*, **14**(2), pp. 98–107.

Richardson, J.T.E. (1991) The menstrual cycle and student learning. *The Journal of Higher Education*, **62**(3), pp. 317–340.

Simon, R.W. (1992) Parental role strains, salience of parental identity and gender differences in psychological distress. *Journal of Health and Social Behavior*, **33**(1), pp. 25–35.

Sistrunk, F. and McDavid, J.W. (1971) Sex variable in conforming behavior. *Journal of Personality and Social Psychology*, **17**(2), pp. 200–207.

Stumpf, H. (1995) Gender differences on tests of cognitive abilities: Experimental design issues and empirical results. *Learning and Individual Differences*, **7**, pp. 275–288.

Tenenbaum, H.R. and Leaper, C. (2002) Are parents' gender schemas related to their children's gender-related cognitions? A meta-analysis. *Developmental Psychology*, **38**(4), pp. 615–630.

Vasilyeva, M., Casey, B.M., Dearing, E. and Ganley, C.M. (2009) Measurement skills in low-income elementary school students: Exploring the nature of gender differences. *Cognition and Instruction*, **27**, pp. 401–428.

Vogel, J.J., Bowers, C.A. and Vogel, D.S. (2003) Cerebral lateralization of spatial abilities: A meta-analysis. *Brain Cognition*, **52**, pp. 197–204.

Willingham, W.W. and Cole, N.S. (1997) *Gender and fair assessment*. Mahwah: Lawrence Erlbaum Associates.

Zimmerman, E. and Parlee, M.B. (1973) Behavioral changes associated with the menstrual cycle: An experimental investigation. *Journal of Applied Psychology*, **3**, pp. 335–344.

Part III
Origins: re-examining some of the core theories of learning

8 Rediscovering Piaget
A fresh perspective on Piagetian theory and method

Claire Lloyd

Introduction

The purpose of this chapter is to explore Piaget's theory of cognitive development. The discussion is framed around two different, but related, strands of his body of work. The first concerns Piaget's study of the nature of knowledge development, also known as his 'epistemological project'. The second looks at his empirical approach to the study of children and explores the methods he used to carry out his research.

Piaget was interested in epistemological questions about the construction and the nature of knowledge, and specifically 'the formation of necessary concepts and intellectual operations' (Bond and Tryphon, 2009: 173). This focus reflects a core belief running through his work, namely, that we cannot investigate the acquisition of knowledge (i.e. learning) without addressing the epistemological assumptions that underlie such an investigation (i.e. assumptions about the nature of knowledge, relations between thought and behaviour, between mind and body) (Müller *et al.*, 2009). This is Piaget's 'genetic epistemology', the first strand of his work we will explore. Although nowadays, the term 'genetic' is typically associated with heredity, for Piaget the phrase meant something closer to 'genesis' or the study of the 'mechanisms in the growth of the different kinds of knowledge' (Piaget, 1957: 14).

Piaget argued that we cannot understand how knowledge is developed unless we carry out empirical investigations to determine the conditions under which the acquisition of knowledge takes place (Campbell, 2006; Smith, 1981). Hence, the second strand of his work we will address concerns the empirical methods he used to inform his study of the development of knowledge: observations of children, interviews and analysis of their speech and actions. For Piaget, epistemology is not the sole purview of philosophers, and he advocated the use of empirical methods in approaching epistemological questions to establish the conditions under which an individual acquires knowledge (Smith, 1981: 14). Common misconceptions about Piaget's work arise from an overly *psychological* interpretation of his theory which pays insufficient attention to its epistemological foundations (Müller *et al.*, 2009). We will see that the fundamental concerns that drove Piaget's work with respect to knowledge construction – the theoretical models he developed and the interpretive approach he used to inform those conclusions – are still relevant and useful today (Bibace, 2013).

It is important to acknowledge from the start that, given both the scope and depth of Piaget's theories, which evolved and developed over several decades and in collaboration with others, it is not possible to do full justice to them all in a single chapter. Indeed, only a glimpse into his theory can be achieved. It is even more difficult to review the vast range of publications his work has spawned over the last six decades, as others have interpreted, reinterpreted and, indeed, mis-interpreted his work.

Reception

Piaget's theory of cognitive development was dominant in the field of psychology throughout much of the twentieth century. It had a profound impact on our understanding of human knowledge acquisition in ways that have been described as revolutionary (Beilin, 1992). In the 1960s and 1970s, Piaget's genetic epistemology, with its focus on understanding the intellectual operations of knowledge construction, was a key reference point for those studying human development (Rodríguez and Martí, 2012).

Throughout the late 1990s, Piaget continued to be one of the most referenced authors in the field of developmental psychology. In reviewing his influence, as reflected in the 4,500 pages of the 1998 edition of the *Handbook of Child Psychology*, Bond and Tryphon (2007: 14) concluded that 'Piaget is by far the most referenced author in the field of child psychology'. Indeed, key Piagetian constructs have now become part of the general vocabulary of human development studies: 'constructivism', 'developmental stages', 'cognitive schemas'; and his stages of development (described in Table 8.1) are likely to be familiar to all who have taken an introductory course in developmental psychology. Indeed, in reviewing Piaget's contribution to the field, Harry Beilin (1992) was not exaggerating when he wrote:

> No one affected developmental psychology more than Jean Piaget (1896–1980). From his ear-liest publications in the 1920s to the time of his death, the influence he exercised was extra-ordinary. His theory ... has no rival in developmental psychology in scope and depth.
>
> (p. 191)

However, this recognition has come at considerable cost. Since the 1980s, Piaget's work has been the focus of severe and sustained critical attention, suffering what Bond and Tryphon (2009: 189) have referred to as 'death by a thousand cuts'. Indeed, it is difficult to identify a theory that has been more debated and critiqued (Valsiner, 2012), with many arguing that his work is no longer useful or relevant and advocating either a partial or wholescale rejection (see Lourenço and Machado, 1996, for a review).

Piaget himself recognised this, and expressed mixed feelings about the attention he had received. For example, toward the end of his career, in a series of conversations about his enduring legacy, Piaget made the following comment: 'I am pleased by it, of course. But it is pretty catastrophic when I see how I'm understood'. When asked if he felt he had been 'badly interpreted', Piaget replied 'Yes, in general .... As to understanding the theory itself' (Bringuier, 1977/1980: 54).

A catastrophic understanding

It is inconceivable that any theory that attempts to conceptualise the entirety of human cognitive development should emerge fully formed. Indeed, Piaget's 30-year research programme

Table 8.1 Summary of Piaget's four stages of development

Stage	Age*	Description**
Sensorimotor	Approx. birth to 24 months	Learning occurs through movement (actions), senses, and reflexes. Growing understanding of the nature of objects, e.g. their existence outside of the perceptual field (object permanence). Logical, intentional actions.
Preoperational	Approx. 24 months to 6–7 years	Symbols are used to represent objects (e.g. signs, gestures, images). Language develops rapidly (also a symbol system).
Concrete operations	Approx. 6–12 years	Growing awareness that something remains stable when redistributed (conservation). Logical thinking when solving in hand-on problems.
Formal operations	Approx. 12–18 years and into adulthood	Growing capacity to reason – considering a hypothetical problem or issue and using deduction to resolve it (hypothetico-deductive reasoning).

Notes

* Substantial variation in individual children is assumed (Feldman, 2004).
** Richards, 1985; Woolfolk, 2016.

underwent what Beilin (1992: 191) describes as 'change from beginning to end'. Key concepts were developed and extended, new terminology was introduced and refined, areas of focus shifted and evolved. Moreover, Piaget did not work alone, collaborating with a vast number of inter-disciplinary specialists at the International Centre of Genetic Epistemology (ICGE), which he estab-lished in 1955 at the University of Geneva (Rodríguez and Martí, 2009). The Genevan School, as the ICGE later became known, brought together a team of scholars including psychology pro-fessors, graduate students and interdisciplinary specialists to build the foundations of genetic epistemology. The 30 volumes of *Studies in Genetic Epistemology* that the ICGE produced speak to the magnitude of its contribution.

Given the vast body of work and its complex evolution, many criticisms stem from partial and narrow readings of Piagetian theory. Indeed, in reviewing his legacy, Bond and Tryphon (2007) have noted that most citations cover only a restricted period, representing a small subset of his 53 books and virtually none of his 523 published papers. Such omissions have led to serious inaccuracies and misinterpretations. Perhaps the most fundamental error underpinning many 'bad interpretations' of Piaget's work is that psychologists as well as philosophers have tended to ignore the epistemological assumptions upon which his research programme is based, namely, understanding the development of knowledge (Lourenço and Machado, 1996). In doing so they fail to attend to the theoretical framework that drove his research programme, and which one of his principal collaborators, Bärbel Inhelder, notes has led to 'important mis-understandings and misses the deep and enduring meaning of Piaget's approach' (Inhelder and De Caprona, 1997: 4).

Piaget recognised this. In addressing the criticisms directed at his theory in a major, and influential, commentary on his work by the psychologist John Flavell, he remarked that insufficient attention was given to its epistemological foundation:

> In short, as regards the entire first set of criticisms – the general trend of which is that, in Professor Flavell's opinion, there is too wide a gap between the facts I describe and the theories I invoke – it could be argued that the differences between us stem from the fact that his approach is perhaps too exclusively psychological and insufficiently epistemological while the converse is true for me.
>
> (Piaget, 1963: viii–ix)

Piaget's epistemological foundation

Piaget's genetic epistemology addressed the same basic questions as all philosophical epistemologists: What is knowledge? Where does it come from? How do we know what we know? However, he rejected the idea that epistemological questions required only philosophical answers. He also rejected the practice, still widespread in cognitive psychology, of theorising about processes such as memory, problem-solving and visual imagery, without considering the manner in which they develop (Campbell, 2006). (See Atkinson and Shiffrin's theory of memory in Chapter 2 as an example of just such a cognitive approach to memory.)

Piaget's epistemological project is based on the assumption that in order to understand what knowledge is, it is first necessary to understand the process through which it is acquired. The fundamental purpose of his body of work was not to discover *what* an individual knows but *how* an individual knows (Bond and Tryphon, 2009). He argued that this discovery was only possible through scientific enquiry into the construction of knowledge. In this way, Piaget's epistemology 'charted a novel course between science and philosophy', providing an empirical resolution to philosophical problems (Smith, 2009: 64).

How an individual knows

Piaget grounded his work in the assumption that the acquisition of knowledge is not passive – knowledge does not pre-exist in the world to be imposed upon individuals, nor is it already innately pre-prepared within them. For Piaget, both practical and conceptualised knowledge is acquired through an individual's actions in the world (Pascual-Leone, 2012; Smith, 1981). In other words, 'in order to know objects, the child must act upon them, and therefore transform them' (Piaget (1970/1983: 104). These actions are always intentional; the individual has a goal in mind and an idea about the action needed to achieve that goal.

Piaget argued that as individuals act upon objects in the world, they are able to coordinate their behaviour at progressively more complex levels. He was interested in studying this 'ontogenetic development', which is to say, studying how knowledge unfolds developmentally as individuals grow older (Pascual-Leone, 2012). He did this through observing children's actions over the course of their development. Thus, the overarching purpose of this genetic epistemology was to generate richer understandings of the acquisition of knowledge through the scientific study of children's intentional, goal-directed actions (Lourenço and Machado, 1996).

Based on his early research in biology, Piaget believed that the development of knowledge required an organising tendency whereby a child's actions are coordinated to make them understandable (Woolfolk, 2016). This tendency occurs through a series of internally related operative structures that enable the child to make sense of the objects and events encountered in his/her world. New structures are constructed and existing structures refined given the success and failure of the child's actions (Smith, 1981). In this way, operative structures are a mechanism for organising the experiences that arise from the actions performed – creating order, bringing meaning and advancing thinking.

The typical representation of Piaget's work as a 'stage theory', found in almost every textbook on education, shows children's cognition developing from sensorimotor to formal operations, but neglects to mention these operative structures which underpin this process of development. This makes it hard, if not impossible, to understand how the developmental milestones described by the stages are achieved. Thus, to properly understand cognitive development from a Piagetian perspective we need to know more about his concept of operative structures.

Reflections

For Piaget, knowledge is operative – it is developed and refined through the success and failure of goal-directed activity. Think back to the last time you learned something new. What were you trying to do? How did your knowledge develop – through success or failure? Did new ways of thinking open up as a result of your developing knowledge?

Piaget's operative structures

With operative structures conceived as a way of coordinating goal-directed action at progressively more complex and advanced levels, different structures come into play as children mature. Furthermore, the logical properties relevant to one structure are qualitatively different from those relevant to another (Smith, 1981). This key point can be illustrated by reviewing the features of two types of operative structure, namely action-schemes and operational structures.

An 'action-scheme' is the most basic type of operative structure, giving rise to practical knowledge (Campbell, 2009). A typical early action-scheme, used in the sensorimotor stage of infant development, comes into play as an infant coordinates its motor movements to push or kick a mobile that hangs over its crib. Kicking and pushing become part of a collection of different actions, all of which are associated with each other owing to the fact that they achieve the same goal: moving the mobile away. Action-schemes are, thus, organised wholes – coordinating a range of actions and giving them meaning (Müller *et al.*, 2009). In this way, they become instruments of generalisation – an infant who knows how to move an object by pushing with its hands or kicking with its feet can do this with an indefinite range of objects even though each is different.

Clearly, this basic, practical knowledge is still possessed by children as they mature. However, over the course of development, more powerful operative structures come into play. 'Operational structures' are one example of a more sophisticated operative structure involved in logical thinking, specifically deductive reasoning (Smith, 1981). As discussed above, sensorimotor action-schemes give rise to practical knowledge. Here, actions are considered separately. Take, for example, the infant who pulls the mobile close to its mouth and then pushes it away. If the infant thinks of this as performing two discrete actions, then it will only develop practical knowledge from those actions. The infant starts to move beyond this basic level of thinking and generates operational structures when it makes deductive inferences that conceptualise the relations between the discrete actions. For example, the infant might begin to understand that the two discrete actions are interconnected, that pushing and pulling are inversely related. Thus, the actions made by two infants might be the same; for example, both infants may push the mobile away, and yet the operative structure behind the action might be different: if one child uses an operational structure and the other an action-scheme. To Piaget, what is crucially different in these cases is the presence or absence of deductive inferences in the thinking of the child (Piaget, 1950).

To take a more complex example, a child could be said to have a practical knowledge of microwaves if they know how to open the door of a microwave and push a button to heat up a snack. The child's practical knowledge is made possible by the use of action-schemes. However, the child would be using an operational structure if they could correctly understand the deductive relations that apply to both the objects and actions, such as knowing that a subclass must be smaller than that of its including class. A child employing this operational structure would know that a microwave is a kitchen appliance but that not all kitchen appliances are microwaves. Hence, the child would not try to heat up a snack by putting it in a fridge (Smith, 1981).

This brings us to an important understanding of Piaget's theoretical commitment – knowledge acquisition involves an active process of growth and development within internal, inter-related operative structures that proceed from less knowledge to a state that is more complex and powerful (Pascual-Leone, 2012). With this commitment, Piaget's theory is clearly structuralist, constructivist and dialectical in nature. It is structuralist in that operative structures are required for knowledge to arise, and new structures are formed out of a child's use of existing structures. It is dialectical in the broad sense of recognising that structures emerge and develop through a system of internal relations whereby the nature of one structure is partly a matter of how it relates to another structure through conflicts and oppositions. It is constructivist in highlighting the qualitative changes that occur within these operative structures over the course of development as a consequence of goal-directed action. It is interesting to note that, of all these aspects of Piaget's epistemology, it is the latter 'constructivist' element that he is best known for. Indeed, in many textbooks Piaget's theory is presented as the foundation of the constructivist teaching movement.

Research focus: constructivism in the classroom

Akpan and Beard (2016) argue that constructivism's key assumptions about the internal, organisational structures of knowledge acquisition and its operative nature have important implications for practice and considerable potential to improve the learning of all students.

Constructivist teaching and learning is based on students actively developing their own knowledge and understanding through engaging in goal-directed activities. Students make sense of the world by integrating new experiences into already existing operative structures: what they have already come to understand about the world (Brooks and Brooks, 1999). In this process, knowledge is developed and refined through the success and failure of goal-directed activity. It is a process of active sense-making and is a result of students engaging in their own experiencing, thinking, reflecting and processing (Von Glasersfeld, 1989; Steele, 2005).

Because knowledge is constructed in action by individual student-knowers, instruction is learner-centred with the teacher taking the role of facilitator, mentor and co-explorer. The teacher creates learning opportunities that encourage students to question, challenge and formulate their own ideas and conclusions (Ultanir, 2012).

Akpan and Beard (2016) acknowledge that some concerns have been raised within the educational community about constructivist teaching strategies. Kirschner *et al.* (2006), for example, point to the perils of approaches that provide minimal guidance during instructional tasks (e.g. constructivist, experiential, discovery and problem-based learning). However, Akpan and Beard cite research which shows that learner-centred teaching with careful teacher guidance and support has considerable potential to benefit all students, including those with special needs (Brooks and Brooks, 1999; Larson and Keiper, 2007).

The mechanisms of growth

Having established the importance of operative structures to help children coordinate their actions, it is important to unpack some of the essential mechanisms through which they adapt to the constant changes in their world in ways that advance their thinking (Woolfolk, 2016).

Equilibration

Piaget argued that the benefits children could gain from their actions depend upon their ability to compensate for any potential sources of disorder and instability caused by their experiences. This assertion reflects his process of equilibration, a core feature of development and a central concept in his genetic epistemology. Equilibration is based on the assumption that the direction of cognitive development is always toward eliminating sources of cognitive disorder and instability (or disequilibrium) that occur as a result of a child's intentional actions in the world (Piaget, 1975/1985). In the following section some of the central features Piaget's theory of equilibration will be reviewed, although due to its complexity this account is necessarily limited.

Piaget makes a key distinction between the *process* of equilibration, involving the development of a child's operative structures, and the *state* of temporary and partial equilibrium, which is the ideal aimed for by the equilibration process (Boom, 2009). Equilibration occurs because Piaget's operative structures carry within them expectations about what should happen next, conditional on what has happened before (e.g. a child learns from dropping things that when it lets go of a toy, the toy falls down). When expectations are violated by experience (e.g. when the child lets go of a helium balloon), a state of incoherence (disequilibration) occurs. The child seeks to avoid incoherence and thus mobilises perceptual and mental attention to resolve anomalies, eliminate resistances, simplify processing and restore equilibrium (Pascual-Leone, 2012). However, even when a state of equilibrium seems to have been reached, the new structure opens up new possibilities that lead to new disequilibrations. As Boom (2009: 136) explains, 'equilibrium must be taken as a dynamic equilibrium: as a property of a process that is constantly changing as far as its elements are concerned but that has found a stable form'.

Knowledge is reconstructed over time in such a way as to maintain a state of partial equilibrium between operative structures and the external environment (Basseches, 1984). Equilibrium is, thus, a way of coping with continual change by enabling something to remain stable, or at least recognisable, for a period of time. (See Chapter 7 for an example of this process in the form of the development of our gender schemas.) It is a way of taking increasing control over experience and achieving higher levels of equilibrium. This corresponds with Piaget's notion of cognitive development as a process of construction and reconstruction that is directed and progressive.

Assimilation and accommodation

Because the re-establishment of higher levels of equilibrium occurs through an active process of equilibration, operative structures are self-organising and dynamic, involving the dialectical interplay of two component processes: assimilation and accommodation. These are two opposite poles of adaptive behaviour (Bennour and Vonèche, 2009).

'Assimilation' refers to the incorporation of new elements into already existing operative structures (Müller *et al.*, 2009). Assimilation always involves adding something to an existing structure since a child assimilates through his/her actions in the world (Basseches, 1984; Smith, 1981). For example, a child may react to a new toy by bringing it to his/her mouth and sucking it. This experience is assimilated into an existing 'grasping and sucking' action-scheme. In doing so 'a scheme of assimilation confers a certain meaning on the objects assimilated and therefore assigns definite goals to the actions which have reference to them' (Smith, 1981: 18). For example, as the new toy is assimilated into the grasping and sucking scheme, it attains the functional meaning of being 'graspable' and 'suckable'. Applying the scheme to reach for the new toy and putting it into its mouth, has achieved the child's goal as expected.

However, in some cases assimilation will be unsuccessful: applying the action will not lead to achieving the expected goal. For example, the new toy (e.g. a large plastic ball) may be different from previous toys that the child has grasped. It presents novel features that the existing action scheme must accommodate: it is not graspable or suckable. When assimilation has not been met with success, the child needs to modify its operative structures in order to accommodate to the environment (Campbell, 2009).

'Accommodation' involves the modification of existing structures to take into account the particular features of a new object or situation. For example, the pre-existing grasping and sucking scheme needs to be modified because the child cannot grasp and suck the new toy. Accommodation is the process through which the operative structure is moderated or transformed to facilitate or encompass a not-yet-assimilated aspect of the environment (Di Paolo *et al.*, 2014). Sometimes the modifications of the child's existing operative structure may be small, putting restrictions on it (e.g. use the grasping and sucking scheme only with small toys) or differentiating it into one or more sub-schemes (e.g. small and large toys). Sometimes entirely new schemes will need to be constructed for successful accommodation to take place. In every case, something new has been constructed as a result of the dialectical interaction of child and environment (Basseches, 1984). For example, Piaget (1932/1985) reported that children's knowledge of 'justice' unfolds developmentally, going through considerable change over the course of their development. For instance, up to age 7–8 years, children's conceptions of what is 'just' is derived from authority figures; by age seven 'equality' is progressively prioritised over authority; beyond age ten 'equity' (in relation to the particularity of the situation) takes precedence over equality.

Reflections

Recall a time when you felt your understanding of justice shifted or evolved. What caused the disequilibrium? How did your understanding develop; can you think of any changes which would be an example of assimilation or accommodation?

Research focus: learning through assimilation and accommodation – evidence from a high school physics lesson

Renner *et al.* (1996) conducted a study to investigate how assimilation and accommodation might operate to facilitate knowledge acquisition during the learning of key concepts in physics. They designed a series of instructional activities around a teaching procedure called 'the Learning Cycle' (Atkin and Karplus, 1962) which consisted of three phases: Exploration, Invention and Expansion.

Assimilation often occurred in the Exploration phase as students interacted with material in the laboratory, conducting experiments and collecting data. These activities enabled students to actively make sense of the concepts and equations introduced during lectures by engaging with tangible evidence. A state of disequilibrium developed when the material presented through the students' experiences could not be assimilated into their existing structures (i.e. there was a disparity between what students thought should happen and what they actually observed/experienced). This triggered a drive to accommodate, which occurred during class in the Conceptual/Invention phase.

Finally, opportunities for reading and reflecting during the Expansion phase allowed students to consider the assimilated/accommodated information in light of their existing operative structures. Here, having experienced the concept in the Exploration phase, and accommodated any new information in the Conceptual/Invention phase, students were able to organise what was read into newly assimilated/accommodated structures, thereby consolidating and/or extending their conceptual knowledge through further reading.

The authors concluded that the Learning Cycle was a powerful tool to facilitate an understanding of physics concepts because it was compatible with Piaget's theory of knowledge acquisition. The instructional strategies worked in synchrony with the students' operative structures – enabling knowledge to be constructed through a self-organising process of equilibration which sought to maintain order and stability (i.e. resolve disequilibrium) through the interplay of assimilation and accommodation.

Connecting epistemology and method

This description of the core assumptions informing Piaget's epistemological project as well as some of his key conceptualisations (i.e. the operative structures and mechanisms of growth) provides a basis from which to consider his method. It enables what Lourenço and Machado (1996: 143) call 'the view from within', namely, considering Piaget's method in light of its underpinning epistemological goals and assumptions.

Piaget investigated children's actions in the world to inform his epistemological project – to achieve the specific objective of 'laying bare the operational mechanism of thought' (Inhelder, 1962: 19). However, considering his vast number of publications, Piaget provided little explanation of his method. Instead, in each volume of work he provided hundreds of protocol extracts to illustrate his theory (see Table 8.2).

These transcripts reveal Piaget interacting with children, often his own, observing their behaviour and reflecting upon their intellectual development. As his method evolved, he presented the children with problems and talked to them about their responses, offering counter-suggestions in what became known as his 'clinical interview method' (Duveen, 2000). However, details regarding how he carried out this data collection, such as descriptions of the research setting and the procedures used to analyse the data, were rarely provided and typically very vague (Bond and Tryphon, 2009). It was this ambiguity that opened up his research to severe critical attention.

Owing to the fact that the scientific method has emerged as the dominant methodology in mainstream psychology, many criticisms have been based on assumptions originating in the positivist tradition, reflecting the pre-eminence given to experimental empiricism (Müller *et al.*, 2009). For example, some have suggested that the problems Piaget presented to children were

Table 8.2 Two Piagetian protocols

Observation 126. – A final behaviour pattern belonging to the present group of schemata ('removing the obstacle') consists in searching under a screen for invisible objects. We shall closely study this behaviour in connection with the development of the concept of the object. ... For example Laurent, at 0:8(29), plays with a box which I remove from his hands in order to place it under a pillow. Although, four days before, he did not react at all in an analogous situation, this time he at once takes possession of the pillow. Though it cannot be stated that he expects to find the box under the pillow (for the behaviour is too undecided), it is nevertheless apparent that Laurent is not interested in the pillow as such and that he lifts it in order to try something. The act of lifting the pillow is therefore not a sure means for the child, but it already constitutes a 'means' for the attempt, that is to say, a separate action from grasping the box.
 	
(Piaget, 1936/1952: 222)
	We hung a metal box from a double string and placed it in front of Vel, in such a way that, on letting go of the box, the string unwound making the box turn round and round.
	   Why does it turn? – *Because the string is twisted.*
	   Why does the string turn too? – *Because it wants to unwind itself.*
	   Why? – *Because it wants to be unwound.* (= it wants to resume its original position in which the string was unwound)
	   Does the string know it is twisted? – *Yes.*
	   Why – *Because it wants to untwist itself, it knows it's twisted!*
	   Does it really know it is twisted? – *Yes. I am not sure.*
	   How do you think it knows? – *Because it feels it is all twisted.*
	   (Piaget, 1947/1960: 175–176)

too abstract and failed to make sense to the child. Others have argued that his clinical interview, with its use of counter-suggestion, involved forms of dialogue that introduced a systematic bias into his investigations (see Duveen, 2000, for further discussion). All of these criticisms reflect a broad concern with Piaget's method, namely that his theory of cognitive development was non-experimental, non-statistical and relied upon description and interpretation without causal explanation (Lourenço and Machado, 1996).

Given these issues, Piaget's findings were called into question. It was suggested that he had seriously underestimated children's intellectual capacity and that his key constructs were merely the artefacts of inadequate methods (Donaldson, 1978; Duveen, 2000). Researchers also argued that if he had used more stringent experimental controls, he would have found greater consistency and continuity in the developmental process and more clearly delineated cognitive stages (Duveen, 2000). These criticisms were given empirical weight in the 1970s and 1980s when a number of experimental studies emerged that sought to address perceived weaknesses in Piaget's method (see Wood, 1988, for a review). Collectively these studies represented a body of evidence purporting to demonstrate that young children were capable of engaging in the forms of thought which Piaget attributed to much later ages.

However, the difficulty with considering these studies from the 1970s and 1980s as a legitimate and credible critique of the Piagetian research project is that they introduced significant changes to his method (Smith, 1992). Many of these researchers developed their own problem scenarios, which they presented to children under controlled, experimental conditions. As such, they operated with a design and procedure that was far removed from that used by Piaget, as Duveen (2000: 80) points out:

> children are presented with a problem ... and asked for a solution. There is not, however, any attempt to pursue the conversation with the child any further, they are not asked to give any justification for their answer, nor are they exposed to any counter-argument from the interviewer.

Perhaps more fundamentally, in problematising Piaget's method and setting up experimental studies to test aspects of his theory, his critics neglected his major goal: to investigate the ontogenetic development of knowledge acquisition – to discover not 'what' a child knows but 'how' the child knows it through investigating his/her goal-directed actions in the world (Pascual-Leone, 2012). Piaget's critics adopted a 'view from without' – separating his method from its epistemological grounding (Lourenço and Machado, 1996: 143). In doing so, they perpetuated a profound misunderstanding of his research programme. Piaget never sought to engage in the experimental investigation of causal variables (Smith, 2009). His work was grounded in qualitative methodology and interpretive in nature. Knowledge claims emerged from an analysis of single cases which were studied systematically. Indeed, his theory should always be read as *interpretive* rather than experimental and *teleological* rather than causal (Smith, 1981), seeking to reveal the operative mechanisms of thought through descriptions of goal-directed, intentional action (Inhelder, 1962).

Reflections

When describing the challenges of learning his clinical interview method, Piaget declared 'at least a year of daily practice is necessary before passing beyond the inevitable fumbling stage of the beginner' (Piaget, 1926/1960: 8–9). Are you surprised that such rigorous training is required? What particular interview skills do you think would be important when using an interpretive approach such as Piaget's? Do you feel that Piaget's clinical interview was a useful method to investigate children's thinking?

Piaget's interpretive method

In response to those who read Piaget's protocols and consider that he developed his theory simply by conversing with his own children, contemporary Piagetian scholars have carefully investigated both his published (but little cited) work and his unpublished documents at the 'Archives Jean Piaget' (see Duveen's [2000] and Mayer's [2005] well-grounded reviews of Piagetian methodology). They have found that the protocols provided in his publications were supported by a much larger, often concealed, epistemologically driven research programme. Drawing on the work of these scholars, it is possible to gain key insights into the Piagetian method, which evolved over time and in different and inconsistent ways across his writings (Bond and Tryphon, 2009).

Piaget began his investigations into the development of children's thinking in the 1920s by observing them in natural settings (i.e. nurseries and schools). Throughout his observations, he kept detailed records of their speech during unstructured periods of play (Piaget, 1923/1926). According to both Duveen and Mayer it was because Piaget found these observations did not always reveal children's understanding of the world, that he introduced interviews. He described his interview technique as 'clinical' – presenting a child with a problem and asking carefully crafted questions in an attempt to understand their comprehension of the situation. Using techniques employed in psychiatric assessment, perhaps learned during the early years of his career which he spent at Alfred Binet's psychometric laboratory, a form of counter-questioning was introduced. Here, the child was presented with a case that contrasted with their initial response – a practice which helped to promote their active engagement with a problem rather than static reflection. Importantly, Piaget did not record the child's responses as an objective feature of their activity. Instead, behaviours and conversations were interpreted through the organising structures articulated in his theory of development. In this way, the data were rendered intelligible through interpretation.

Almost a decade later, in the 1930s, the nature of the clinical interview remained. However, rather than presenting children with a simple problem, a dilemma presented through a short vignette was introduced. Duveen (2000) has suggested Piaget felt that this allowed for greater exploration of children's thinking. Piaget also entered into the children's activities/games, questioning them as a participant observer. He later used this method when studying sensorimotor development during infancy. However, since a verbal interview was not feasible, an active element was created which paralleled the interview by rearranging objects in the child's environment to produce a new situation.

By the 1940s, Piaget had shifted his focus back to the intellectual development of older children. In these studies, the child was first presented with a practical problem and, when they had given an answer, was asked to provide a justification. Throughout the conversation the interviewer always responded to the child's answers, posing questions, seeking justifications, rearranging materials and presenting counter-arguments. Piaget retained this clinical interview method throughout his active career, which lasted until his death in 1980 (Bond and Tryphon, 2009).

As can be seen from the above review, Piaget's method was always qualitative in nature (Smith, 2009). Duveen (2000) goes so far as to characterise it as 'ethnographic' given Piaget's use both of thick descriptions of children's responses to inform his work and the generalisation of descriptive data to an abstract model to reveal the operative structures of knowledge. This ethnographic engagement enabled a dialectic between the data collected and the theoretical constructs employed by the researcher in the interpretation of the data (Duveen, 2000). This relationship between the child's response and the researcher's interpretation is illustrated in the extract below, where Piaget describes the assimilation of another's hand into a child's action scheme:

> It may be thought strange that we should assert with regard to Observation 74 that at 0:3 Laurent manages to assimilate my hand to his, despite differences in size and position. But a good reason impels us to this interpretation. Beginning 0:3(4) I have been able to establish that Laurent imitates my hand movements; he separates, then joins his hands in response to my suggestions. This imitative reaction recurred at 0:3(5), 0:3(6), at 0:3(8), at 0:3(23), etc. Now if there is assimilation of such a movement, to the exclusion of so many others, it is obvious that there is assimilation. That his assimilation is entirely synthetic, without objective identification, is evident; it does not yet involve either the distinguishing of another's body and his own body or the concept of permanent and comparable objects grouped in categories, and it is doubtless even based upon a confusion rather than an actual comparison. But no more than this is needed to enable us to speak of assimilation. Assimilation, which is the source of imitation as it is of recognition, is an earlier mechanism than objective comparison and, in this sense, there is no obstacle to asserting that a 3-month old child can assimilate another's hand to his own.
>
> (Piaget, 1936/1952: 108)

As this extract shows, Piaget justifies his interpretations by satisfying himself that the cognitive mechanisms which he proposed are adequate to make sense of the action observed (i.e. the hand movements) (Duveen, 2000). Here, his initial interpretation regarding the reasons for the hand movements is made and is then interrogated through further observation. It is also possible to see Piaget's ongoing internal dialogue – questioning/evaluating his own interpretation and persuading himself that there are no obstacles to the authenticity of his conclusions. A similar pattern is followed during the clinical interviews, with initial interpretations explored through further dialogue that is embedded within a broader interpretive framework. With this ongoing, systematic dialectic between data and interpretation, Piaget's method becomes a powerful tool for revealing the internal structures involved in the acquisition of knowledge. As he suggests:

> The clinical examination is thus experimental in the sense that the practitioner sets himself a problem, makes hypotheses, adapts the conditions to them and finally controls each hypothesis by testing it against the reactions he stimulates in conversation. But the clinical examination is also dependent on direct observation, in the sense that the good practitioner lets himself be led, though always in control, and takes account of the whole of the mental

context, instead of being the victim of 'systematic error' as so often happens to the pure experimenter.

(Piaget, 1929: 8)

This quote perhaps lends support to Bond and Tryphon's (2009) claim that although Piaget may have been interested in quantitative investigations into his key ideas, it is likely that he would consider the data gathered through his own clinical method to be scientifically compelling. That said, Piaget did not believe that his theory provided a definitive answer to the question 'How an individual knows'. Indeed, he recognised that his theory was partial and that subsequent research was needed to fill in the missing pieces and adapt and refine key ideas (Lourenço and Machado, 1996). The important point, to build effectively from his scientific work, is to begin with a sound understanding of the goals and assumptions driving his epistemological project and informing his methodological approach.

Conclusion

This chapter has provided an introduction to Piaget's epistemological project, with its overarching goal to investigate the emergence of new, progressively more advanced forms of thinking and the construction of practical and conceptual knowledge. The organisational structures of knowledge acquisition and their underlying cognitive mechanisms, which help children adapt to a world of constant change, have been set out. In doing so, the constructivist, structuralist and dialectical nature of Piaget's theory has been highlighted, and conceptualisations such as equilibration, assimilation and accommodation have been introduced and explained.

It has been argued that the core components of Piaget's theory continue to have a place in contemporary educational psychology more than 30 years after his death, making an important contribution to our understanding of the way children construct knowledge over the course of their development. Indeed, instructional approaches grounded in the principles of his theory are potentially powerful tools to advance children's learning as they are fundamentally responsive to *how* children acquire knowledge (i.e. the internal mechanisms of thought).

It has been suggested that many current criticisms of Piaget's research operate outside an understanding of its epistemological foundations – critiquing his ideas with a positivist rationality and experimental logic that separates an individual's actions from the world and seeks causal answers to teleological problems. Such interpretations serve only to perpetuate widespread misunderstandings of Piaget's theoretical constructs and research methods. When his work is interpreted with its major goals and purposes in mind, it is argued that Piaget's qualitative, broadly ethnographic research method demonstrates how an interpretive approach, which is both rigorous and systematic, can provide enduring insights into the development of knowledge.

Key points

- Piaget's epistemological project is based on the assumption that in order to understand what knowledge is, it is first necessary to understand the process through which it is acquired, i.e. how the child knows.

- As children act upon objects in their world, they are able to coordinate their actions at progressively more complex levels – knowledge unfolds developmentally.
- The organisation of actions occurs through a series of internally related operative structures that enable the child to make sense of the objects and events encountered in his/her world.
- Action-schemes are the most basic type of operative structure, giving rise to practical knowledge. Operational structures are a more sophisticated operative structure involved in logical thinking, specifically deductive reasoning.
- Equilibrium and equilibration, assimilation and accommodation are essential cognitive mechanisms through which children adapt to the constant changes in their world in ways that further advance their thinking.
- Piaget's method was qualitative in nature and has been described as 'ethnographic' given his use both of thick descriptions of children's responses to inform his work and the generalisation of descriptive data to an abstract model to reveal the operative structures of knowledge.

Recommended readings

Duveen, G. (2000) Piaget ethnographer. *Social Science Information*, **39**, pp. 79–97.
Lourenço, O.M. (2016) Developmental stages, Piagetian stages in particular: A critical review. *New Ideas in Psychology*, **40**, pp. 123–137.
Lourenço, O. and Machado, A. (1996) In defense of Piaget's theory: A reply to 10 common criticisms. *Psychological Review*, **103**(1), pp. 143–164.
Martí, E. and Rodríguez, C. (eds) (2012) *After Piaget*. London: Transaction Publishers.
Müller, U., Carpendale, J. and Smith, L. (eds) (2009) *The Cambridge companion to Piaget*. New York: Cambridge University Press.

References

Akpan, J.P. and Beard, L.A. (2016) Using constructivist teaching strategies to enhance academic outcomes of students with special needs. *Universal Journal of Educational Research*, **4**(2), pp. 392–398.
Atkin, J.M. and Karplus, R. (1962) Discovery of invention. *The Science Teacher*, **29**(5), pp. 20–22.
Basseches, M. (1984) *Dialectical thinking and adult development*. New York: Ablex.
Beilin, H. (1992) Piaget's enduring contribution to developmental psychology. *Developmental Psychology*, **28**(2), pp. 191–204.
Bennour, M. and Vonèche J. (2009) The historical context of Piaget's ideas. In U. Müller, J.I.M. Carpendale and L. Smith (eds) *The Cambridge companion to Piaget*. Cambridge: Cambridge University Press.
Bibace, R. (2013) Challenges in Piaget's legacy. *Integrative Psychological and Behavioral Science*, **47**, pp. 167–175.
Bond, T. and Tryphon, A. (2007) Piaget's legacy as reflected in The Handbook of Child Psychology [1998 edition]. Available at www.piaget.org/news/docs/Bond-Tryphon-2007.pdf (Accessed 20 May 2017).
Bond, T. and Tryphon, A. (2009) Piaget and method. In U. Müller, J.I.M. Carpendale and L. Smith (eds) *The Cambridge companion to Piaget*. Cambridge: Cambridge University Press.
Boom, J. (2009) Piaget on equilibration. In U. Müller, J.I.M. Carpendale and L. Smith (eds) *The Cambridge companion to Piaget*. Cambridge: Cambridge University Press.
Bringuier, J.C. (1977/1980) *Conversations with Jean Piaget*. Chicago: University of Chicago Press.
Brooks, J.G. and Brooks, M.G. (1999) *In search of understanding: The case for constructivist classrooms*. Alexandria, VA: Association for Supervision and Curriculum Development.
Campbell, R. (2006) *Jean Piaget's genetic epistemology: Appreciation and critique*. Available at http://campber.people.clemson.edu/piaget.html/ (Accessed 20 May 2017).
Campbell, R. (2009) Constructive processes: Abstraction, generalization, and dialectics. In U. Müller, J.I.M. Carpendale and L. Smith (eds) *The Cambridge companion to Piaget*. Cambridge: Cambridge University Press.
Di Paolo, E.A., Barandiaran, X.E., Beaton, M. and Thomas, B. (2014) Learning to perceive in the sensorimotor approach: Piaget's theory of equilibration interpreted dynamically. *Frontiers in Neuroscience*, **8**, pp. 1–16.

Donaldson, M. (1978) *Children's minds.* London: Fontana.

Duveen, G. (1997) Psychological development as a social process. In L. Smith, P. Tomlinson and J. Dockerell (eds) *Piaget, Vygotsky and beyond.* London: Routledge.

Duveen, G. (2000) Piaget ethnographer. *Social Science Information,* **39**, pp. 79–97.

Feldman, D.H. (2004) Piaget's stages: The unfinished symphony of cognitive development. *New Ideas in Psychology,* **22**, pp. 175–231.

Inhelder, B. (1962) Some aspects of Piaget's approach to cognition. *Monographs of the Society for Research in Child Development,* **27**(2), pp. 19–40.

Inhelder, B. and De Caprona, D. (1997) What subject for psychology? *The Genetic Epistemologist,* **25**, pp. 4–5.

Kirschner, P.A., Sweller, J. and Clark, R.E. (2006) Why minimal guidance during instruction does not work: An analysis of the failure of constructivist, discovery, problem-based, experiential, and inquiry-based teaching. *Educational Psychologist,* **41**, pp. 75–86.

Larson, B.E. and Keiper, T.A. (2007) *Instructional strategies for middle and high school.* Abingdon: Routledge.

Lourenço, O.M. (2016) Developmental stages, Piagetian stages in particular: A critical review. *New Ideas in Psychology,* **40**, pp. 123–137.

Lourenço, O. and Machado, A. (1996) In defense of Piaget's theory: A reply to 10 common criticisms. *Psychological Review,* **103**(1), pp. 143–164.

Mayer, S.J. (2005) The early evolution of Jean Piaget's clinical method. *History of Psychology,* **8**, pp. 362–382.

Müller, U., Carpendale, J. and Smith, L. (2009) Introduction: Overview. In U. Müller, J.I.M. Carpendale and L. Smith (eds) *The Cambridge companion to Piaget.* Cambridge: Cambridge University Press.

Pascual-Leone, J. (2012) Piaget as a pioneer of dialectical constructivism: Seeking dynamic processes for human science. In E. Martí and C. Rodríguez (eds) *After Piaget.* New Brunswick: Transaction Publishers.

Piaget, J. (1923/1926) *The language and thought of the child.* London: Kegan Paul Trench Trubner.

Piaget, J. (1929) *The child's conception of the world* (J. Tomlinson and A. Tomlinson, Trans.). London: Routledge and Kegan Paul.

Piaget, J. (1932/1985) *The moral judgement of the child* (M. Gabain, Trans.). Glencoe, IL: The Free Press.

Piaget, J. (1936/1952) *The origins of intelligence in children.* New York: International University Press.

Piaget, J. (1947/1960) *The psychology of intelligence.* New York: Littlefield Adams.

Piaget, J. (1950) *The psychology of intelligence.* London: Routledge.

Piaget, J. (1957) Epistèmologie gènètique, programme et mèthodes. In W. Beth, W. Mays and J. Piaget (eds) *Epistèmologie gènètique et recherche psychologique.* Paris: Presses Universitaires de France.

Piaget, J. (1926/1960) *The child's conception of the world.* (J. Tomlinson and A. Tomlinson, Trans.). London: Routledge and Kegan Paul.

Piaget, J. (1963) Foreword to J. Flavell (1963), *The developmental psychology of Jean Piaget.* London: Van Nostrand.

Piaget, J. (1970/1983) *Genetic epistemology.* New York: Columbia University Press.

Piaget, J. (1975/1985) *The equilibration of cognitive structures: The central problem of intellectual development.* Chicago: University of Chicago Press.

Renner, J.W., Abraham, M.R. and Birnie, H.H. (1996) The occurrence of assimilation and accommodation in learning high school physics. *Journal of Research in Science Teaching,* **23**(7), pp. 619–634.

Richards, B. (1985) Constructivism and logical reasoning, *Synthese,* **65**(1), pp. 33–64.

Rodríguez, C. and Martí, E. (2009) The fertility of Piaget's Legacy. In E. Martí and C. Rodríguez (eds) *After Piaget.* New Brunswick: Transaction Publishers.

Rodríguez, C. and Martí, E. (2012) Introduction. In E. Martí and C. Rodríguez (eds) *After Piaget.* New Brunswick: Transaction Publishers.

Smith, L. (1981) Piaget's genetic epistemology: A theoretical critique of main epistemic concepts. Unpublished doctoral dissertation, University of Leicester.

Smith, L. (ed.) (1992) *Jean Piaget: Critical assessments.* London: Routledge.

Smith, L. (2002) Piaget's model. In U. Goswami (ed.) *Blackwell handbook of childhood cognitive development.* Oxford: Blackwell.

Smith, L. (2009) Piaget's developmental epistemology. In U. Müller, J.I.M. Carpendale and L. Smith (eds) *The Cambridge companion to Piaget.* Cambridge: Cambridge University Press.

Steele, M.M. (2005) Teaching students with learning disabilities: Constructivism or behaviorism? *Current Issues in Education,* **8**(10). Available at http://cie.ed.asu.edu/volume8/number10/ (Accessed 25 May 2017).

Ultanir, E. (2012) An epistemological glance at the constructivist approach: Constructivist learning in Dewy, Piaget, and Montessori. *International Journal of Instruction,* **5**(2), pp. 195–212.

Valsiner, J. (2012) Series editor's preface. In E. Martí and C. Rodríguez (eds) *After Piaget*. New Brunswick: Transaction Publishers.

Von Glasersfeld, E. (1989) Cognition, construction of knowledge, and teaching. *Synthese*, **80**, pp. 121–140.

Wood, D. (1988) *How children think and learn*. Oxford: Blackwell.

Woolfolk, A. (2016) *Educational psychology: Global edition*. Harlow: Pearson.

9 Rats, reinforcements and role models

Taking a second look at behaviourism and its relevance to education

Cathal Ó Siochrú

Introduction

The work of theorists such as Watson and Skinner in developing some of the first behaviourist learning theories is relatively well known in education, although the extent of its relevance is not always fully appreciated. To many educators, the early research by behaviourists using rats and other animals is seen as a useful illustration of basic learning principles but too simplistic to describe learning in humans, which we like to think of as being a far more sophisticated process. Furthermore, behaviourist learning theories are often characterised as 'black box' theories which fail to acknowledge any internal mental processes that might influence learning. Where behaviourist learning theories are applied by educators they tend to be focused mainly on behaviour management: maintaining discipline and influencing behaviours that are only indirectly related to 'real' learning.

This chapter seeks to challenge that view, to show that the behaviourist model of learning is capable of helping us to understand and influence almost any kind of learning. In order to achieve this we take a fresh look at well-known behaviourists like Skinner and Watson, while also shedding some light on work done by lesser known early behaviourists such as Edward Thorndike. Following this we will explore some of the developments of the behaviourist model of learning, ranging from the well-regarded social learning and self-efficacy theories of Albert Bandura to the less widely known but nonetheless significant work done on topics such as intentionality and behaviour. We will also consider educational practices including 'token economies' or 'gamification', as well as important social issues such as the effects of video games on children's behaviour, all of which draw on the behaviourist model of learning to achieve their insights. Ultimately this chapter aims to show that the behaviourist model of learning is a sophisticated tool which can help us to understand and predict people's learning in a large range of educational contexts.

What is the behaviourist model of learning?

Before we can talk about the behaviourist learning theories we need to establish the parameters of the behaviourist model of learning, the set of fundamental assumptions about learning which are common to all behaviourist learning theories.

Clues to these assumptions can be found in the various behaviourist definitions of learning. Gerrig *et al.* (2012) define the behaviourist perspective on learning as 'a process that results in a relatively consistent change in behaviour or behaviour potential [which] is based on experience' (p. 194). Two key features of this definition are its description of learning as a change in behaviour and that this change happens in response to our experiences. Other behaviourist theorists, such as Bloom (1956), extended the core definition of learning to encompass everything from simple to complex behaviours, with the view that complex behaviours are comprised of many simpler parts which can be learnt in turn. Finally, researchers like Thorndike (1910) define learning as 'the modifications of instincts and capacities into habits and powers' (p. 11). A consequence of that definition, according to Thorndike, is that we need to use comparative studies of learning in other animals as a basis for understanding human learning, since instinctive behaviours are extremely difficult to study directly in humans.

You may notice that none of these definitions make any reference to learning in terms of knowledge, information, understanding or any other mental construct. One common misunderstanding of the behaviourist model of learning is the belief that behaviourists deny the existence of mental processes or dismiss mental processes and structures as irrelevant in relation to learning. This is not true. It is true to say that the behaviourist perspective on learning is based on the premise that psychology should focus only on observable phenomena, which is to say 'behaviour' (Watson, 1913). They see the study of unobservable phenomena such as the mind as unscientific. The claim that we can never directly observe or measure the mind doesn't mean that behaviourism is denying its existence; but it does preclude the scientific study of mental processes since the scientific method requires objective measurement to function. In other words, the behaviourist sees no point in speculating on mental processes, which are invisible and thus unknowable and so excludes these processes from the behaviourist model of learning.

As a result of this review of definitions, we can now see the basic assumptions of the behaviourist model of learning, which are as follows.

- Learning is a relatively permanent change in behaviour as a consequence of experience.
- General laws govern all learning. These laws apply to all situations and all species, including humans. This means that learning in humans can be compared to learning in other animals.
- All learned activities, no matter how complex, evolve from simpler ones.
- It is not necessary to understand mental processes to understand learning.

If we wish to understand how the behaviourist model of learning came to have such assumptions, then we need to know a little about the context in which behaviourism first emerged, as well as those factors and major figures in the field of behaviourism that influenced its development.

Context

Behaviourism as we know it could be seen as a product of a number of philosophical and scientific movements. Early influences range from British and American empiricist philosophy (e.g. Thomas Hobbes, John Locke, William James) and the scientific approach to psychology championed by the German physiologists (e.g. Gustav Fechner, Wilhelm Wundt) to Darwinian evolutionary theory and of course the pioneering research by Ivan Pavlov. A major influence on the methodology of behaviourism was the scientific approach to psychology championed by the psychophysicists such as Hermann von Helmholtz, Fechner and Wundt. Wundt is credited with being one of the most influential psychologists of his era (Mandler, 2011) and his application of empirical methods to the study of sensory phenomena became the template for much of modern experimental psychology including behaviourism. That being said, the behaviourists rejected a number of key elements of Wundt's approach, such as his use of introspection, and while they might emulate his use of the scientific method, they sought to apply it with what they saw as an even greater sense of empirical rigour.

Almost as significant an inspiration for behaviourism was the psychoanalytic perspective, which was a key element of the dominant paradigm in psychology in the early twentieth century. In many ways behaviourism can be seen as the antithesis of the psychoanalytic perspective, which was dominated by a study of purely mental phenomena and structures. For example, the psychoanalytic methods of dream analysis and free association used to study the unconscious mind which can never be known or studied directly, would be anathema to any behaviourist; they would reject such methods as unscientific and circular in their reasoning. Behaviourism was to find its antidote to the structuralism and mentalism of both Freud and Wundt in a form of a radical functionalism, grounded more than anywhere else in the work of Ivan Pavlov.

Pavlov

With the exception of Sigmund Freud, Ivan Pavlov is probably the best known 'psychologist' of all time. This is somewhat ironic as Pavlov would have considered himself first and foremost a physiologist, not a psychologist. His primary research interest, which would eventually earn him a Nobel Prize, was concerned with the *digestion* of dogs and not their learning or behaviour. His discovery of conditioned responses in his dogs' behaviour was an accidental by-product of experimental control in his digestion study which required the dogs to be fed at the same time each day. By observing production of saliva, first in response to the presence of the technician and then later in response to other stimuli, such as the now famous ringing of a bell, Pavlov established the principles of what would become known as 'classical conditioning' and the core of the behaviourist model of learning (Pavlov, 1927).

In this model a person or animal is presented with a stimulus, known as the 'unconditioned stimulus', and experiences an innate (i.e. not learned) response to that stimulus, known as an 'unconditioned response'. In his original study, food is the unconditioned stimulus and salivation is the unconditioned response. At the same time that the unconditioned stimulus is being presented, a second stimulus is also presented to which the animal has no natural response, making it a neutral stimulus initially. The presentation of the food was paired with what was initially a neutral stimulus, such as the ringing of a bell. However, after the pairing of conditioned and neutral stimulus has been repeated often enough, the previously neutral stimulus starts to produce the same response as the unconditioned stimulus, even if presented on its own. At this point the neutral stimulus has become a 'conditioned stimulus' and the response it produces is known as a 'conditioned response'. Thus, after enough repetitions you can ring the bell on its own without any food present and the dogs will salivate. Salivating in response to a bell is now a conditioned response or, to put it in other words, the dog has 'learned' to salivate in response to a bell.

Although Pavlov laid the theoretical foundations for the behaviourist model, it wasn't until his work was publicised by John B. Watson that his theories became widely known in the West. It could be said that without Pavlov the behaviourist model might have been very different but equally, as we will see, without Watson there might not have been a behaviourist movement at all.

Watson, 'little Albert' and the power of myth

John B. Watson worked as an academic and researcher at Johns Hopkins University during the early 1900s and 1910s. His early writings (1903) focused on instincts as the explanation for much behaviour, especially behaviour that was thought to be unlearned. He did acknowledge that instincts would later be replaced by learned habits but at first he lacked a comprehensive model to explain how this replacement took place. He had also begun to explore the importance of association in learning, using what he and others would later call the theory of contiguity. This theory suggested that all that was required for an association to form between a stimulus and a behaviour was for them to occur in close temporal proximity (Guthrie, 1930).

However, what seems to have crystallised Watson's theories on learning was the initial introduction of Pavlov's work to an American audience by Yerkes and Morgulis (1909). Watson was inspired by Pavlovian theories and research methods; he championed the Pavlovian model of learning in his writing and speeches, such as his presidential address to the APA in 1915 (Watson, 1916). Apart from championing the Pavlovian model of learning, Watson's other significant contribution was to establish behaviourism as a movement. The starting point for this is thought by many to be Watson's 1913 article 'Psychology as the Behaviorist Views It', which is often referred to as the 'Behaviourist Manifesto'. Apart from this, Watson's own research does not appear to have produced many enduring concepts or discoveries. His most famous study, carried out by Watson and Rayner in 1920, explored the conditioning of a boy known only as 'little Albert'. In this case study Watson and Rayner claim to have successfully created an association between the colour white and a fear response in a small child who was referred to with the pseudonym 'Albert B' in Watson and Rayner's article on the case. This was done by associating white objects, which are neutral stimuli and cause no innate response, with a loud and sudden noise behind the child which is an unconditioned stimulus as it produces an innate fear response in most children (and many adults too). By repeatedly associating the noise with the colour, eventually the white objects produced a conditioned fear response on their own.

Critics of the case study question the validity of the methods used and raise numerous potential confounds and limitations (Samelson, 1980). However, the degree to which these critiques should be considered consequential is somewhat limited given that a case study does not typically seek to establish experimental control or validity and is not intended as vehicle to provide empirical evidence. Indeed, the conclusion of Watson and Rayner's 1920 article makes it clear that their main purpose is to pose an alternative to the psychoanalytic paradigm which they claim traces all emotional disturbances back to sex. That being said, even if we acknowledge the case study on its true merits, the level of historical interest seems out of proportion to its impact. This was no 'body blow' to the credibility of psychoanalysis nor does it appear to be a great inspiration for the behaviourist research that followed. In fact, as Hilgard and Marquis (1940) reported, those studies that attempted to reproduce the 'little Albert' case study were unable to replicate its findings. I would argue that it remains so well-known not so much for its scientific merits as much as its unsavoury reputation as a cautionary tale of unethical research. It has become the research ethics equivalent of a good horror story, told mainly for its spine-chilling or unnerving effect on the listener. Indeed, some historians of psychology have questioned the nature of our enduring interest with this minor case study, suggesting that the telling and retelling of the 'little Albert' story is often more of interest in terms of what it reveals about changes in the prevailing paradigm in psychology each time it is retold (Harris, 1979).

Reflections

How could we test Watson and Rayner's claim of phobias being rooted in association in an ethical and empirical manner? Given that even the most ethically rigorous research design carries some risk of long-term effects on the well-being of the participants, how can we justify such risks?

As with any story told many times, it changes with the telling and certain myths have grown up around it, including such hair-raising claims as Albert's mother not being told what was happening or that Watson and Rayner deliberately neglected to undo the conditioned fear. In one of these mythical narratives 'Albert' grows up with a long-term and serious phobia of all things white and ends up in therapy. In truth, no one is certain what the long-term effects were, since 'Albert's' identity remains unknown. Some have claimed to have uncovered 'Albert's' true identity but even these candidates fail to lend any credence to the myth of long-term harm; they suggest instead that the real 'Albert' either died while still a child of an unrelated illness (Beck *et al.*, 2009) or lived a long and relatively normal life without any obvious phobias (Powell *et al.*, 2014). It's likely that the phobia/therapy myth comes from a speculation by Watson and Rayner (1920) that if Albert were to grow up with a phobia of white things he might end up seeking therapy from a psychoanalyst. Watson and Rayner fancifully speculated that the psychotherapist would end up interpreting one of 'Albert's' dreams to indicate that the phobia was a product of being scolded at age 3 for attempting to play with his mother's pubic hair. To some, this comment feeds the myth of Watson and Rayner as callous behaviourists, unconcerned about to the potential for long-term harm to the child. A more likely interpretation is that Watson and Rayner were highlighting what they perceived as the lack of scientific rigour or validity of the dominant therapeutic methods of the time, which were based on psychoanalysis.

In many ways the story of 'little Albert', the myths surrounding it and its inclusion as a staple of any history (including this one) of behaviourism or psychology is very telling regarding the significance of Watson's contributions to behaviourism. I would argue that 'little Albert' is included in all these histories, not because it represents a significant finding for Watson but rather to add some much needed depth and colour to what would otherwise be a rather sparse story of Watson's contribution to the field. Although Watson did contribute his own research and theories to the early formation of behaviourism, his enduring theoretical legacy appears to be as a champion of the work of other researchers such as Pavlov. As such, we might see Watson as a man whose importance to psychology and behaviourism is undeniable, but his importance is as an organiser and advocate for the behaviourist movement rather than as a researcher or theorist.

While this focus on Watson as an important figure and colourful character in the history of behaviourism is not undeserved, it may serve to distract us from some of his contemporaries whose contribution to behaviourism and psychology of education is just as worthy. One such example is the often underappreciated figure of Edward Thorndike.

Thorndike and the birth of educational psychology

Thorndike was a contemporary of Watson's and another pioneer of the functionalist approach to psychology through a focus on behaviour. Although he studied animals at first (chickens, cats, dogs, monkeys and even fish), his primary research interest was always in human learning and education. He believed that many of the sample principles that apply to animal learning could be applied to human learning. His best known research was on cats using his 'puzzle box' (which predates Skinner and his box), and from research such as this Thorndike established a number of 'laws', the best known being the laws of readiness, exercise and effect (Thorndike, 1932).

The law of readiness states that learning is more likely to occur when the individual is adequately prepared. To Thorndike this preparation could be physical or mental: a student needs to be rested, healthy and focused on their learning to make the most of it but they also need to be motivated and view the learning as necessary and purposeful. The law of exercise appears to borrow from Pavlov in that it originally stated that learning occurs through repetition, whether that is repeated association or practice. Thorndike would later abandon this law, claiming that repetition had little effect on learning (Thorndike, 1932). Finally, the law of effect was a precursor to Skinner's operant conditioning theory, as it states that learning is likely to endure if accompanied by a positive or pleasurable experience. One area where Thorndike disagreed with Skinner was that he felt that reward alone had an effect on learning and that punishment was not effective in undoing or preventing learning.

Even though Thorndike was his contemporary, Watson seems to have almost completely ignored his model of learning in favour of Pavlov's. Historians of psychology have speculated that one reason for this was that Watson may have objected to Thorndike's 'deviation' from a strictly functionalist approach in his laws through references to mental constructs such as 'satisfaction' and 'dissatisfaction' (Gewirtz, 2001). Thorndike's theories may also have been unpalatable to Watson for being teleological in the sense that Thorndike talked about behaviour as operant (i.e. purposeful) rather than sharing Watson's view of all behaviour occurring in response to a stimulus (Gewirtz, 2001).

While his impact on behaviourism was far less than he deserved, Thorndike still managed to leave an indelible impact on psychology as a whole. Through his writings and his research, Thorndike established the field of educational psychology as a credible science, and in doing so he changed the landscape of education. Before Thorndike, those who wrote about the nature and practice of education offered insights and theories based either on practical experience or philosophical reflection. In 1910 Thorndike was involved in founding one ofthe first and most influential journals in the field, the *Journal of Educational Psychology*. In the first edition of this journal was the paper 'The Contribution of Psychology to Education', which is Thorndike's manifesto for educational psychology. In it Thorndike reveals that his main aim was to make the study of learning and pedagogy more scientific. Educational psychology was to be an applied science whose findings would inform practice. However, the practical experience of teachers and research findings of academics were to be valued equally. Educational psychology would not seek to tell teachers what to do if they had already found a method that worked. Instead, educational psychology could help by finding out why the successful methods were successful. To this end, Thorndike studied the education system in America, publishing a large number of books and articles on practical and pedagogical issues ranging from methods to evaluate the reading difficulty of books to the merits of streaming students based on ability.

Thorndike's contribution to educational psychology goes beyond being a founder and advocate of the field. Thorndike's own research made important contributions to our understanding of education. One example of this is the considerable emphasis in Thorndike's research on the importance of positive motivation in learning. You can see this at its most basic level in his Law of Effect, where he states that rewards are what motivate and reinforce learning. It is interesting to note that while the original law of effect saw equal benefit to both reward and punishment, later in his career Thorndike's research would lead him to modify this, stating that reward alone (*not* reward and punishment) influenced learning. In practical terms, educators had long been aware of the impact of both reward and punishment in the classroom. However, around the turn of the twentieth century the prevailing pedagogical advice to teachers advocated fault-finding and punishment as the primary methods of instruction. Thorndike's research lent vital support to those like John Dewey who were proponents of more progressive education methods. Together, their efforts ultimately shifted the paradigm in Western education away from punishment and towards reward as the primary method of instruction.

Reflections

Can we still use rewards and avoid using punishments if the students never demonstrate the desired behaviour so that we can reward it? How could we defend Thorndike's views in the face of educators who claim that certain students only respond to punishment or the threat of punishment?

Thorndike's research also challenged other prevailing views in education such as the doctrine of formal discipline, which claimed a universal transfer of learning skills from the study of the classics (Latin and Greek) to study in completely unrelated disciplines in later life. Research by Thorndike and others showed that in most cases there was no universal transfer of skills from one area of learning to all others and that transfer of learning is only likely to occur if the new situation shares elements which are identical to those in the original learning situation (Thorndike, 1906; Thorndike and Woodworth, 1901). Finally, Thorndike was an advocate of standardised testing, and his efforts here were a major influence on the emergence of standardised testing and as a core element of the American education system, later to be copied by many other education systems across the world.

In conclusion, it could be said that Thorndike's legacy lies with his foundation of educational psychology as a field of study and his own research in this area, rather than his contribution to the foundation of behaviourism. Snubbed by Watson, it then appears that Thorndike's second misfortune was to be overshadowed by the person whose theories seem to borrow most heavily from Thorndike: the other great name in early behaviourism, B.F. Skinner and his theory of operant conditioning.

Skinner and operant conditioning

Operant conditioning had been studied by Thorndike as far back as 1901, and it involves a model of learning which looks at behaviour as being purposeful, not reflexive, and argues that it is the consequences of that behaviour which determine what it is we learn from it. Skinner would adapt Thorndike's theories, removing all references to mental elements such as 'satisfaction' and instead, taking a leaf out of Watson's book, strip back the process of operant conditioning to its essentials (i.e. those things we can see), the behaviour and the outcome.

Thus, Skinner took as the starting point for his model of learning the basic principles of reward and punishment which would be familiar to any educator or parent as the foundations of learning. Learning occurs when a behaviour produces an outcome which influences the chances of that behaviour being reproduced by the same individual in similar circumstances in the future (Skinner, 1938). Rewards were relabelled as 'reinforcements' and used to describe any outcome which makes it more likely for the behaviour to be reproduced. Most students who get a good mark see it as an endorsement (i.e. reinforcement) of the study techniques which produced the mark. This is an example of positive reinforcement: the outcome seen as a reward, thus making the behaviour which produced that outcome more likely.

Another, less obvious example of reinforcement is the student who experiences anxiety when they think about an upcoming exam and so avoids thinking about (or preparing for) the exam until the last minute. Although this behaviour will almost certainly result in a poorer exam performance it also reduces the period that the student is experiencing any exam-related anxiety to a very short period just before the exam. Furthermore, the outcome makes it more likely that the student will reproduce that behaviour and wait until the last minute to prepare for other exams in the future. Here, the reinforcement is occurring not because something good has been introduced but because the behaviour reduced or eliminated something bad (i.e. the anxiety). It's this removal of something negative that leads this form of reinforcement to be termed 'negative reinforcement' (Skinner, 1953).

Research focus: effective rewards

Praising a student can be one of the most simple and yet effective methods of reinforcement available to an educator. However, there are a number of factors which can alter the effectiveness of praise as a reward and whose impact can be better understood using the behaviourist model. In their review of effective praise techniques O'Leary and O'Leary (1977) highlighted the importance of promptness, suggesting that praise must occur as soon as possible after the desired behaviour for an association to form. This appears to draw on the principle of contiguity, thought to be an important element of the formation of associations (Watson, 1913). O'Leary and O'Leary also argued that there was a need to specific about what it is that was praiseworthy about the behaviour. This would be very much in line with the concept of 'shaping', where reinforcement is given to ever more specific behaviours in order to guide or 'shape' the development of that behaviour toward a specific goal (Skinner, 1953).

However, there are limitations to the behaviourist model's ability to explain the impact of rewards. For example, Sears and Pai (2012) found that the negative effect on learning which normally occurs when educators stop rewarding a learning behaviour is less dramatic if the reward was a group reward rather than an individual one. They suggest that the social bonds of the group help to mitigate negative effects of reward-removal and that mental and social factors like 'relatedness' may interact with rewards to determine their effect on levels of motivation. Another mental phenomenon which might interact with the effect of a reward is how the reward will be interpreted by the recipient. Dweck (2007) found that offering praise to students which focuses on intelligence unintentionally promotes a 'fixed mindset'. Students with this mindset viewed intelligence as an innate trait and would engage in ineffective learning activities (e.g. fixate on performance, avoid challenges which might invite failure) and be less likely to admit failure or seek assistance. Dweck argued that teachers should be praising effort, which would promote a growth mindset and healthier learning activities. These findings highlight one of the limitations of the behaviourist model; that mental and social structures, not typically included in the behaviourist model, could be key factors in determining the impact of a reward and the behaviours it reinforces.

According to operant conditioning, punishment is any outcome which makes the behaviour less likely to occur. Detentions or exclusions are the most dramatic examples of punishment, but a poor mark can be seen as punishment by some students. Many educators would dispute the interpretation that they are giving a poor mark as a 'punishment', instead preferring to see it as formative feedback which recognises (i.e. rewards) the positive elements in the submitted piece while also signposting where there is room for improvement. However, whether the students see a lower mark or critical feedback as encouragement or punishment can depend on their level of self-confidence (Young, 2000). The perceived punishment of a low mark can deter the wrong behaviour. Walker (2005) claimed that students who put in a high level of effort but receive a low grade can lose faith in the relationship between effort and rewards in assignments, which could result in them putting in lower levels of effort on future assignments. Also, ideally punishment should do more than simply deter the undesired behaviour but also steer the student toward the desired behaviour. Thorndike (1932) and others dispute whether punishment does any of this and claim instead that reward and not punishment is the only truly effective method for producing lasting learning.

In conclusion, Skinner's theory of operant conditioning was a critical development in the behaviourist model of learning. Its view of learning, driven by reinforcement and punishment, remains influential to this day, although it owes an unacknowledged debt to the prior work of Thorndike on operant learning. While the theory of operant conditioning has a lot to offer educators who wish to be more effective in their use of rewards, the radical behaviourist approach (disregarding purely mental phenomena) does represent a limitation for this theory. This is demonstrated when we consider one of the challenges in the application of both reinforcement and punishment: the potential for mental concepts such as self-efficacy to result in a lesson being learned by the student which is a very different one from that intended by the educator.

Token economies

One application of behaviourist learning theory which may be more familiar to most people than they realise is the token economy. A token economy is a system of behaviour modification based on 'points' or 'tokens' that are earned in response to target behaviours and which can be exchanged for rewards (Kazdin, 1977). The tokens act primarily as a means to obtaining a reward which reinforces target behaviours; however, earning tokens can itself also become a secondary reinforcement. A secondary reinforcement is a neutral object like a token, which can become a reinforcement on its own as a result of regular association with primary reinforcements (i.e. things we already find pleasurable and rewarding) (Miller and Drennen, 1970). In essence, we start to take pleasure in just earning tokens before we ever spend them.

Tokens offer a number of benefits over direct rewards. They are more flexible than a direct reward as they give the person earning the tokens a chance to choose their reward or save up for a bigger reward. Although initially devised for use in clinical environments, token economies are now used in numerous different contexts (e.g. supermarket 'loyalty' schemes). In education, token economies can be recognised in the system of gold stars, dojo points or numerous other similar systems for rewarding appropriate behaviour and academic success. There are numerous studies which have demonstrated the beneficial impact of token economies on learning behaviour (Doll *et al.*, 2013) as well as providing insights into their effective use. For example, while many token economies use virtual tokens (i.e. points), with younger students or those with developmental delays, tangible items like coins or cards can be more effective (McLaughlin and Williams, 1988). Concerns about token economies tend to be less about their effectiveness and more about the administrative overheads and certain ethical concerns about token economies as 'bribery'. However, both concerns have been addressed in the literature (see Chance, 2006; McGoey and DuPaul, 2000) and neither represents an insurmountable obstacle. As such, token economies remain a popular tool among educators and can be found at the heart of even the latest teaching techniques and trends such as in 'gamification'.

Research focus: gamification in education

Gamification is the application of computer game design techniques to other activities. In essence you take the things that make video games so appealing and addictive and you use them to make those other activities appealing/addictive too. Typical game elements that educators can attempt to build into their courses include treasures, achievements, quests, checklists and levelling. The effect of these elements can all be understood through the lens of behaviourism.

Treasures and achievements are typical reinforcements. A treasure is a direct reinforcement for any desirable behaviour. By contrast, quests and achievements are something you 'unlock' only when you do a specific behaviour or series of behaviours. This is an example of 'shaping' behaviour since you are guiding the person towards engaging in ever more specific behaviours. Checklists are used in both achievements and quests to break up a bigger task into smaller steps. Although a major part of the appeal of crossing off items on the list is derived from the big reward at the end, research suggests that crossing things off can itself become a secondary reinforcement, triggering a biological reward in the form of dopamine release (Herd *et al.*, 2010). Ultimately, these in-game mechanisms translate to game points, which can be spent in an in-game token economy, providing primary reinforcements in the form of access to exclusive resources or enhancing our enjoyment by making it easier for us to do something.

While there is a considerable positive 'buzz' surrounding gamification in education, the research evidence is more equivocal. In a recent meta-analysis of studies on gamification in education by Dichev and Dicheva (2017) the reviewers expressed concern that many of the reported benefits from gamification could be a 'novelty effect' and that there was insufficient evidence of long-term benefits. They also observed that similar implementations of gamification produced a benefit in one educational context while also producing a deficit in another. This suggests that compatibility between elements of gamification and the learning context is an issue which could benefit from further research. Neither of these concerns is intended to dismiss the value of gamification but it does caution us to be wary of the hype and approach its application to our learning environments from a critical perspective.

In conclusion, the research on token economies adds practical insights as to how the behaviourist model of learning could be applied to reinforcing and shaping a wider variety of different aspects of learning. Despite this, there are still a number of unresolved issues with the behaviourist model. The most significant of these issues is that directly learning through association and reinforcement does not appear to be sufficient to explain the variety and speed of human learning. A development of behaviourist learning theory was needed which could marry behaviourist principles to the social element of learning to be found in the work of Lev Vygotsky and others. (See Chapter 10 for more on the socio-cognitive perspective on learning.)

Bandura and social learning

A serious issue for the behaviourist model based on classical and operant conditioning is that people can show evidence of learning without visible reinforcement or association. An example of this can be found in Chomsky's critique of behaviourist theories of language acquisition. This critique makes the case that levels of language-related reinforcement are insufficient to explain the speed and diversity of children's language development (Chomsky, 1980) (see Chapter 5 for a more detailed discussion of Chomsky's critique). However, a line of research by Albert Bandura and colleagues led them to propose what would become the next great leap forward in the behaviourist model of learning: social learning. In his outline of the Social Learning theory, Bandura (1965) brought together the findings of several of his studies from the preceding five years to show how children can learn from observing the behaviour of those around them and the consequences of that behaviour.

The best known study in that first body of research was the study by Bandura *et al.* (1961) which looked at what they called the 'transmission' of aggressive behaviour through the imitation of aggressive models. In their study, Bandura and colleagues asked children to watch a video of an unknown adult 'model' interacting with a number of toys including acting aggressively towards a particular toy (the eponymous Bobo doll). The children were divided into three conditions; they either saw the model's aggression being praised, reprimanded or experiencing no consequences. The children were then introduced to the same toys and their behaviour was monitored to determine whether they imitated the aggressive behaviour of the model. The findings showed that in all conditions boys were more likely to imitate aggressive behaviour than girls, and that all the children who witnessed the model being reprimanded were less likely to imitate the aggressive behaviour than either of the other two conditions.

Reflections

Why were the boys more likely to imitate the aggressive behaviour? Why was there no difference in levels of imitation between the children who saw the model rewarded and those who saw the model experience no consequences?

It's a common misconception that the 'Bobo doll' study was a breakthrough which led Bandura and colleagues to 'realise' the existence of social learning. The reality is that in their 1961 article, Bandura *et al.* did their best to make their findings 'fit' the traditional behaviourist model. The children seemed to be 'learning' the behaviour of the model as they watched the video but without engaging in any behaviour themselves and without receiving any rewards. To get around these glaring contradictions to the behaviourist model, Bandura and colleagues tried to suggest that the children might be mentally copying the model and mentally rewarding themselves as their imagined behaviour 'succeeds'. It's possible that this rather far-fetched speculation is an example of confirmation bias, where researchers try to make their results fit the model they are testing, no matter what (Snyder, 1984). Then again, we need to remember that at the time there was no other model available to explain what they were seeing. Four years and several studies later, Bandura (1965) had realised that his findings were pointing towards a new model, a social learning model. Social learning meant observing the behaviour of certain specific others (role models) as well as the outcomes of that behaviour (successes and failures); the observer would then learn from that observation in the same way traditional behaviourism would have predicted if the observer had been the one to engage in that behaviour and experience that outcome.

One unanswered question from the 'Bobo doll' study, arising from the fact that the data was collected immediately, is what the long-term impact might have been. It's unclear how long the newly 'learned' behaviour would last or whether the learned aggressive behaviours would cross over from toys into aggression towards people. Both of these questions remain of interest to researchers and parents alike in the present day, prompting numerous studies and reviews, such as the Byron Review of the effects of video games and the internet on children's behaviour.

Research focus: the Byron Review

In 2008 and again in 2010, the UK government commissioned Dr Tanya Byron to lead a team that conducted an extensive review (i.e. a meta-analysis) of all the existing studies that had looked at the impact of video games and the internet on children's behaviour.

The review found only a short-term causal effect for video games on aggression: game players were more aggressive for a short time (minutes usually or a few hours at most) before reverting to their normal levels of aggression. There was no reliable evidence of long-term negative effects of video games. No increase in violent behaviour, no desensitisation and no increase in anti-social behaviour. The review found that children were quite capable of distinguishing between what was acceptable behaviour in a game and what is acceptable in real life. This was even true in those children with a troubled past and who had previously been violent themselves.

In contrast to the supposed negative effects, there was evidence for beneficial effects from playing video games in terms of improved perception, decision making and problem solving abilities. Some studies even suggested that playing games might help children to learn impulse control, an important factor in reducing levels of aggressive behaviour. In order to achieve some of these positive effects, helping children to interpret the violence as they see it happen in the game or directly afterwards is important. Kids are able to learn on their own the lesson that violence in real life isn't acceptable, but for parents who are worried, Bryon's review showed that discussing with your kids the implications of violence in the real world has a positive effect.

In conclusion, we can see that social learning theory represents an important development of the behaviourist model for learning. By allowing learning to occur vicariously through the observation of key others (role models) social learning theory has helped to tackle certain limitations of the original behaviourist model while also recognising a more social dimension to learning and education. This was just the beginning. In this next section we will see how this new area of research would now seek to explore how concepts related to social learning, such as confidence and social understanding, would impact on levels of both social learning and learning in general.

Social learning and social understanding

A common misrepresentation of social learning is to reduce it to little more than children learning to copy the behaviour of their role models, as expressed in the adage 'Monkey see, monkey do'. But this representation misses out a key element, that the social learner is copying the behaviour with the intent of achieving the same outcome as the model. Thus not everyone who copies the behaviour of another fulfils this important requirement. Michael Tomasello and Malinda Carpenter explore this very question in a long history of studies with various collaborators looking at intentionality and behaviour in both children and apes (for a review, see Tomasello and Carpenter, 2007). Their research identifies important differences between what might be classed as 'mimicry', 'imitation' and 'emulation'. Mimicry describes when we do what the role model does for no other reason than to copy them. Imitation describes when we do what the role model does to achieve the same outcome as they achieved. Finally, emulation describes doing a different behaviour in order to achieve the same outcome as the one the role model achieved with their behaviour.

An observation that was common to several studies in this area was that 12 months of age in children was a key turning point, both in terms of their awareness of others as intentional beings and the emergence of imitative behaviours (Carpenter *et al.*, 1998). This suggests a connection between the emergence of imitation and the beginning of awareness of the intentions of others. In other words, we can only begin to imitate others once we have become aware of their intentions: before I can attempt to copy your behaviours in order to achieve the same outcome I first need to know what outcome you intended your behaviour to have. More recent research has continued to advance our understanding of this area and, while there is still broad agreement on there being a specific point at which awareness of intentions begins to emerge, that point is now thought to occur at around 6 months of age (Behne *et al.*, 2005).

Whatever the age, these findings suggest that there may be a lower age limit, before which children may not be able to engage in social learning due to a lack of social understanding (see Chapter 6 for a more complete discussion on the nature and development of social understanding). This could have relevance to any attempt to employ social learning in an early-years educational context. Thus, the ability to understand the goals and intentions of others becomes a prerequisite of social learning. It also raises the possibility that levels of ability in social understanding may predict effectiveness at social learning; for example, through a person's ability to differentiate between rational and irrational methods of achieving an outcome (Gergely *et al.*, 2002).

Social learning and self-efficacy

As Bandura and others continued to explore social learning they came to the conclusion that, although social learning enables us to learn a vast number of behaviours, we don't perform them all (Bandura, 1999). While it may not sound like much to suggest this, it is another example of the way that social learning was breaking with behaviourist traditions. To a traditional behaviourist, learning a behaviour and demonstrating it were one and same thing, you couldn't have one without the other. To suggest that there were learnt behaviours lying undemonstrated inside the person's head carried implications of structuralism which was incompatible with the traditional behaviourist model. But the social learning perspective was open to the possibility of mental structures and so found no contradictions in the suggestion that we pay attention, observe the behaviour, interpret the outcome, store the behaviour in memory and perform it later if or when the time is right.

While this process sounds simple, there are many examples in everyday education where this sequence is not followed through to the end. For example, two students sit in the same class, both watch the teacher demonstrate the best method to solve a certain type of problem and yet when the test begins only one of them demonstrates learning by putting the method they saw the teacher use into action. In order to explain situations such as this, Bandura and others identified a number of factors which have an impact on the way we learn from observing the behaviour of another. Some of these are cognitive factors like attention and retention (Bandura, 1999): do we notice the behaviour and the outcome when the role model does the behaviour and do we remember the behaviour when we find ourselves in a similar situation? As well as cognitive factors there are also factors relating to motivation and ability that affect social learning; does the reward associated with the outcome appeal to us and do we think we would achieve the same outcome if we repeated the same behaviour ourselves?

This last question, as to whether we would achieve the same outcome, may be as much about confidence as it is ability. It could be said that before an individual will attempt to imitate another they must first have a certain level of confidence or self-belief in their ability to successfully imitate the other's behaviour and achieve the same outcome. This was an idea that Bandura (1986; 1994) and others captured in the concept of 'self-efficacy'.

Bandura (1999) defined self-efficacy as 'people's beliefs in their capabilities to perform in ways that give them some control over events that affect their lives' (p. 46). Thus, self-efficacy can be thought of as our level of belief in our own competence in relation to a specific behaviour or ability (i.e. to socially learn).

Reflections

What kind behaviours do you find the hardest to imitate even after you've witnessed others demonstrate the behaviour for you? Why do you think those behaviours are so challenging for you to learn in this way?

The specificity of self-efficacy is critical to understanding the concept, as it means that we will have separate levels of self-efficacy for different behaviours (e.g. you might have high self-efficacy for writing essays but low self-efficacy when it comes to exams). This is one way in which self-efficacy is different from self-esteem. Self-esteem is a 'global' value, an overall estimate of your worthiness and ability across all situations, whereas self-efficacy is a 'local' value and applies to one specific ability or situation (Bandura, 2006). The relationship between self-efficacy and self-esteem is likely to be complex. For example, when Di Giunta *et al.* (2013) looked at the relationship between self-esteem, self-efficacy and academic performance among Italian schoolchildren they suggested that although self-efficacy was one of many factors which contributed to self-esteem, the relationship between self-esteem and academic performance was entirely mediated by self-efficacy. What all this suggests is that self-efficacy, and not self-esteem, is the concept that should be of the greatest interest to educators in terms of understanding the learning of their students.

We can see then that, in addition to affecting how we approach social learning, self-efficacy has been found to interact with many different kinds of learning in a wide variety of contexts. Levels of self-efficacy appear to predict how we engage in a variety of academic behaviours from essay writing to participating in classroom discussions. For example, Adetimirin (2015) found that self-efficacy in computer use was a significant predictor of postgraduate students' use of course-related online discussion forums. Self-efficacy can be a factor before the course has even begun, with Britner and Pajares (2006) finding that lower levels of enrolment by female students in science courses was predicted by lower levels of science self-efficacy in female students compared to male students (see Chapter 7 for a discussion on factors like self-efficacy and gendered subjects explaining such apparent gender differences in education). The effects of self-efficacy on learning are not limited to the students. For example, Bandura *et al.* (1996) found that levels of parental self-efficacy in their ability to support their children's academic development had an impact on the aspirations of those children.

The level of self-efficacy we have in relation to a given ability is likely to be a product of a number of factors; chief among them are previous personal success, social learning from the successes of others, and emotional states, as well as encouragement and feedback from others (Bandura, 1994). The relationship between self-efficacy and the last of these, feedback, is perhaps the most complex. Unsurprisingly, feedback has been found to have an impact on self-efficacy, with feedback from parents and teachers in relation to a subject having a significant influence on a student's level of self-efficacy in that subject (Bandura, 1994; Walker, 2005). What makes the relationship more complex is that it may well be reciprocal: feedback may influence self-efficacy but surprisingly self-efficacy may affect feedback by affecting the way we engage with it. The feedback itself may not change, but as Garcia (1995) found out, students may interpret feedback in such a way as maintain positive self-efficacy. For example, a student might attribute a poor mark as being the result of tutor bias rather than their own poor performance on the assessment and thus be less likely to engage with the feedback that tutor provides (Carless, 2006). Research by Young (2000) found that even when they did engage with the feedback, the student's level of self-efficacy changed how they interpreted it. Students with higher self-efficacy saw the feedback as focused on the work, helpful, constructive and so motivational, whereas students with lower self-efficacy were likely to see the feedback as aimed at them personally, critical and so de-motivational.

In conclusion, with the addition of the concept of self-efficacy, social learning theory makes a clean break with the radical functionalism of classical and operant conditioning. Self-efficacy is an important mental structure/concept which mediates between observing a behaviour and demonstrating social learning by putting that behaviour into practice. Moreover, self-efficacy is a concept whose relevance has been found to extend far beyond social learning alone and instead can be applied to a large variety of learning situations and educational contexts.

Conclusion

In summary, we can see now how behaviourism and the theories associated with it have a lot more to offer in terms of helping us to understand and influence learning than classroom management alone. We gained a fresh perspective on the pioneering work of Pavlov, Thorndike, Watson and Skinner and those that followed them. Between them, they established educational psychology as a field of scientific study, developing applied theories which both inform and are informed by practice. We saw how even the familiar principles of operant conditioning can be given a new spin through their application in token economies and effective rewards. We also saw how the traditional behaviourist model of learning became a social learning model by adding a social dimension, connecting with research on social understanding and reintroducing mental concepts like self-efficacy in order to broaden the model's scope of relevance in education. Ultimately, we see that at its heart the behaviourist model is an applied model and that the core purpose of behaviourism is, and has always been, to enable educators to better understand and positively influence the education of others.

Key points

- Behaviourism believes that all learning can be characterised as changes in our behaviour which can be explained through the study of that behaviour and the manner in which it interacts with the environment.
- Watson and Thorndike made important contributions to psychology by establishing the fields of behaviourism and educational psychology respectively.
- Classical conditioning believes that learning occurs through associating new stimuli with existing stimulus–response pairs, whereas operant conditioning believes learning occurs through the reinforcement or punishment that occurs as an outcome of behaviour.
- The principles of operant conditioning can be used to promote learning through token economies and gamification.
- Social learning theory established that it was possible to learn vicariously by observing the outcome of behaviour by significant others known as role models.

- Self-efficacy describes our level of self-confidence in relation to specific abilities and is an important factor in explaining levels of social learning and other aspects of education.

Recommended readings

Bandura, A., Ross, D. and Ross, S.A. (1961) Transmission of aggression through imitation of aggressive models. *Journal of Abnormal and Social Psychology*, **63**(3), pp. 575–582.

Dweck, C.S. (2007) The perils and promises of praise: Educational leadership. *Early Intervention at Every Age*, **65**(2), pp. 34–39.

Thorndike, E.L. (1910) The contribution of psychology to education. *Journal of Educational Psychology*, **1**, pp. 5–12.

References

Adetimirin, A. (2015) An empirical study of online discussion forums by library and information science post-graduate students using Technology Acceptance Model 3. *Journal of Information Technology Education: Research*, **14**, pp. 257–269.

Bandura, A. (1965) Influence of models' reinforcement contingencies on the acquisition of imitative response. *Journal of Personality and Social Psychology*, **1**, pp. 589–595.

Bandura, A. (1986) *Social foundations of thought and action: A social cognitive theory.* Englewood Cliffs: Prentice-Hall.

Bandura, A. (1994) Self-efficacy. In V.S. Ramachaudran (ed.) *Encyclopedia of human behavior.* Vol. **4**. New York: Academic Press.

Bandura, A. (1999) A social cognitive theory of personality. In L. Pervin and O. John (eds) *Handbook of personality.* 2nd edn. New York: Guilford Press.

Bandura, A. (2006) Guide for constructing self-efficacy scales. In T. Urdan and F. Pajares (eds) *Self-efficacy beliefs of adolescents.* Greenwich, CT: Information Age Publishing.

Bandura, A., Barbaranelli, C., Caprara, G.V. and Pastorelli, C. (1996) Multifaceted impact of self-efficacy beliefs on academic functioning. *Child Development*, **67**, pp. 1206–1222.

Bandura, A., Ross, D. and Ross, S.A. (1961) Transmission of aggression through imitation of aggressive models. *Journal of Abnormal and Social Psychology*, **63**(3), pp. 575–582.

Beck, H.P., Levinson, S. and Irons, G. (2009) Finding Little Albert: A journey to John B. Watson's infant laboratory. *American Psychologist*, **64**, pp. 605–614.

Behne, T., Carpenter, M., Call, J. and Tomasello, M. (2005) Unwilling versus unable: Infants' understanding of intentional action. *Developmental Psychology*, **41**, pp. 328–337.

Bloom, B.S. (ed.) (1956) *Taxonomy of educational objectives, Handbook 1: The cognitive domain.* New York: McKay.

Britner, S.L. and Pajares, F. (2006) Sources of science self-efficacy beliefs of middle school students. *Journal of Research in Science Teaching*, **43**(5), pp. 485–499.

Byron, T. (2008) *Safer children in a digital world: A report of the Byron review.* http://webarchive.nationalarchives.gov.uk/20120106161038/https://www.education.gov.uk/publications/standard/publicationDetail/Page1/DCSF-00334–2008 (Accessed 31 May 2017).

Carless, D. (2006) Differing perceptions in the feedback process. *Studies in Higher Education*, **31**(2), pp. 219–233.

Carpenter, M., Nagell, K. and Tomasello, M. (1998) Social cognition, joint attention, and communicative competence from 9 to 15 months of age. *Monographs for the Society of Research in Development*, **63**(4), pp. 1–174.

Chance, P. (2006) *First course in applied behavior analysis.* Long Grove, IL: Waveland Publishing.

Chomsky, N. (1980) *Rules and representations.* New York/Oxford: Columbia University Press/Blackwell.

Di Giunta, L., Alessandri, G., Gerbino, M., Kanacri, P.L., Zuffiano, A. and Caprara, G.V. (2013) The determinants of scholastic achievement: The contribution of personality traits, self-esteem, and academic self-efficacy. *Learning and Individual Differences*, **27**, pp. 102–108.

Dichev, C. and Dicheva, D. (2017) Gamifying education: What is known, what is believed and what remains uncertain: A critical review. *International Journal of Educational Technology in Higher Education*, **14**(9). doi:10.1186/s41239–017–0042–5.

Doll, C., McLaughlin, T.F. and Barretto, A. (2013) The token economy: A recent review and evaluation. *International Journal of Basic and Applied Science*, **2**(1), pp. 131–149.

Dweck, C.S. (2007) The perils and promises of praise: Educational leadership. *Early Intervention at Every Age*, **65**(2), pp. 34–39.

Garcia, T. (1995) The role of motivational strategies in self-regulated learning. In P.R. Pintrich (ed.) *Understanding self-regulated learning*. San Francisco: Jossey-Bass.

Gergely, G., Bekkering, H. and Király, I. (2002) Rational imitation in preverbal infants. *Nature*, 415, 755. doi:10.1038/415755a.

Gerrig, R.J., Zimbardo, P., Svartdal, F., Brennen, T., Donaldson, R. and Archer, T. (2012) *Psychology and life*. Harlow: Pearson.

Gewirtz, J.B. (2001) Watson's approach to learning: Why Pavlov? Why not Thorndike? *Behavioural Development Bulletin*, **1**, pp. 23–25.

Guthrie, E.R. (1930) Conditioning as a principle of learning. *Psychological Review*, **37**(5), pp. 412–428.

Harris, B. (1979) Whatever happened to Little Albert? *American Psychologist*, **34**, pp. 151–160.

Herd, S., Mingus, B. and O'Reilly, R. (2010) Dopamine and self-directed learning. In *Proceedings of the 2010 conference on Biologically Inspired Cognitive Architectures*. First Annual Meeting of the BICA Society. Amsterdam: IOS Press.

Hilgard, E.R. and Marquis, D.G. (1940) *Conditioning and learning*. New York: Appleton-Century.

Kazdin, A.E. (1977) *The token economy: A review and evaluation*. New York: Plenum Press.

Mandler, G. (2011) *A history of modern experimental psychology: From James and Wundt to cognitive science*. Cambridge, MA: MIT Press.

McGoey, K.E. and DuPaul, G.J. (2000) Token reinforcement and response cost procedures: Reducing the disruptive behavior of preschool children with attention-deficit/hyperactivity disorder. *School Psychology Quarterly*, **15**, pp. 330–343.

McLaughlin, T.F. and Williams, R.L. (1988) The token economy in the classroom. In J.C. Witt, S.N. Elliot and F.M. Gresham (eds) *Handbook of behavior therapy in education*. New York: Plenum.

Miller, P.M. and Drennen, W.T. (1970) Establishment of social reinforcement as an effective modifier of verbal behavior in chronic psychiatric patients. *Journal of Abnormal Psychology*, **76**, pp. 392–395.

O'Leary, K.D. and O'Leary, S. (eds) (1977) *Classroom management: The successful use of behaviour modification*. 2nd edn. Elmsford, NY: Pergamon.

Pavlov, I.P. (1927) *Conditioned reflexes*. London: Oxford University Press

Powell, R.A., Digdon, N., Harris, B. and Smithson, C. (2014) Correcting the record on Watson, Rayner, and Little Albert: Albert Barger as 'Psychology's lost boy'. *American Psychologist*, **69**(6), pp. 600–611.

Samelson, F. (1980) J.B. Watson's Little Albert, Cyril Burt's twins, and the need for a critical science. *American Psychologist*, **35**, pp. 619–625.

Sears, D.A. and Pai, H. (2012) Effects of cooperative versus individual study on learning and motivation after reward-removal. *Journal of Experimental Education*, **80**(3), pp. 246–262.

Skinner, B.F. (1938) *Behavior of organisms*. New York: Appleton-Century-Croft.

Skinner, B.F. (1953) *Science and human behavior*. New York: Macmillan.

Snyder, M. (1984) When belief creates reality. In L. Berkowitz (ed.) *Advances in experimental social psychology*. Vol. **18**. New York: Academic Press.

Thorndike, E.L. (1906) *Principles of teaching based on psychology*. New York: Seiler.

Thorndike, E.L. (1910) The contribution of psychology to education. *Journal of Educational Psychology*, **1**, pp. 5–12.

Thorndike, E.I. (1932) *The fundamentals of learning*. New York: Teachers College Press.

Thorndike, E.I. and Woodworth, R.S. (1901) The influence of improvement in one mental function upon the efficiency of the other function. *Psychological Review*, **8**, pp. 247–261.

Tomasello, M. and Carpenter, M. (2007) Shared intentionality. *Developmental Science*, **10**(1), pp. 121–125.

Walker, C. (2005) Reflective teaching in post compulsory education: Casting wide the net but coming up short. *Higher Education Review*, **38**(1), pp. 68–89.

Watson, J.B. (1903) *Animal education: An experimental study on the psychical development of the white rat, correlated with the growth of its nervous system*. Chicago: University of Chicago Press.

Watson, J.B. (1913) Psychology as the behaviorist views it. *Psychological Review*, **20**, pp. 158–177.

Watson, J.B. (1916) The place of the conditioned reflex in psychology. *Psychological Review*, **23**, pp. 89–116.

Watson, J.B. and Rayner, R. (1920) Conditioned emotional reaction. *Journal of Experimental Psychology*, **3**, pp. 1–14.

Yerkes, R.M. and Morgulis, S. (1909) The method of Pavlov in animal psychology. *Psychological Bulletin*, **6**, pp. 257–273.

Young, P. (2000) I might as well give up: Self-esteem and mature students' feelings about feedback on assignments. *Journal of Further and Higher Education*, **24**(3), pp. 409–442.

10 Learning as a shared process

Vygotsky and the socio-cultural theories of learning

Catherine O'Connell

Introduction

When we talk about the development or use of mental processes like memory, decision-making and problem-solving we tend to think of these things as located within each individual. Socio-cultural theories in psychology ask us to reconsider this viewpoint and show us that our cognition is not just influenced by other people; it's actually a shared process that takes place among the group rather within each individual. In a sense, it is suggesting that we don't make decisions and learn as individuals, we make decisions and learn as a group.

As an illustration of the way the socio-cultural context shapes individual actions, Holland and Skinner (Holland *et al.*, 1998) describe a startling incident during their ethnographic study of cultural practices of the Naudada community in rural Nepal. Debra Skinner had invited one of the community members, a 50-year-old woman, to come to the house where she was staying to participate in an interview. Located on the first floor, the room where the interview would take place was accessible only through the kitchen. Within local cultural norms, a community member of lower social standing would not normally be permitted in this part of the house. The response of the woman (of a lower caste than the house-owner) was to climb up the wall of the house and over the balcony. In this example, we see a woman solving a problem (a cognitive process) and her solution, while it may seem strange to us in our cultural context, makes complete sense within the woman's own cultural context. In fact, her solution only makes sense when you think of it as the right solution for her as part of a larger socio-cultural group. Holland and Skinner emphasise the significance of the woman's unusual improvisation and emphasise the importance of examining human action in relation to its cultural context.

> ### Reflections
>
> As a researcher, what research questions and methods would be of particular interest to develop a fuller understanding of the woman's action?

In this chapter, we will examine some of the reasons why this 'socio-cultural' perspective is gaining increasing attention as a way of understanding learning and education. Our exploration of the socio-cultural viewpoint will begin with one of the best known theorists in the area, Lev Vygotsky. We will look at key elements of his theoretical framework and show how it has contributed to further branches of socio-cultural theory in psychology. Alongside Vygotsky we will also explore the work of Engeström and his collaborators, whose 'activity systems theory' (AST) model seeks to expand on the Vygotskian perspective that learning is mediated by cultural tools and resources. The AST model aims to show us how collective goals, divisions of labour and social rules can all shape our learning. In this way, they draw attention to the broader societal system that provides the context and conditions of our own learning experiences. Toward the end of this chapter, we will turn to the 'figured worlds' theory proposed by Holland *et al.* (1998) who focus on different social contexts of education and the identities associated with these contexts. We will explore the way particular cultural practices and tools that exist within a specific context both enable and constrain learning activity and shape learner identities in that context. Ultimately, I aim to demonstrate that if we hope to understand the thinking of any learner we must view that learner and their cognitive processes through the lens of their cultural context.

Vygotsky's perspective on learning

Vygotsky in context

It is important to locate Vygotsky historically and culturally in order to give insight into some of the influences on his work. Although more widely known than many other socio-cultural theorists, Lev Vygotsky (1896–1934) is often presented in introductory texts as a counterpoint to Piaget rather than a fully fleshed out theorist with a fundamentally different view on the nature of cognition. (See Chapter 9 for more on Piaget and his theories.) Vygotsky is widely credited with introducing a new approach to both theorising and researching about learning which draws attention to the social and cultural context of learning and the way this context interacts with individual cognition.

Psychology, as a discipline, addresses a broad range of questions relating to mind and behaviour. The theoretical and empirical approach to these broad matters of mind and behaviour is framed differently by the behaviourist and cognitive traditions within psychology. There is a tendency in the behaviourist approach to limit itself to considering behaviour alone, dismissing the study of the mind as unscientific and thus irrelevant. (See Chapter 3 for a more critical discussion of this part of the behaviourist model.) By contrast, the cognitive paradigm, which has been a mainstay of psychological research in recent decades, studies the mind extensively, seeking to better understand those mental process which are seen as key elements of what most people would call 'thinking' (e.g. attention, memory, problem-solving). From the mainstream cognitive perspective though, the mind (or human cognition) is conceptualised as being entirely the property of the individual. However, from the socio-cultural perspective, exemplified in Vygotsky's work, the mind is conceptualised as a combination of individual and social processes. From this theoretical standpoint, individual cognition is not separable analytically from the social and cultural context.

The psychological research conducted in these different traditions tends to contribute to our understanding of education in different ways. There are those studies that attempt to understand learning in terms of individual acquisition processes (such as perception, attention, memory, imitation) and then there are those which view learning as an interactional process, learners and teachers producing learning through interacting with each other (Illeris, 2007). The mainstream cognitive research tradition has tended to focus on the 'individual' approach, seeking to understand the constituent processes of knowledge acquisition and particular forms of learning which are implicit and informal. Within this mainstream cognitive tradition, the developmental cognitivist perspective (as reflected in Piaget's work) investigates the key periods or phases in which cognitive capacities develop within the individual. In research like this, the role of education is of secondary interest; the primary goal of the research is to identify universal patterns in human development.

Vygotsky's research orientation can be located at the interactional end of this spectrum, as his perspective conceptualises human cognition primarily in social (rather than individual) and cultural terms (Kozulin, 2003). Consequently, this perspective reflects an explicit interest in education and the role of instruction. As an educational scholar and practitioner working during the Soviet political and economic regime, his work was both influenced and constrained by the political and social context of the time. During a period when the behaviourist paradigm was predominant in psychology, the conceptual ideas he proposed were radical and challenging, both politically and to the norms of the discipline

Through a programme of theoretical and empirical work, Vygotsky formulated some central ideas on both the nature of learning through an emphasis on concept acquisition and on the processes of learning through a focus on tools and symbolic mediators. Moreover, the ideas were developed through a particular set of methods which presented a different way of examining mind and behaviour from existing psychological research traditions. Vygotsky's research focused largely on play and academic learning. The primary focus was upon interactions between the learner and the instructor in the immediate learning context, and on the nature of that interaction. As such, the focus of Vygotsky's empirical work is seen to give greater priority to instructor-led learning and consequently is criticised in some quarters for representing education as a relatively 'friction-free' process of cultural transmission from instructor to learner (Illeris, 2007). This theoretical and empirical focus is regarded as a limitation of the theory, in its neglect of the broader institutional framework in which education takes place. As we shall see later in the chapter, more recent theorists have extended Vygotsky's theoretical framework to give more focus to the societal and political contexts of education.

Vygotsky's concept of the zone of proximal development

Of all Vygotsky's theoretical ideas, the 'zone of proximal development' (ZPD) is probably the one that is best known among educators. It is commonly defined, in introductory psychology texts, as the difference between what a learner can do without external assistance and what they can do with external assistance. Through the concept of 'zone of proximal development' Vygotsky draws attention to the socially-situated context of learning. The ZPD is actually the relationship between two zones of development, the 'objective' zone and the 'subjective' zone. The objective zone represents all those cultural tools (abilities and knowledge) which might be expected of a learner of that age, as determined by institutional demands and the social and historical context (Chaiklin, 2003). For example, a school-age child is expected to have mastered various stages of literacy and numeracy by certain ages. The zone of proximal development is conceptualised then as the relationship between this 'objective' zone and the individual's 'subjective' zone, which is their current level of mastery of these cultural tools. As such, the ZPD is a diagnostic means of establishing the learning potential of the individual as determined through interaction with an instructor. In that sense, through the support of their instructor the student should be able to master all those cultural tools in their 'objective' zone which aren't already part of their 'subjective' zone. The purpose of learning, therefore, is to support the acquisition of conceptual and symbolic tools that make higher level forms of understanding possible (Kozulin, 2003: 5). Thus, Vygotsky presents us with a key claim of his model of education: that 'learning is a necessary and universal aspect of the process of developing culturally organized, specifically human psychological function' (1978: 90). From this perspective, learning drives development. It contrasts strongly with Piaget who believed that development occurred independently of learning and that learning abilities were unlocked by reaching developmental stages.

Researchers and practitioners have highlighted several conceptual and practical challenges in applying the concept of the ZPD. On the one hand, there are concerns that it can be misinterpreted as endorsing a form of entirely teacher-centred instruction, where the teacher's choices regarding how they support the learner will determine what the student learns (Illeris, 2007). One the other hand, Vygotskian theory has also been misinterpreted as endorsing an entirely student-centred form of learning, where all viewpoints which exist within the ZPD are equally valid and so the teacher should avoid correcting the students or directing their learning. If true, this approach would pose some serious dilemmas for teachers in meeting the demands of a prescribed curriculum (Derry, 2013). Instead, Derry would argue that neither extreme fully reflects the broader facets of Vygotsky's theory. A more accurate representation of Vygotskian theory lies somewhere in the middle, but achieving that middle ground is by no means easy. Derry (2013) illustrates the difficulties in achieving this balance in an example which occurred in the context of a secondary-level maths lesson. In this case study, Derry (2013: 55) describes the experience of a teacher working with two 11-year-old boys looking at diagrammatic representation of triangles which include shapes with right-angled triangles and scalene triangles. One of the boys dismisses the second example as 'not being a triangle'. The teacher was then faced with the dilemma of whether to respond and explore the boy's conception of triangle or to address the misconception, emphasising the relevant field of knowledge of Euclidian geometry. Derry would argue that to fully reflect the broader facets of Vygotsky's ZPD theory the teacher should acknowledge the student's current view as a starting point but then introduce them to the Euclidian interpretation and the contributions of the mathematical community to the ZPD on questions such as this.

The Vygotskian perspective on cognition, as demonstrated in the ZPD, draws significant attention to the impact of the external environment on the learner, and for this reason can be seen as a deterministic view of human development (Woolfolk Hoy, 2013). However, it is important to note that, to Vygotsky, learning is not a one-way process of cultural shaping of the individual. His empirical work focused also on ways that children create their own 'cultural tools' to enable their learning and performance. Rather than viewing the learner as an 'object' to be filled with knowledge, this socio-cultural perspective represents the learner as the agent and society as the mediator of learning activity (Williams, 2012: 83). From this standpoint, the potential always exists for change and transformation in both the learner and the context as well.

In conclusion, we can see that Vygotsky provides a new metaphor of 'learning as mediation' which draws attention to the ways in which learning is influenced by the external environment. In contrast to the prevailing behavioural and cognitive perspectives which share an orientation towards the biological basis of behaviour, Vygotsky emphasised the way in which human behaviour is culturally shaped. From this perspective, it does not make sense to separate learning from environmental context analytically. Through the concept of the ZPD, in emphasising how the objective zone is shaped by local culture and context, Vygotsky is proposing that there is no single biologically-determined, universally appropriate way to learn (Engeström and Sannino, 2012). The theory, therefore, draws particular attention to the context of learning and the strategies which enable it. In order to better understand how our context can shape our learning as well as the strategies we use, we can turn to another important element of Vygotskian theory, namely his explanation of the way in which we acquire new concepts, also known as 'conceptual learning'.

Vygotsky's emphasis on conceptual learning

For Vygotsky, there is no such thing as pure thought. Development of higher-level conceptual understanding is not just a matter of biological maturation but relies on the mastery of culturally-created tools (Wells and Claxton, 2002). From this perspective, physical and symbolic tools (including language) are important mediators of learning and development. Through his research studies, Vygotsky characterised the way we draw on tools in the external environment to develop our own cognitive processes. These tools, physical or symbolic, may vary in different cultures. Literacy and number systems are examples of culturally produced tools.

In his empirical research, Vygotsky (1978) was interested in the processes by which we acquire higher-level conceptual understanding of various concepts, scientific concepts in particular. Vygotsky drew a distinction between everyday concepts that we develop through direct experience (e.g. the concept of a 'cat') and scientific concepts that are more distant from our everyday experience (e.g. the concept of a 'prime number'). The concept of a prime number does not arise spontaneously; it requires a process of formal instruction. The ability to acquire concepts represents a higher-level cognitive ability: the ability to create abstract representations and to internalise our understanding of these representations in ways that can be applied in new contexts. In this way, Vygotsky sees learned concepts not just as propositional and abstract knowledge (i.e. facts) but as conceptual tools which can be used to mediate further understanding. Bakhurst (2015) explains the idea of scientific concepts through the metaphor of using a map to understand our surrounding environment. The map is an abstract representation of key features of the environment. However, the real value of the map is that it enables us to look more closely at salient features (i.e. places and objects) in the environment and to gain a deeper understanding of the relations between those features. Thus, once we have represented the environment as a map we can use that map to better understand the environment. Similarly, once we have acquired scientific concepts which can be used to represent the world around us we can use those concepts to better understand that world.

Conceptual learning forms a significant part of formal education. Vygotsky was critical of the general field of psychology for a lack of attention to the processes by which scientific concepts are acquired and the instructional processes which can facilitate such concept acquisition (1978: 366). The implication from the socio-cultural perspective is that education has a key role in helping learners to acquire and become proficient in the use of tools (including conceptual ones). Socio-cultural theorists have given significant attention to the ways conceptual learning can be achieved. Subsequent research addressing conceptual learning has highlighted the need for a systematic approach to support concept acquisition. Increasingly, there is a recognised need for an appropriate educational approach to such learning, where learning about scientific concepts is linked to learning about the way those concepts are used. The Vygotskian perspective cautions against a piecemeal approach of exposure to isolated pieces of information (such as individual rules and facts), but rather encourages the integration of new forms of knowledge to broader conceptual frameworks and the identification of ways of using new knowledge in different contexts. An example of such an orientation applied to elementary mathematics instruction would involve an initial educational focus on how numerical systems have evolved historically and in relation to particular forms of activity such as their use in engineering or commerce. Through this emphasis on the uses of mathematical tools for meaningful practices and practical tasks, students gain a deeper conceptual understanding of number systems, including how they can use those systems to better understand the world around them (Stetsenko and Vianna, 2009).

Because Vygotsky talks a lot about scientific concepts in his theories on conceptual learning, some critics believe he is a rationalist, someone who thinks we can make sense of the world in purely abstract ways without considering context. Derry (2013) disagrees and suggests such viewpoints misunderstand Vygotsky. She emphasises the need for a deeper understanding of the philosophical foundations of Vygotsky's ideas, which Vygotsky attributes to Spinoza and Hegel. Far from having a decontextualised view of abstract rationality, Vygotsky's conception of scientific concepts is one that is derived and developed through environmental interaction:

> Thus, the concept does not arise from this as a mechanical process of abstraction – it is the result of a long and deep knowledge of the object … Psychological research is disclosing that in a concept we always have an enrichment and deepening of the content that the concept contains.

> (Vygotsky, 1998: 54)

In conclusion, what we can see from this exploration of Vygotsky's views on conceptual learning is that more than any other branch of psychology of the time, Vygotsky's approach sought to understand how and why educational instruction could and should support this kind of learning. Through his empirical work, Vygotsky drew considerable attention to the processes that enable concept formation and, as we shall see in the next section, proposed a new scientific method to investigate these processes.

Vygotskian methodology

Drawing on Marx's philosophy, which proposes that human nature is shaped by the prevailing social conditions, Vygotsky is identified as the first scholar to pursue this perspective within the discipline of psychology (Cole and Scribner, 1978). This perspective rests on a different philosophical stance from traditional cognitive theory. It rejects the so-called 'Cartesian idea' underpinning much philosophical and psychological thought that mind and body are analytically separable entities. Instead, it saw the body, which in Vygotskian theory is represented by the person located in their social context, as an extension of the mind. (See Chapter 5 for a discussion on a similar perspective based on the concept of embodiment.) Also, by proposing the use of conceptual tools as cultural mediators, Vygotsky is regarded as offering a new formulation of psychological research on cognition, which is more culturally than biologically defined. These novel conceptualisations represented a significant break from traditional thinking of the time and were accompanied by a similarly different approach to conducting research in this area of psychology.

Vygotsky favoured a naturalistic form of empirical observation which drew attention to the way learners use a range of cultural tools. These cultural tools are often obscured within patterns of habitual and skilled behaviour, so Vygotsky employed particular techniques of disruption to help make these processes more visible through the use of more demanding and novel tasks. In studying children's language development, for example, Vygotsky created situations where children had to co-operate in activities with others who did not speak the same language (e.g. foreign-language-speaking and deaf children). In other studies, Vygotsky provided a range of different tools with which to solve problems in order to observe the different uses of the tools by children of different ages in in different task conditions (Cole and Scribner, 1978).

Inspired by the historical materialism proposed by Marx, Vygotsky has contributed significantly to a field of educational research which embraces a socio-material approach (Fenwick *et al.*, 2011) and a unit of analysis which examines individual action in the broader cultural and historical context. In this approach to research there is a particular emphasis on naturalistic and qualitative methods (e.g. ethnographic and participant observation) due to the theoretical focus on how social practices are shaped by culture. An example of this would be the use of documentary analysis to identify the origins of classroom procedures (Fenwick *et al.*, 2011). Vygotsky's work has stimulated diverse areas of research, and the conceptual ideas have been further developed, modified, contested and extended. There is also, as we shall see later in this chapter, a significant interest in interventionist methodologies.

Developments in Vygotskian theory

The penetration of Vygotsky's ideas into mainstream educational research and practice has been observed in a series of waves which is, in part, due to constraints on accessing his work due to the political isolation of the Soviet regime and the sporadic translation of his work into English. However, due to the many challenges present in contemporary educational environments, such as the need to support equitable learning in multicultural contexts, effectively integrating technology and achieving fit-for-purpose testing, his work is achieving a greater profile and resonance today (Kozulin, 2003).

Vygotsky's original research centred primarily on learning processes in formal educational environments. Since their publication, there has been a significant interest in applying his theoretical ideas to the types of learning that occur beyond formal instruction. Over the past 40 years a broad field of research has developed, inspired by Vygotskian ideas, and labelled within the broad term of Cultural Historical Activity theory ('CHAT'). Research in this area has led to significant development, reformulation and expansion of Vygotsky's original theories in different domains and contexts. Although broad and diverse, as shall be seen in two branches of this area examined below, all of these new approaches have been inspired by Vygotsky's socio-cultural approach and employ many of the concepts he pioneered. This includes a desire to contextualise educational practices historically, to focus on the functions of cultural and symbolic tools within educational processes, and to examine the cultural practices which surround the learner. However, these developments of Vygotskian theory add to socio-cultural theory by drawing greater attention to the broader social context in which learning takes place.

Activity systems theory

Following his untimely death at the age of 37, a number of Vygotsky's close colleagues and collaborators went on to elaborate and empirically investigate the culturally-mediated aspects of
complex, collective activity. In what is described commonly as the second generation of socio-
cultural theory, Leontiev played a significant role in expanding the level of analysis from the individual
to community, particularly in respect to the issue of motivation. Leontiev argues that there is no
activity without an object and that the object provides a motivating force for the activity. However,
Leontiev (1978) also distinguished between the goal-oriented motivations of individuals and the
object-oriented motivations of the collective. This perspective helps us to see that the motives,
intentions and goals of individuals only make sense when we consider the broader activity and
motivation of their social group as a whole.

Leontiev demonstrated the value of this perspective with the historical example of the organisation of a primeval tribe in the context of hunting. In such a context, the role of one of the hunters
is to beat the bushes in order to frighten the animals and drive them towards the group of catch-
ers. This individual action only makes sense in relation to the broader social formation of activity in
which other members of the hunt have their specific roles as well. In this context, all participants
are engaged in the shared object of hunting game and are participating in a complex activity
involving a division of labour, which in turn is reliant on particular types of role specialisation within
the broader community. We can translate these principles to a contemporary education setting.
Thus, to understand the organisation and behaviour of staff in a contemporary school in relation to
standardised testing, we need to understand not only goals of the individuals but also the object or
'purpose' of testing as far as the school is concerned. Of course, to understand the purpose of
testing from the school's perspective it may also be necessary to consider the purpose of education itself in the broader social and historical context (Fenwick *et al.*, 2011).

The point of an activity systems analysis, therefore, is to identify the object orientation of the
collective. From this broader perspective, collective activity is the appropriate unit of analysis
rather than individual plans, motives and goals. This perspective has been further developed by
Yrgo Engeström and collaborators through a programme of research over the past 30 years
known as 'activity systems theory' (AST). The theory views individual human action as being
embedded in collectively organised, artefact-mediated activity systems. Through a more developed
and systematic modelling of the surrounding activity systems (including community, division of
labour and the rules mediating the activity), Engeström aims to provide an explanation for the
durability of some forms of individual activity. AST also directs attention to the tensions and contradictions which can build up in activity systems over time, as well as considering the difficulties
faced by the individual alternating between two activity systems with very different objects or
purposes.

Applications of AST in education

For education practitioners and researchers, the AST model can be very useful when investigating
issues in education in varied contexts, including inter-professional learning, early-years education,
and in specific curriculum areas. This way of researching the teaching-learning environment highlights the extent to which the objects of activity are aligned (or mis-aligned) for different groups.

The AST model has been used by researchers in educational settings to unpick the mix of different activities which take place in a single context as students and teachers pursue different objects. By making these differences in the object of pursuit more explicit, AST research helps to identify particular tensions and contradictions within a context as well as identifying obstacles in transferring learning across contexts.

Applying this AST model in the context of a nursery setting, Hakkarainen (1999) found that the object of a play activity differs for young children and their day care staff. Children constructed the object of their play as a collaborative endeavour, whereas staff oriented and prioritised their interventions towards individual play skills. This research perspective has also been applied to studies in the higher education context. Solomon *et al.* (2014) drew on the AST model as a means to explore issues surrounding collaborative learning involving mathematics undergraduates where higher than expected failure rates were occurring. Prior research had demonstrated inherent problems in undergraduate mathematics teaching. Solomon *et al.* drew on AST concepts to articulate the different objects of the collaborative learning activity for staff and students. For the academic staff the object of the activity was the transmission of knowledge, changing the learner or meeting institutional requirements. For the students the object of the activity was the acquisition of discipline knowledge and gaining academic credit. The results of the analysis were then used to promote dialogue between staff and students and to encourage reconceptualisation of their different objects into one shared object. In addition to looking at conflicts within existing systems, AST has been used to examine the way organisations respond to the introduction of new cultural tools. An example of this is the introduction of university ranking systems, where research by O'Connell showed how the introduction of this new type of artefact into the HE context created new tensions and contradictions between individual and collective motivations (O'Connell and Saunders, 2013; O'Connell, 2015). This suggested the need for opportunities for reconceptualisation among the staff similar to those described by Solomon *et al.* in their study.

In addition to its use in resolving obstacles to learning within a single context, the AST model has also been used to examine obstacles to the transfer of learning from one context to another. Williams and Wakefield (2007) used the model to better understand the particular difficulties of learning-transfer for undergraduate mathematics students when they were on work placements. The study highlighted the different conventions of graphical representation used in academic and workplace environments which reflected the differing historical and social objectives for these conceptual tools in the two different contexts. The research highlighted the need to make explicit to the students how these mathematical tools are products of different social practices with different object orientations in each context. Williams and Wakefield suggested that doing this would help support students in their ability to make sense of these tools and, as they move into new contexts, assist them in re-aligning their individual goals with the object goals of their new collective.

Research focus: reconceptualising different objects into a shared object in an interagency working project

In their work with groups of interagency professionals in a 'children's services' setting, Daniels *et al.* (2010) offer a good example of what is actually required to achieve the reconceptualisation of different objects into a shared object. Their project, titled 'Learning in and for interagency working' (LIW), sought to support education and social care professionals in identifying new ways of working together to meet complex and diverse client needs in a safeguarding context. The project's main objective was to identify points of tension and contradiction in existing work patterns of the different professional groups and to develop a collective understanding of the ways in which the tensions were a product of historical formation of the activity. The aim of the project was to act as a basis for the community of practitioners to engage in dialogue in order to redefine a shared object. To achieve this aim, the education and social care professionals involved were guided through a series of workshops where a problem was identified, and they were provided with tools with which to solve the problem or means by which they could construct tools with which to solve the problem.

In the initial workshops, working practices of team members were discussed. Tensions and dilemmas were highlighted and alternative ways of working were proposed. One way of interrogating practice was for a practitioner to be invited to present a case based on a child who had been supported by these different groups of professionals. The purpose of such activities was to discuss the differing objects of professional activity for the different groups.

Later workshops were aimed at identifying how expertise was distributed across diverse specialisms and professional groupings. This drew attention to the ways in which expertise was claimed, owned and shared. This process helped to highlight problematic areas where there was a need to work more collaboratively to co-ordinate efforts around the child's case.

Finally, through the use of developmental workshops, the historical boundaries between the school team and other professional groupings were weakened. Many structural changes were implemented. Participants identified ways of mediating the effects of legacy rules which had constrained different professional groups from working collaboratively. The development of new objects associated with interagency work emerged as part of the process.

Reflections

Consider the role of the researcher in this context. What is their role in these various workshops? How does this role compare with the role of a researcher in other forms of research you are familiar with?

In conclusion, the development of the AST model gives us a new way of understanding human behaviour in a number of contexts including education. Through AST we can see that education is a collective endeavour which has a shared object, and that we can only understand the behaviour of the individual by first understanding the nature of that shared object. It also tells us that issues can sometimes arise in education when different groups have different objects. Finally, this model presents us with transformational activities that can be used to redefine these shared objects or enable us to adapt our personal goals as we move from one activity system to the next. In the next section we will move away from considering shared motivations and instead considered shared identities and the way that context-defined learner identities can influence the learning process.

Figured worlds

The 'figured worlds' model examines more explicitly the place of the learner identity, acknowledging that learning often relates to the whole person, including their identity. This model was developed through the study of informal learning contexts where there is no curriculum; however, it has become increasingly valued by practitioners and researchers in relation to formal learning environments as well.

The figured worlds model explores how identity is closely interrelated with the social and cultural context. There was already some recognition of this in the original social-cultural theories of Vygotsky and others, where it was recognised that identity is given by the social group but also taken by the individual (Williams, 2012). Thus, social and structural factors can impose particular identities upon us; for example, identities which are determined by formal grade structures (e.g. 'model' student, 'underachieving' student). (See Chapter 7 for a related discussion on gender identity being 'imposed' through society's gender roles.) In the figured worlds model these identities are described as 'positional identities' but they are only one part of the puzzle. The figured worlds model also proposed the concept of 'relational identities' that are formed through the local dynamics between people who all belong to the same context. Thus, an example of a relational identity would be a 'popular' student, since their popularity is a local and subjective phenomenon. From the perspective of figured worlds, both types of identities are a product of culturally-produced 'worlds', social-cultural groups that are defined and shaped by the group's norms, practices and values. If we belong to one of these 'worlds' then we express our identities within that group through the cultural resources and symbols that are available.

Holland *et al.* (1998) develop the figured worlds model through examination of culturally constructed worlds in diverse contexts: for example, the social worlds of Alcoholics Anonymous, of romantic courtly love in the medieval era, and the world of self-care in a mental health context. The research examines how individuals negotiate their identities in these pre-figured worlds of social norms and symbolic practices and specialised discourses. In a sense, the figured worlds model takes the Vygotskian concept of using cultural tools to make sense of the world around us and turns it inwards. This perspective emphasises the dynamic ways in which we engage with cultural tools provided by the socio-cultural worlds we inhabit and use those tools to define ourselves. However, this process is not limited to established 'worlds'. On occasion, in a collective effort with others, we can engage in the making of new worlds of meaning and thus create new spaces for authoring identities.

Holland *et al.* provide us with an example of this model in an educational context in their case study of the social and cultural resources drawn upon to define attractiveness and prestige on an American college campus where women significantly outnumbered men. Through interviews and ethnographic work, the researchers illustrate how men could draw on a broader range of resources to define their identity in a way that enhanced their prestige and perceived attractiveness (e.g. through prestigious positions in campus societies, sporting prowess and through displays of charm and attentiveness). By contrast, academic performance and campus society positions offered little added prestige to a woman's identity in this particular environment. Therefore, the way that male students defined their own attractiveness, an important relational identity, was very different because of perceived differences in the relevant cultural tools that were available to their gender. (See Chapter 7 for further discussion on the impact of gender expectations on both gender identity and experiences in education.) Thus, if we wanted to understand why any one of these students valued a particular symbol of attractiveness, figured worlds theory suggests we need to look at the local culture of the university.

While Holland's study shows how the culture of a figured world might influence the way in which we express our identities, that same culture might even cause us to view certain identities as not relevant to us under any context. Barron (2014) examined an example of this in the way in which identities relating to a religious holiday were negotiated and defined in a kindergarten setting. In an ethnographic study of social and educational practices, in particular those which centred on class craft activities relating to the Eid festival, Barron explored how young children negotiate and make sense of their ethnic and religious identities in relation to the social practices in this setting. In the class activity centred on making Eid celebration cards, a young white British boy responded to a question from the white British researcher about why Eid would not be celebrated in at their home: 'Because we're not dark are we, silly? We'll be having Christmas' (2014: 258). This close-up research demonstrates the complex ways in which even young children recognise which identities are available to them in response to social and educational practices, thus leading them to improvise their own identity from the available cultural resources.

For Holland *et al.* (1998), the figured worlds model provides us with a method of identifying those cultural tools (e.g. routine practices, interactions and identities) which are privileged (i.e. accorded high status) within different learning environments. It also shows how the process can be controlled when there is a collaborative effort to redefine both the cultural tools and their value. In an example of this, Michael *et al.* (2007) demonstrated how teachers and students can work collaboratively to 'figure success' in a US high school which admits a high proportion of students who have been turned away from other high schools. In contrast to the implicit deficit model in the American education system, where students learning English as a second language are disadvantaged through educational norms and testing regimes, the school takes an alternative approach in acknowledging students' cultural and linguistic resources as an asset. The research demonstrates the transformative effect of prioritising students' linguistic and cultural resources as resources for learning and thus promoting the development of positive learner identities in those studying English as a second language.

Research focus: redefining success in a bilingual high school

According to Michael *et al.* (2007), redefining success in the figured world of Gregorio Luperón High School in New York City depended on three things: treating students' Spanish language and literacy proficiency as a resource; relationships of 'authentic caring' between teachers and students, and a discourse of opportunity.

Of the 405 enrolled students, 381 were classified as English Language Learners (ELLs). Ninety-nine per cent of the student body qualified for free lunch. From the moment that students first enrol at Luperón, they receive Spanish instruction in all subject areas as well as instruction in English as a second language (ESL). Spanish is granted a high status. Many of the authority figures in the school (including the principal, more than half of the teaching staff, the office staff, and the custodial staff) were native Spanish speakers. Efforts were made to provide a bilingual aural and print environment. Upon entering the school visitors were greeted by copies of the bilingual school newspaper and weekly and monthly calendars.

The school sought to develop a local culture that repositioned bilingual students as successful. In contrast to the dominant trend, Luperón maintained bilingual education. Set against a broader context in which learners were both linguistically and culturally disadvantaged by traditional tests the school took advantage of the fact that, in the New York area, exams are available in Spanish. More importantly, in the figured world at Luperón, bilingualism was linked with success, and so having Spanish as first language was reimagined as an asset, not a deficit. Through these repositioning strategies, students began to see bilingualism and by extension the Spanish language in terms of their benefits, as this quote illustrates: 'Spanish is the language in which you communicate with your culture. English is like improving oneself. If you don't know English, you're not getting anywhere' (Michael *et al.*, 2007: 176).

Strong, constructive relationships with teachers helped to affirm students' identities as bilingual people and as individuals. Teachers were actively engaged with students, knew them by name, and often grew to know their families. Teachers at Luperón demonstrated authentic caring, in part, through the high standards they held for their students.

Even by conventional measures, Luperón achieves considerable success with its students. The school achieved a 92.4 per cent attendance rate. It has a 10.2 per cent dropout rate, half the rate of comparable schools and less than the national average. The graduation rate of 80 per cent far exceeded the citywide graduation rate. The reason the Luperón approach is so successful can be made clearer if we view it from the figured worlds perspective. Viewed through the figured worlds model, the school is drawing on educational tools and resources which validate the learner's culture and identity and this will, according to figured worlds theory, enable learners to develop a more positive academic identity.

Reflections

What are the implications of Michael *et al.*'s study of the figured world of Gregorio Luperón for education practitioners and policy makers?

Studies like that of Michael *et al.* (2007) show how the figured worlds model can identify the routine practices that can enable or suppress success. The emancipatory concern is to identify cases where particular cultural resources are privileged in ways that exclude some learners. The figured worlds model emphasises the value of cultural modelling so that learners can recognise and use their cultural resources in the classroom, redefining their identity as a learner in the process.

> When students see the validation of their culture and language hence of themselves, in their schooling, they combine their home or community identities within an academic identity.
>
> (Moll, 2010: 456)

As we face increasing cultural and social diversity in almost all aspects of the education system, this approach encourages us to acknowledge these cultural differences. It also offers up examples of 'culturally compatible pedagogies' (Kozulin, 2003) as seen in the Luperón example. Finally, this approach raises questions about any educational policy approaches which promote universalist solutions that seek to suppress or ignore these cultural differences and thus benefit some while disadvantaging others.

Conclusion

Ultimately, this chapter sought to introduce you to the socio-cultural perspective on cognition, namely that cognitive processes are not entirely the property of the individual but are shared between the individual and their socio-cultural context. From the work of Vygotsky and others we have learned that our culture provides us with a selection of conceptual tools with which we make sense of the world around us and ourselves. From the work of Leontiev and Activity Systems Theory (AST) we have learned that individual action only makes sense when considered in light of the collective goal and that conflict can arise when two groups have different goals or when we try and translate our cultural tools from one context to another. Finally, through the work of Holland and others on the figured worlds model we were introduced to the idea that locally defined cultures or worlds provide us with the cultural tools for self-definition, and that possession of a healthy or unhealthy identity can depend on the culture and the tools those worlds provide us.

However, the value of the socio-cultural theories runs deeper than the findings of these specific studies and models. The socio-cultural approach challenges us to see learning as part of a broader social, cultural and historical context rather than separate from it. Bruner cautions against isolating education in our research investigations from the contexts in which it takes place (Bruner, 2009). Jarvis emphasises the need to explore the psychological and sociological aspects of learning in tandem, recognising the 'inter-subjectivity of social living and human learning' (2009: 32). This perspective is particularly compatible with interdisciplinarity, which may be a product of the career trajectories of some of the more influential socio-cultural researchers who hail from very different research traditions and discipline orientations (Bruner was a cognitivist, Jarvis was a sociologist). It may be this interdisciplinary nature that leads the socio-cultural approach to attempt to deconstruct education in such a critical but reflective way. With so many disciplines contributing to the socio-cultural approach itself there is no one paradigm, no unspoken assumptions or holy cows. Socio-cultural research often finds itself focused around breakdowns in sense-making, events which make visible the implicit rules and norms which shape our actions. As often as not, the socio-cultural researcher will apply this critical approach to themselves as researchers as much as the thing they are researching. Rather than attempting to pursue research framed around our own understanding of the teaching and learning environment, the socio-cultural perspective challenges us to question and critically evaluate our own underlying assumptions and cultural traditions in relation to education every time we engage in research.

Finally, the empirical orientation of these socio-cultural theories highlights the need for reflexivity on the part of the researcher in terms of the research questions that are formulated and pursued. Fenwick et al. (2011) describe the theoretical and empirical commitments this entails for both researchers and research participants as an 'epistemology of praxis'. Thus, rather than merely seeking to observe the system, this approach ultimately encourages the socio-cultural researcher to engage with and potentially help to transform the system they study.

Key points

- The socio-cultural perspective encourages us to see learning as part of a broader social, cultural and historical context.
- It contrasts with cognitive theories such as Piaget's, which propose that cognitive development precedes learning, by suggesting instead that the social and cultural practices in which we engage lead our learning and shape our cognition.
- In socio-cultural theories our attention is drawn to the tools (both physical and cognitive) and the cultural practices that can enable and constrain learning.
- The socio-cultural orientation influences the research questions that we ask and the research methods that we apply. Our attention is drawn to the social context that underpins education and we explore its historically shaped norms, rules and artefacts.
- Socio-cultural research highlights the role of education in enabling learners to negotiate and sometimes contest the identities that are imposed on them.
- Ultimately, the socio-cultural researcher is motivated by emancipatory concerns, to research with communities to better understand the contextual factors that shape activity and to identify tools to support new practices.

Recommended readings

Daniels, H., Edwards, A., Engeström, Y., Gallagher, T. and Ludvigsen, S.R. (eds) (2010) *Activity theory in practice: Promoting learning across boundaries and agencies.* Abingdon: Routledge.

Michael, A., Andrade, N. and Bartlett, L. (2007) Figuring 'success' in a bilingual high school. *The Urban Review,* **39**(2), pp. 167–189.

Vygotsky, L.S. (1978) *Mind in society: The development of higher psychological processes.* Cambridge, MA: Harvard University Press.

References

Bakhurst, D. (2015) Understanding Vygotsky. *Learning Culture and Social Interaction,* **5**, pp. 1–4.

Barron, I. (2014) Finding a voice: A figured worlds approach to theorising young children's identities. *Journal of Early Childhood Research,* **12**(3), pp. 251–263.

Bruner, J. (2009) Culture, mind and education. In K. Illeris (ed.) *Contemporary theories of learning: Learning theorists … in their own words.* Abingdon: Routledge.

Chaiklin, S. (2003) The zone of proximal development in Vygotsky's analysis of learning and instruction. In A. Kozulin (ed.) *Vygotsky's educational theory in cultural context.* Cambridge: Cambridge University Press.

Cole, M. and Scribner, S. (1978) Introduction. In L.S. Vygotsky, *Mind in society.* Cambridge, MA: Harvard University Press.

Daniels, H., Edwards, A., Engeström, Y., Gallagher, T. and Ludvigsen, S.R. (eds) (2010) *Activity theory in practice: Promoting learning across boundaries and agencies.* Abingdon: Routledge.

Derry, J. (2013) *Vygotsky: Philosophy and education.* New York: John Wiley and Sons.

Engeström, Y. and Sannino, A. (2012) Whatever happened to process theories of learning? *Learning, Culture and Social Interaction,* **1**(1), pp. 45–56.

Fenwick, T., Edwards, R. and Sawchuk, P. (2011) *Emerging approaches to educational research: Tracing the socio-material.* Abingdon: Routledge.

Hakkarainen, P. (1999) Play and motivation. In Y. Engeström, R. Liettinen and R L. Punamaki (eds) *Perspectives on activity theory.* Cambridge: Cambridge University Press.

Holland, D., Lachicotte, W., Skinner, D. and Cain, C. (1998) *Identity and agency in cultural worlds.* Cambridge, MA: Harvard University Press.

Illeris, K. (2007) *How we learn: An introduction to learning and non-learning in school and beyond.* New York: Routledge.

Jarvis, P. (2009) Learning to be a person in society: Learning to be me. In K. Illeris (ed.) *Contemporary theories of learning: Learning theorists … in their own words.* Abingdon: Routledge.

Kozulin, A. (2003) *Vygotsky's educational theory in cultural context.* Cambridge: Cambridge University Press.

Leontiev, A.N. (1978) *Activity, consciousness and personality.* Engelwood Cliffs: Prentice Hall.

Michael, A., Andrade, N. and Bartlett, L. (2007) Figuring 'success' in a bilingual high school. *The Urban Review,* **39**(2), pp. 167–189.

Moll, L.C. (2010) Mobilizing culture, language and educational practices: Fulfilling the promises of Mendez and Brown. *Educational Researcher,* **39**(6), pp. 451–460.

O'Connell, C. (2015) Close up examination of discourses associated with global university rankings: Counter-narratives in the UK context. *Higher Education Quarterly,* **69**(3), pp. 279–294.

O'Connell, C. and Saunders, M. (2013) Mediating the Use of global university rankings: Perspectives from education facilitators in an international context. *Journal of Studies in International Education,* **17**(4), pp. 354–376.

Solomon, Y., Croft, T., Duah, F. and Lawson, D. (2014) Reshaping understandings of teaching–learning relationships in undergraduate mathematics: An activity theory analysis of the role and impact of student internships. *Learning, Culture and Social Interaction,* **3**(4), pp. 323–333.

Stetsenko, A. and Vianna, E. (2009) Bridging developmental theory and education practice: Lessons from the Vygotskian project. In O. Barbain and B. Hanna Wasik (eds) *Handbook of child development and early education.* London: Guilford Press.

Vygotsky, L.S. (1978) *Mind in society: The development of higher psychological processes.* Cambridge, MA: Harvard University Press.

Vygotsky, L.S. (1998) *The collected works of L.S. Vygotsky, volume 5: Child psychology.* R.W. Reiber (ed.). New York: Plenum Press.

Wells, G. and Claxton, G. (2002) *Learning for life in the 21st century: Sociocultural perspectives on the future of education.* Oxford: Blackwell.

Williams, J. (2012) The learner, the learning process and pedagogy in social context. In H. Daniels, H. Lauder and J. Porter (eds) *Educational theories, cultures and learning: A critical perspective.* Abingdon: Routledge.

Williams, J. and Wakefield, G. (2007) Metaphors and models in translation between college and workplace mathematics. *Educational Studies in Mathematics,* **64**(3), pp. 345–371.

Woolfolk Hoy, A. (2013) *Educational psychology.* Boston: Pearson.

Index